FIGHTING POVERTY IN THE US
AND EUROPE

The Rodolfo Debenedetti Lectures

Public lectures by leading academicians on issues at the forefront of economic research

The main purpose of the Rodolfo Debenedetti Lectures is to present to a non-technical readership new and evolving research on topical issues, such as:

- the implications of the ageing of populations;
- long-term trends in income distribution;
- the changing size and composition of welfare states in an integrated Europe;
- labour market reforms and transitions in employment, unemployment and inactivity, and the spread of temporary work;
- international and regional migration;
- the future of trade unions and collective bargaining; and
- the political economy of social welfare reform.

The Scientific Committee in charge of selecting the authors of the Rodolfo Debenedetti Lectures is composed of Giuseppe Bertola (University of Turin), Olivier Blanchard (M.I.T.), Tito Boeri (Bocconi University), and Stephen Nickell (London School of Economics).

fondazione RODOLFO DEBENEDETTI
Via Salasco 5, 20136 Milano
Telefono: (39)-02-58 36 33 41/2
Fax: (39)-02-58 36 33 09
E-mail: info@frdb.org
Internet: www.frdb.org

FIGHTING POVERTY IN THE US AND EUROPE

A World of Difference

Alberto Alesina and Edward L. Glaeser

OXFORD
UNIVERSITY PRESS

OXFORD
UNIVERSITY PRESS

Great Clarendon Street, Oxford OX2 6DP

Oxford University Press is a department of the University of Oxford.
It furthers the University's objective of excellence in research, scholarship,
and education by publishing worldwide in

Oxford New York

Auckland Cape Town Dar es Salaam Hong Kong Karachi
Kuala Lumpur Madrid Melbourne Mexico City Nairobi
New Delhi Shanghai Taipei Toronto

With offices in

Argentina Austria Brazil Chile Czech Republic France Greece
Guatemala Hungary Italy Japan Poland Portugal Singapore
South Korea Switzerland Thailand Turkey Ukraine Vietnam

Oxford is a registered trade mark of Oxford University Press
in the UK and in certain other countries

Published in the United States
by Oxford University Press Inc., New York

British Library Cataloguing in Publication Data

Data available

Library of Congress Cataloging in Publication Data

Data available

Typeset by Newgen Imaging Systems (P) Ltd., Chennai, India
Printed in Great Britain
on acid-free paper by
Ashford Colour Press, Gosport, Hampshire

ISBN 978–0–19–926766–8
ISBN 978–0–19–928610–2 (Pbk.)

10 9 8 7 6 5 4 3 2

To our mothers.

Contents

Acknowledgments

Our greatest debt is toward Bruce Sacerdote, who coauthored a paper published in the Brookings Papers on Economic Activity that started our thinking on these issues. We could not have done it without his hard work, intelligence and good humor. For comments on parts of this book we are very grateful to Tito Boeri, Sam Engerman, Claudia Goldin, and Andrei Shleifer. We presented parts of this book in many seminars and lectures and we thank all of the many participants who offered comments.

Arnaud Devleeschauwer, Pryianka Malhotra, and Neil Mehta provided excellent research assistantship. We are also very grateful to Neil Mehta for creating the indices. Lorenza Negri helped us to put together the reference list. Lauren LaRosa did heroic things throughout the project, including proofreading, editing, and generally organizing the mayhem. Roberta Marcaletti and Giovanna Albano were very helpful in organizing the Lecture at Università Bocconi in November 2002. The NSF supported this research with a number of research grants. The Taubman Center for State and Local Government provided generous funding.

Finally, we are extremely grateful for our wives for their continuing patience and support.

List of Figures

List of Tables

Chapter 1

Introduction

In the United States, public policies that redistribute from the rich to the poor are much more limited than in continental Western Europe. Both the United States and Europe are democratic societies. Both have common cultural and religious roots. Both are wealthy. Why did Europe develop such a different attitude toward redistribution than the United States?

This question is intrinsically important. After all, the European welfare state touches almost every aspect of its economy and society. But trying to understand the transatlantic differences in this area can also shed light on other U.S.–Europe differences. Recent conflict between the United States and several European countries, especially France and Germany, has suggested again that there is an Atlantic divide which is often summarized by the term "American exceptionalism," a term made famous by Lipset (1996). But, is this divide grounded in economic realities, political institutions, or national psyches? Is it permanent and immutable or the result of changing political or economic forces?

In this volume, we follow in the footsteps of Friedrich Engels, Werner Sombart, and more recently Seymour Martin Lipset, and try to understand the roots of American exceptionalism by focusing on the welfare state. More precisely, our focus is on why Americans are much less willing to redistribute from the rich to the poor than Europeans.

Redistribution can occur by means of certain types of government spending that favor the poor and disadvantaged (health, unemployment subsidies, transfers to low income families, disability, etc.), by means of progressive taxation to collect revenues for the government, and also by certain types of labor and goods market regulation.

We begin in the next chapter by documenting the remarkable differences between the United States and Europe in many aspects of government spending, tax policy, and regulation. As a whole, government spending in the United States is about 30 percent of Gross Domestic Product (GDP). In continental Europe, government spending is about 45 percent of GDP and in Scandinavia is more than 50 percent of GDP. Almost two-thirds of this difference comes from spending on welfare. Therefore, if we want to understand why Europe has big governments and the United States appears more laissez-faire, we must understand why the Europeans have a welfare state.

Not only does government spending in Europe favor the poor much more than in the United States, but government tax policy as well is much more redistributive. Income tax rates are more progressive in Europe than in the United States. Labor market regulations, which are at least presented as being pro-poor and are certainly strongly supported by labor unions, are more favorable to workers in Europe than in the United States. If one were born (and remained) at the bottom end of the income distribution, one would be much better taken care of by government policies in Europe than by those in the United States.

The welfare state, of course, comes at a price. It requires high taxes and extensive regulation, which may discourage work and reduce economic growth. This is important, but it is not, we repeat, not, the point of this book. Our interest is in the explanation of why the welfare state, not in its costs and benefits. We hope free marketeers can read this book and understand how America avoided (what they perceive as) the creeping, intruding socialism of the European continent. We also hope that social democrats can read this book and understand how Europe managed to avoid (what they perceive to be) the shamefully unjust American system.

1.1. Economic explanations

After a description of the differences in public policies concerning redistribution in Chapter 2, in Chapter 3 we begin our exploration of possible reasons for cross-Atlantic differences by looking at economic variables. In particular, we focus on those variables that economists believe "should" create more redistribution. We conclude that economic considerations alone do not go very far in explaining American exceptionalism.

One natural explanation of differences across democracies in the level of redistribution is the pre-tax distribution of income. It would seem natural that places that start off with more pre-tax inequality should redistribute more. If democracies desire equality, then more intrinsic inequality should lead to more aggressive government redistribution. Furthermore, high levels of inequality might be expected to change the political situation, as a large majority of the relatively poor will vote to tax the few rich.

This theory cannot explain the differences in redistribution between the United States and Europe. Pre-tax income inequality is higher in the United States than in Europe. Both aggregate indices of inequality, such as the Gini coefficient, and more specific measures of wage dispersion, indicate higher levels of inequality in the U.S. Recent discussions of "excessive" compensation for CEOs and of the "winners take all" society are highly publicized examples of wage dispersion in America. As Europe is more equal than the United States before taxes and redistribution, the European welfare states widen the gulf in the level of inequality between the United States and Europe.

A variation on this theory is that the data on American inequality overstate the true level of inequality within the United States, because they don't consider the high levels of American social mobility. This variant suggests that the United States is actually an egalitarian society, because the poor will be rich tomorrow and the rich will be poor. Conversely, according to this theory, at a point in time Europe looks more equal, but since European society is so immobile, lifetime inequality is greater. This theory suggests that in the United States, the poor can more easily escape from poverty and therefore they do not need help from the government.

Indeed, there is no doubt that, according to many surveys, Americans believe that their society is mobile and Europeans believe that the poor are "trapped." According to the World Values Survey (an attitudinal survey conducted on about forty countries in the world), 71 percent of Americans believe that the poor could escape poverty if they worked hard enough, and only 40 percent of Europeans think the same.[1] While these surveys provide us with a fascinating glimpse at the differences in attitudes and ideology, their differences across countries do not seem to have much to do with any real differences in social mobility.

Certainly, there are enormous difficulties in making mobility comparisons across countries, but a fair reading of the technical literature suggests that social mobility (i.e. movement up and down the income ladder) is quite similar in the United States and Europe. The tendency of middle-income individuals to move upwards is slightly higher in the United States than in Europe. But the mobility of the poor (the bottom fifth, for example) is lower in the United States than in Europe. If anything, the American poor seem to be much more "trapped" than their European counterparts. Even the most pro-American reading of the evidence cannot conclude that the strong differences in opinions across continents reflect equally strong differences in mobility. As such, we are led to believe that the differences between the United States and Europe are not the result of greater American mobility (although conceptions of mobility might have something to do with it, and we will discuss that later).

The truly die-hard advocate of the view that America is the land of equal economic opportunity has one last argument. It might be that the observed measures of mobility do not reflect opportunity but rather the initiative taken by the poor. According to this view, the poor in Europe strive and climb out of poverty (despite notable barriers), while the poor in the United States stay poor out of laziness (despite abundant opportunity). Indeed, a majority of Americans do indeed believe that the poor are lazy. However, the American poor work just as much or more than their European counterparts.

[1] The World Value Survey, which we will use extensively in this volume is a collection of surveys conducted in about 40 countries in the world. Between 600 and 2,000 individuals are interviewed in each country.

We cannot say whether the American survey respondents or the Europeans are correct (after all, we can't figure out what trapped or lazy means in terms of hours worked or social mobility), but we can say that these differences in opinion do not reflect differences in economic reality across countries.

Another simple explanation of U.S.–Europe differences in redistribution is that tax collection is more efficient in Europe. If European tax collection involved fewer social losses, then the cost of the welfare state would be lower in Europe. Indeed, the efficiency of tax collection is an important determinant of the size of government. For example, improvement in tax collection may explain part of the secular growth in the size of government in industrial countries. Before the twentieth century, the only large-scale taxes that could be efficiently collected were taxes on visible, immobile property (especially real estate) and import taxes at ports. In the twentieth century, as the ability of the state to monitor private activity has risen, a much larger range of tax options has emerged and these new taxes have provided the revenues needed for expanding the size of government. Naturally, there is two-sided causality here as well, where the increasing size of government has also led to a wider range of tax instruments.

However, it is quite unlikely that differences in the efficiency of the tax system can explain the large transatlantic differences in the size of the welfare state. Even the most casual consideration of this hypothesis suggests its implausibility. Could it really be possible that the tax collectors in Italy are so much more effective than the American Internal Revenue Service? In addition, the tax systems within Europe are very different from each other. Despite those differences, everywhere in continental Europe redistributive policies are larger than in the United States. Furthermore, the available evidence on the efficiency of tax collection confirms casual observation: Tax evasion is much higher in continental Europe than in the United States. Higher levels of tax evasion suggest that it is more difficult to collect taxes in many countries in Europe than in America.

Another theory is that European countries may be more redistributive because they are inherently more unstable. After all, one view is that the welfare state basically exists to provide insurance for citizens buffeted by the changing economy. As such, if the small size of

European economies and their openness to external shocks made them more volatile, we would expect a larger welfare state to cushion workers from these shocks. The evidence does not support this view. The U.S. economy has been less stable than the European ones in terms of variability of GDP growth and unemployment rates. Furthermore, if this argument were important, then as European economies became more and more integrated in one big common market economy, the European welfare state should have shrunk quickly to an American level since the U.S. economy is about as open as Europe as a whole. This contraction of the welfare state has not happened and we see no evidence that European integration is leading towards a decline in redistribution.

One last "economic" explanation is simply that Americans are less generous and altruistic than Europeans, and as a result they want to redistribute less. This view does not square well with two other observations. When it comes to private charity Americans are much more generous than Europeans. As we discuss below, we do not think that this has to do with tax deductibility rules, but it may be related to the fact that Europeans, feeling highly taxed, do not have a stronger incentive for charity. Also, Americans are much more likely than Europeans to participate in social activities in groups, an observation that questions the view of extreme American individualism. One interesting possibility is that Americans may prefer private charity to public redistribution because with the former they can choose the beneficiary. Aversion to public redistribution in the United States may not be a result of general stinginess, but rather a reduced desire to contribute to some disadvantaged American. Perhaps Americans dislike government transfers because they (like most people) prefer giving money to people of their own race, religion, and ethnicity.

1.2. Political institutions and the welfare state

Given that economic factors cannot solve our puzzle, we turn to politics and institutions in Chapter 4. Perhaps the differences in the degree of redistribution reflect differences in political structure.

After all, while the United States and the countries of western Europe are all democracies, they have very different rules for implementing the desires of the populace. One particularly striking difference is that almost all European countries have proportional representation systems (England and, currently, France are notable exceptions). These systems have generally facilitated the growth of left-wing parties (socialists and communists) that are primarily oriented towards increased redistribution and an enlarged welfare state. One very plausible explanation for why socialism succeeded in Europe but failed in the United States is that the American majoritarian system made it difficult for a new, fringe party to elect any representatives.

A second difference between the United States and Europe is that the U.S. Constitution places heavy emphasis on checks and balances, which deter large changes in all government policies, and in particular have limited large increases in the level of redistribution. In different time periods, the American Supreme Court and Senate stopped the expansion of the welfare state.

A third difference is American federalism. The United States is more decentralized than all of Europe, except for Switzerland. Small jurisdictions within a mobile society have strong incentives not to redistribute, since such redistribution tends to push away industry and the rich.

There is broad empirical support for the idea that proportional representation leads to greater levels of redistribution. We find that the difference between welfare spending in majoritarian and proportional systems is large, and this institutional feature may "explain" in our estimation about half of the difference between the United States and Europe in welfare spending. Of course this explanation begs the question of why electoral systems are different, an issue which we address later.

Checks and balances also matter. Countries with judicial review of legislature spend less of their GDP on social services than countries without judicial review. But, these institutions are often of recent vintage, and in some ways they are more a result than a cause of U.S.–Europe differences.

In Chapter 5, we turn to the causes and history of institutional differences between the United States and Europe. In a number of smaller European countries (Belgium, Finland, Sweden, the Netherlands, and Switzerland), before the World War I, the labor movement was able to use general strikes to hobble the country. Electoral reform was a direct response to these strikes, and in most cases proportional representation was a specific demand of the strikers. These smaller countries had tiny armies and were sufficiently small so that concentrated labor uprisings effectively threatened the entire nation.

In the larger European countries (Germany, Austria, and Italy), proportional representation was implemented in the period after World War I when the army was in disarray and labor uprisings dominated the country. Amidst the chaos of defeat or withdrawal, socialist and communist groups were able to impose constitutions that favored their needs. France introduced proportional representation after World War II, when the right was tarred by its connection with Vichy and the left was triumphant.

The history of Europe helps us to understand why proportional representation never made much headway in the United States. In the United States, the socialist and communist movements were never able to push their desired constitutional reforms. The majoritarian, American constitution with its manifold checks and balances was stacked against any fringe parties pushing major change. But, we could say the same thing about the political rules of the Kaiser's Germany. The difference between the United States and Germany is that the United States was never defeated on its own territory. The devastation of World War I, and the large number of desperate men in close contact for years in fighting armies, was a fertile ground for the diffusion of communist ideas concerning redistribution from capitalists to workers. This did not happen in the United States. As a result, the generally victorious U.S. army was a much more reliable tool against leftist uprisings than the more dispirited armies of mainland Europe.

Of course, Sweden has not lost a war on its home territory either, because of her long tradition of neutrality. America's large size and ethnic diversity provides the explanation for why the Constitution was not changed lacking a military defeat. While strikes in Liège could threaten the government in Brussels, strikes in Chicago could not rattle the U.S. Senate in far off Washington. Even in Sweden, the population is concentrated over a small area, and as such, it was possible for general strikes to impact the entire nation. Density also mattered because poor American workers in the cities of the east could search for fortune in the vast and almost unexplored west.

Furthermore, while Swedes are remarkably homogeneous and can't be split along ethnic, racial, or religious lines, in the United States, the white majority was afraid that proportional systems would give more representation, and thus political power, to racial minorities (especially blacks). The U.S. polity is still shaped by the impact of slavery and immigration. Successive waves of immigration to the United States of ethnically diverse members of the working class created cleavages across racial and ethnic lines, which "confused" and diluted the classic class line of Marxism. An Irish worker in Boston, say, felt Irish first and then "worker" and often viewed, say, the new Italian immigrant workers with just as much animosity as he viewed capitalists. Marx and Engels were aware of this problem in the United States and considered it a critical obstacle for the formation of an American Communist Party.

Another possible impact of immigration is the self-selection of those who choose to leave Europe to move to the United States. These immigrants may have had a propensity to find an individual (or individualistic) solution to adversity rather than fomenting a social revolution at home.

American political stability (which is itself the result of American isolation, military strength, and size) implies that the U.S. Constitution is of much older vintage than those of European countries. Many European countries have relatively recent constitutions, which are often the result of revolutionary periods in which the large mass of workers had a voice in the political arena. The American Constitution has obviously been amended, but it is still the same document approved by a minority of wealthy white men in 1787. In his famous "Economic Interpretation of the Constitution" Charles Beard shows how one motivation of the Constitutional Convention was to write a document that managed to protect wealth against expropriation. Historically, the Supreme Court was a major obstacle to progressive policies and was a bastion of the defense of property. In some ways, the role of the Supreme Court in the United States (an issue to which we devote considerable attention) can be compared with that of the House of Lords in England, until the latter lost its political power.

1.3. Race and redistribution

Our evidence suggests that European institutions can explain approximately one-half of the difference in social spending between the United States and Europe. Thus, we do not believe that even if Europe had the same political institutions as the United States, attitudes towards redistribution and welfare policies would be identical. In Chapter 6, we argue that one important reason for the differences between the United States and Europe that cannot be explained by institutions is racial and ethnic fractionalization. America's immigrants and the descendants of its slave population ensure that the United States is a much more racially fragmented society than anywhere in western Europe.

Moreover, while European governments strove to eradicate ethnic and cultural differences over the past four centuries (with differing levels of success; compare homogeneous France and ethnically diverse Spain), American governments put much less effort into this task, which would have surely been impossible in such a diverse country. As a result, it is much easier to convince a white middle class person in the United States to think that the poor are "different" (read black) than to convince a white middle class person, say, in Sweden.

Racial divisions and racial preferences appear to deter redistribution, especially when poverty is concentrated in minority groups. A vast body of experimental and survey evidence shows that individuals are more generous towards members of their own racial or ethnic group than to members of other groups. Of course, these attitudes are not innate, instead they reflect cultural and political conditioning. Race hatred is often used strategically by politicians whose main objective is to avoid redistributive policies; precisely by using the racial animosity of distrust, political entrepreneurs can gain support from even relatively poor whites against redistribution.

Places with natural ethnic, religious, or racial divisions facilitate this sort of divide and conquer strategy. It therefore follows that redistributive policies should be more limited in more fragmented societies where generosity across people is limited by racial cleavages. This effect is likely to be much more important when minority groups are over-represented among the poor.

Empirical evidence across countries and within the United States shows that racial heterogeneity tends to support the political importance of fractionalization. Research on American cities shows that participation in social activities, interpersonal trust, redistributive policies, and provision of public goods are lower in more racially fragmented communities. Within the United States, we find that states with a lower share of African-Americans offer more generous welfare benefits. Across countries, racial fractionalization is a strong predictor of the degree of redistribution. Indeed, our estimates suggest that racial fractionalization can also explain about half of the difference in redistribution between the United States and Europe.

One natural implication of our conclusion that fractionalization reduces redistribution is that if Europe becomes more heterogeneous due to immigration, ethnic divisions will be used to challenge the generous welfare state. We have already seen some of this happen in the political success of Joerg Haidar, Jean-Marie LePen, Umberto Bossi, and Pim Fortuyn. All of these politicians (and there are many others) both favor less redistribution and emphasize the flaws of recent immigrants. The rhetoric of many of these politicians has already emphasized that immigrants become citizens of European countries to take advantage of the generous European welfare system.

1.4. Culture and attitudes

In Chapter 7, we turn to the cultural differences across the Atlantic regarding the perception of the poor. Survey evidence shows that Americans think that the poor are lazy and Europeans think that the poor are unfortunate. A larger fraction of Americans than Europeans think that one can escape poverty with hard work;

those who think that poverty is due to lack of effort will be less sympathetic to redistributive policies. This impression is confirmed by the analysis of survey responses in the United States: Americans who are more firmly convinced that poverty is due to lack of effort are also more strongly opposed to redistribution. The same applies to other countries: The larger the proportion of respondents to surveys who believe that poverty is due to lack of effort, the lower the redistributive role of government.

While we believe that these opinions are an important influence on the level of welfare spending, we also believe that they are fundamentally a result of American politics, not a cause. American institutions have strengthened the political right and given anti-redistribution politicians the ability to push their world view—and this world view emphasizes economic opportunity. European institutions, to the contrary, have empowered the left; as a result, leftist leaders have been able to indoctrinate Europeans with Marxist ideas about class solidarity and the capriciousness of the capitalist system. Moreover, racial heterogeneity in the United States has been an important factor enabling American politicians to emphasize the moral failings of the poor. As such, we think beliefs about the nature of poverty are important because they reflect deeper forces, which have ensured the relatively greater strength of the right in the United States and the left in Europe.

Our work emphasizes the importance of institutions and race, but we do not mean to rule out other factors, which may also have had a lesser influence on the development of the United States and Europe. The Calvinist, Protestant ethic is also a strong cultural force that leads Americans to view success as a sign of "goodness," at least more so than Catholic Europe. Indeed, Catholic parties in Europe have been (together with Socialist parties) strongly supportive of redistributive policies. Immigrants who left the old continent to travel to the new continent might have been those less prone to worry about risks, and more likely to believe in the value of individual initiative. Less aversion to risk implies lower demand for social insurance and redistribution. Once again, survey evidence suggests that individual risk aversion is indeed related to demand for redistribution. Americans may, therefore, be less averse to the inequality that they see as a result of different abilities and different comfort levels in risk taking than Europeans.

1.5. Summary

The reasons why Americans and Europeans differ on their choices over the welfare state and redistribution run very deep into their different history and culture. No simple economic theory provides a one-line answer.

Instead, we have to touch upon a wide range of considerations, involving economic, political, social, and attitudinal variables, and, of course, history. In particular, ethnic heterogeneity and political institutions seem to explain most of the differences, and these political institutions are themselves the legacy of the chaotic first half of the twentieth century.

As we have been pondering our question, we have come to the view that the differences across the two sides of the Atlantic are quite deeply ingrained in culture and attitudes. It is therefore unsurprising that tensions and animosity between the two sides of the Atlantic occasionally reach the surface. Most recently, we have seen these tensions in the debate surrounding war with Iraq. These divisions are unfortunate, but if our analysis is correct, this divide has deep roots. However, sometimes friendships work best when group members use their different strengths to compensate for one another's weaknesses. Let us hope that this applies to America and Europe.

Chapter 2

Redistribution in the United States and Europe: The Data

2.1. Introduction

How much do different countries take from the rich to give to the poor? This is not an easy question to answer because net flows of income and services to various income groups are multi-faced, complex, and different countries have a variety of welfare systems. The poor benefit not only from transfer programs directly targeted to them but also take advantage, more than the rich, of publicly provided goods. The poor pay proportionately less in taxes since the total burden of taxation is progressive. Finally, various regulations in the labor and goods market may favor low income groups.

On the other hand, certain government programs redistribute not only between rich and poor, but also across non-income based lines. Primary examples are "pay-as-you-go" pension systems, in which the pensions of the retirees are paid by the contributions of the currently employed. These systems redistribute from the workforce to the retirees. However, they also imply income redistribution, since the poor retirees generally receive proportionally more than rich ones. Another example is labor market regulation. These regulations often favor the "insiders," already employed and union members, but may have negative effects for the unemployed or those outside the labor force, who, in fact, are generally poorer than the protected labor force. From all the above it follows that measuring and comparing across countries the redistributive flows from rich to poor is not an easy task. For instance, to what extent is it true that, as commonly believed, the poor are better treated in Europe than in the United States, the basic premise and the *explanandum* of this volume?

In this chapter, we reassure the readers that two commonly held views are, indeed, correct: (*a*) there are indeed heavy redistributive flows from the rich to the poor and (*b*) these flows are much larger in western Europe, especially in continental western Europe, than in the United States. However, we go well beyond this and discuss various nuances around these two basic facts. For instance, we will show how certain groups of citizens are relatively well protected even in the United States, and we investigate in which areas the differences between the United States and Europe are larger.

We look at the data in three different and complementary ways. First, we analyze macroeconomic variables on the spending side of the government budget. Second, we examine several specific programs that are redistributive in nature, looking at the laws and regulatory prescriptions. Finally, we consider the Luxembourg income study, which provides a survey of income sources for a sample of several thousand households in various countries. These data allow us to estimate the amount of government transfers received by different income groups in different countries based on the respondents' answers. After having analyzed the spending side of the government budget, we consider the revenue side. Finally, we examine labor and goods market regulations that may create policy induced effects on the distribution of income.

2.2. Government spending: The macro data[1]

2.2.1. The current data

Table 2.1 summarizes the magnitude and composition of government spending in Europe and the United States, using the latest available data from the Organization for Economic Cooperation and Development (OECD). In addition to reporting the average for the countries in the European Union, we provide separate data on the United Kingdom (the E.U. country with the smallest government and in many ways most similar to the United States), France and Germany (the two largest E.U. countries), and Sweden (as the prototype of a country with an especially large welfare state). In the

Table 2.1. Composition of General Government Expenditure (as % of GDP) in 2000

Country	Total[a]	Consumption		Subsidies	Social benefits and other transfers[b]	Gross investment
		Goods and services	Wages and salaries			
United States	29.9	5.3	9.2	0.4	10.6	3.3
Continental						
Europe[c]	44.9	8.3	12.4	1.5	17.6	2.5
France	48.7	9.7	13.5	1.3	19.6	3.2
Germany	43.3	10.9	8.1	1.7	20.5	1.8
Sweden	52.2	9.8	16.4	1.5	20.2	2.2
United						
Kingdom	37.3	11.4	7.5	0.4	15.6	1.1

Notes:

[a] Totals also include interest payments and some categories of capital outlays.

[b] Includes social security.

[c] Simple average for Austria, Belgium, Denmark, Finland, France, Germany, Greece, Italy, Netherlands, Norway, Portugal, Spain, and Sweden.

Source: Authors' calculations based on data from OECD Economic Outlook Database (No. 71, Vol. 2002, Release 01), June 2002.

[1] This section heavily draws on Alesina, Glaeser, and Sacerdote (2001).

Appendix of this chapter we provide a more detailed description of the data sources used in this chapter.

General government spending in the countries in the European Union averages about 45 percent of GDP; it is 37 percent in the United Kingdom and 52 percent in Sweden. General government spending in the United States is smaller than any of these, at less than 30 percent of GDP. General government includes both central and local governments and the OECD devotes much effort to making these data compatible internationally.

The composition of spending is also instructive. The largest differences between the United States and Europe are to be found in transfers to households (including social security) and subsidies. In fact, the sum of these two categories of spending is almost twice as large, as a share of GDP, in Europe as in the United States (about 18 percent in the European Union, more than 20 percent in Sweden, versus 11 percent in the United States). Public consumption of goods and services and government wages are also higher in Europe, but the difference relative to the United States is smaller than that for transfers. Public investment is actually higher in the United States than in the average E.U. country. Of course, military spending is higher in the United States than in Europe (data not shown), even today when U.S. defense spending is low by post-World War II standards. Western Europe since World War II has been a free rider on defense provided by the United States.

Clearly, not all public spending is redistributive and not all transfers go to the poor. However, given that the United States spends on transfers half of continental Europe's expenditures, the U.S. system of transfers would have to be exceptionally well-targeted for the U.S. poor to receive more than the continental European poor. We return to these issues in more detail below. On the other hand, even public goods can be redistributive to the extent that the rich pay (more than proportionally) for them, although they may use higher quality private goods. Think for instance of public versus private transportation, public versus private schools, or public versus private providers of healthcare.[2] Public employment can also be used

---

[2] See Besley and Coate (1991) and (1995) for a formal discussion of redistribution through the public provision of goods.

Table 2.2. Government Expenditure on Social Programs (as % of GDP) in 1998

Country	Total	Old-age, disability, and survivors[a]	Family[a]	Unemployment and labor market programs	Health[b]	Other[c]
United States	14.6	7.0	0.5	0.4	5.9	0.9
Continental Europe[d]	25.5	12.7	2.3	2.7	6.1	1.7
France	28.8	13.7	2.7	3.1	7.3	2.1
Germany	27.3	12.8	2.7	2.6	7.8	1.5
Sweden	31.0	14.0	3.3	3.9	6.6	3.2
United Kingdom	24.7	14.2	2.2	0.6	5.6	2.0

Notes:
[a] Includes cash benefits and in kind services.

[b] Includes, among other things, inpatient care, ambulatory medical services, and pharmaceutical goods.

[c] Includes occupational injury and disease benefits, sickness benefits, housing benefits, and expenditure on other contingencies (both in cash or in kind), including benefits to low-income households.

[d] Simple average for Austria, Belgium, Denmark, Finland, France, Germany, Greece, Italy, Netherlands, Norway, Portugal, Spain, and Sweden.

Source: Authors' calculations based on data from OECD Social Expenditure Database 1980–98 (3rd edn.), 2001.

for redistributive purposes and to support the income of poorer regions.[3]

The OECD offers a different breakdown of government social spending; these data are presented in Table 2.2 for 1998, the latest year for which they are available. Apart from the fact that the two tables refer to different years, the definitions of the two items differ. For instance, health benefits in Table 2.2 include the wages of government workers in the health sector, which would be included under "Wages and salaries," in Table 2.1. Total social spending in Table 2.2 is not meant to coincide with the item "Social benefits and other transfers" in Table 2.1.

[3] As shown by Alesina, Danninger, and Rostango (2001). Italy offers a prime example of this mechanism.

Fighting Poverty in the US and Europe

In all categories, the United States spends a smaller portion of GDP than the European average. The differences are particularly large in family allowances, unemployment compensation, and other labor market programs. By this accounting, social spending in the United States was less than 15 percent of GDP in 1998, whereas the European average was 25.5 percent.

2.2.2. Historical trends in the size of government

Understanding the reasons for these striking differences between the United States and Europe requires that we know something of the history of redistribution in both regions. In particular, we want to know *when* the size of government, and especially the size of the welfare state in Europe, diverged from that in the United States. Did the two share a similar size of government for a while and then diverge, or has the difference always been present?

Figure 2.1 provides a clear answer: From the very beginning of the expansion of the public sector in the late nineteenth century, the United States and Europe show very distinct patterns. Although the ratio of welfare spending was already high at the end of the

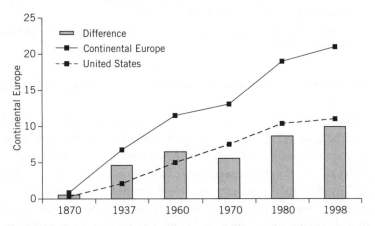

Fig. 2.1. Government Expenditure on Subsidies and Transfers (% of GDP) During 1870–1998 (Obtained from Table 2.4)

Source: Alesina, Glaeser, and Sacerdote (2001); original source Tanzi and Schuknecht (2000) and OECD.

nineteenth century, the absolute difference grew as the welfare state expanded both in Europe and the United States, especially in the 1960s and 1970s. The observation that the difference is long-standing is important, because it allows us to exclude explanations of the difference that are specific to a certain period or event.

2.3. The "micro" evidence

2.3.1. Income support policies and safety nets

We consider a representative household in Germany, Sweden, and the United States; specifically we investigate to what extent are existing welfare programs beneficial to such a household when it experiences needs such as the costs of raising a child, of sickness, of disability, and of extreme poverty.

Our representative household is composed of two adults and two children. The adults, both aged thirty-five, are average production workers with fifteen years of work experience. The two children are aged eight and twelve (to take a benchmark often used by social security administrations). The monthly before-tax earnings of an average production worker in the three countries, in 1999 dollars adjusted for purchasing power parity (PPP), are $2,498 in the United States, $2,561 in Germany, and $1,880 in Sweden.

Family benefits. Child benefits are available in Germany and Sweden for every parent, without regard to income, until the child reaches eighteen (in Germany) or sixteen (in Sweden), but those limits can be extended if the child pursues higher education. By contrast, family allowances do not exist in the United States. The United States does have a fixed child tax credit ($600 per child in 2001), and the amount of the earned income tax credit increases with the number of children in the family (but is available only to low-income work-ers). In addition, special allowances for children of low-income fam-ilies are allocated under the Temporary Assistance for Needy Families program (TANF, which replaced the Aid to Families with Dependent Children, or AFDC, program in the mid-1990s), as discussed below.

Thus, each child entitles the representative household to monthly benefits (again in 1999 PPP-adjusted dollars) of $136 in Germany, $87 in Sweden, and zero in the United States.

Healthcare. The public healthcare systems of Germany and Sweden also differ significantly from that of the United States. Both Germany and Sweden provide universal coverage, with unlimited benefits including payments for doctors' fees, hospitalization, and the cost of pharmaceutical products. The United States, on the other hand, relies on two programs, Medicare and Medicaid, which target mainly the elderly and low-income households, respectively. If one of the members of our representative U.S. family became sick and had to visit a doctor or stay in a hospital, he or she would not be eligible for public funds or services (although a large proportion of employers offer health insurance as part of their compensation package). In contrast, the representative German or Swedish household would have most of these expenses covered by the public healthcare program. A small part of the cost is borne by the household in the form of a deductible. In Germany the household pays a deductible of $9 for each day of hospitalization; in Sweden the hospitalization deductible is $8, and in addition there is a deductible of $10–14 for medical treatment, again in 1999 PPP dollars.

Sickness and accidental injury benefits. Sickness benefits are intended to replace the loss of earnings due to sickness of a household's income earners. Once again, the coverage and the extent of benefits differ radically between the United States and the two European countries examined here. Indeed, only five states in the United States offer any kind of sickness benefit (there is no federal benefit), whereas German and Swedish legislation guarantees benefits for all persons in paid employment; these benefits replace up to 70 percent and 80 percent of gross earnings, respectively. If the head of our representative U.S. household fell sick (and was fortunate enough to live in one of the five states that offer sickness benefits), he or she would receive (in 1999 PPP dollars) between $452 and $1,576 a month (between 18 and 63 percent of the average wage); the representative household head in Germany would receive $1,793 a month, and his or her Swedish counterpart would receive $1,504 a month. The U.S. household's benefits would last for a maximum of fifty-two weeks, whereas those of the German household would expire only after seventy-eight weeks, and those of the Swedish household could continue indefinitely.

Accidental injuries occurring in the enterprise or in connection with the working situation of the employee are covered in all three countries, including every state in the United States, and these benefits are quite comparable. German and Swedish workers who suffer on-the-job injuries see their income replaced according to the amounts allocated by sickness benefits, whereas American workers receive the equivalent of two-thirds of their average weekly earnings, up to a maximum of between $270 and $714 a week, depending on the state.

Disability benefits. All three countries also have provisions to replace income lost due to inability to engage in any gainful activity. Participation is compulsory in all three systems, and coverage is based on work history. The United States and Germany require at least five years of employment before a worker can receive benefits; in Sweden the requirement is three years. But, the extent of coverage differs dramatically across the three countries. Whereas in the United States the disability pension is based on the worker's average monthly earnings, the Swedish scheme provides a basic minimum pension, augmented by an income-based supplementary pension, care allowances, and handicap allowances; German pensions are computed using the level of income and the number of years of contribution. For the representative production worker, disability benefits amount to $1,063 in the United States and $1,504 in Sweden (again in 1999 PPP dollars). These correspond to 43 percent and 80 percent of the average wage, respectively.

Poverty relief. In all three countries, certain government programs are directed at persons who are unable to support themselves but are not covered under the schemes described above. These persons may fail to meet eligibility criteria because of insufficient past contributions, or their incomes may be too low to allow them to take part in insurance schemes. The programs that provide these pure case transfers differ in structure across the three countries. Germany and Sweden rely on unlimited and unconditional plans (called Sozialhilfe and Socialbidrag, respectively), which are meant primarily to alleviate poverty. Additional plans covering the costs of housing and heating are also available for German residents. The United States, on the other hand, offers an array of plans targeting different groups in the population, as opposed to the general category of "the poor." Supplemental Security Income (SSI) targets aged, blind, and disabled persons with annual gross income below about $14,500; the federal payment can be augmented by a state supplement. The TANF program, mentioned above, is limited to two years of assistance; recipients who are able to work must find employment at the end of that period. Other plans, such as those for food and nutrition assistance and those for housing assistance, also provide relief to low-income households.

A representative U.S. household that has zero income and has exhausted all other claims to regular benefits could be eligible for $1,306 in monthly benefits under these programs ($726 from SSI, or 29 percent of the average monthly wage, and $580 from TANF, or 23 percent of the average wage).[4] Its German counterpart would be eligible to receive $1,008 a month, and its Swedish counterpart $892 a month (47 percent and 39 percent of the average wage, respectively, again in 1999 PPP-adjusted dollars). These amounts do not include benefits available under additional programs such as house allowances.

2.3.2. The pension systems

A sizeable and growing fraction of measured welfare spending is allocated in most countries for pensions. Table 2.3 shows the share of pension spending over GDP. Note how the United States spends about half in terms of the share of GDP on public pensions, relative to France and Germany. Also, while that share shows a tendency to increase in France and Germany, it is stable in the United States.

Pay-as-you-go systems, in which pensions of current retirees are paid out of contributions of the current young, create a complex web

---

[4] This value refers to the state of Massachusetts, which pays the highest TANF benefits among states in the program.

Table 2.3. Public Pension Expenditure, 1985–95

As % GDP			
France	Germany	United Kingdom	United States
1985 6.14	6.9	4.04	3.31
1995 7.59	7.71	4.68	3.27

Source: OECD Social Expenditure Database, OECD Statistical Compendium 2002.

of redistributive flows. First, they redistribute from the current young to the current old. Second, and more relevant for our purposes, the pension systems redistribute in favor of the "poor old." In fact, public pension systems give much more as a share of income to the poor retirees than to the wealthy retirees, both in terms of total income after retirement and in terms of share of labor income before retirement. In fact, it is an explicit goal of public pension systems to reduce inequality among the old, and several studies evaluate European programs from the point of view of how successful they are at reaching this goal.[5] Therefore, pensions are not neutral from the point of view of income redistribution among the population currently alive. Finally, in many cases pension systems redistribute in favor of certain overprotected groups, often public employees who manage to achieve special privileges because of various political distortions.[6] We are concerned here specifically with the redistributive flow that goes from the rich to the poor.

The structure of public pension systems is often rather complex and involves several parameters, from the retirement age to the

---

[5] See Kohl (1992), Hauser (1997), Heinrich (2000), and Disney and Johnson (2001) for surveys and Boeri and Perotti (2002) for a detailed study of some European countries.

[6] These kinds of special interest favors through the pension systems are particularly common in developing countries. The typical problem of pension systems in these countries is that very few privileged insiders are well protected and many others are not. Especially until recent reforms, in Italy certain groups, particularly public employees, received extremely privileged treatment and the public pension system was (and partly still is) a jungle of special provisions granted for political patronage. In France the first step of a broader pension reform was to eliminate some privileges of public servants, in 2002. For more discussion see Boeri (2000).

computation of the base salary to which the pension is applied, to the share of salary that the pension covers, to the nature of pensions for survivors, to the number of years of contribution necessary, etc. For this reason, a complete comparative study of pension systems of OECD countries would require a book in itself. In fact, we are not aware of a comprehensive comparative study of all OECD pension systems, which compares the overall degree of rich to poor redistribution implied by these systems. It would be an important project to pursue.

Incidentally, one may argue that some of this complication in the rules of pension systems is strategic: The more complicated the system, the easier it is to "hide" special privileges for certain groups, including the poor. For instance, a change in the computation of the salary over which the pension is computed, a rather obscure parameter in the structure of pensions, can generate very large differences in the pension received.

If we compare the pension systems of European countries and the United States, we reach several conclusions. First, European countries spend more on publicly provided pensions than the United States. The poor in Europe receive much more than the poor in the United States as a share of their salary when they retire. In some countries in Europe, the rich also get more than in the United States, but in both cases proportionally less than the poor. The bottom line is that pension systems in Europe imply some redistribution from rich workers to rich retirees in addition to redistributions from rich workers to poor retirees. The poor are better treated when they retire in Europe than in the United States. If somebody with an income below average could choose where to retire, he would choose Europe rather than the United States.

Table 2.4 compares, according to our best understanding of the pension systems, the amount of public pensions received by different income levels in the countries we are focusing upon. Essentially, we have applied the parameters prescribed by law to a hypothetical single male with an average labor income indicated in the first column of the table.

The critical comparison from our perspective is among the pensions received by the poor, say below $10,000 of pre-retirement income

Table 2.4. Annual Public Pension for a Single Male with the Following Characteristics for a Given Average Annual Wage

Average annual wage ($U.S.)[a]	France (incl. ARRC)	France (incl. AGIRC)	Germany (West)	Germany (East)	Sweden	United Kingdom	United States
2,000	8,770	8,770	1,617	1,403	6,435	5,383	5,904
5,000	8,770	9,531	4,044	3,509	9,022	6,133	5,904
7,000	8,770	11,903	5,662	4,912	10,747	6,633	6,384
10,000	10,930	15,459	8,089	7,018	13,334	7,383	6,384
12,000	12,396	17,831	9,707	8,421	15,059	7,883	6,804
17,000	16,059	23,758	13,752	11,930	19,371	9,133	8,404
20,000	18,257	27,315	16,179	14,036	21,959	9,883	9,364
50,000	29,943	31,211	40,449	35,090	32,778	17,383	15,701
70,000	29,943	44,923	56,629	41,787	32,778	22,383	18,701
100,000	29,943	65,491	57,130	41,787	32,778	29,883	23,201
200,000	29,943	134,049	57,130	41,787	32,778	54,883	38,201

Notes:

[a] Using 1995 exchange rates.

Source: Authors' calculations based on the official laws governing old age pension calculations in France, Germany, Sweden, the United Kingdom, and the United States.

Data Source: Gruber and Wise (2002) and Social Security Bulletin (2000). Details about the construction of this table are in the Appendix of this chapter.

across countries. Remember that we are talking about the total income of a single male; that of a two-income family would be around $20,000. The table shows that as a share of their pre-retirement income, the American poor retirees receive much less than their counterparts in Europe and slightly less than their German counterparts. Wealthy retirees also receive more in Europe than in the United States but this is the result of larger contributions of the current young, so it implies a flow from rich young to rich old which is roughly orthogonal to our concerns here. A comparison between the United States and Sweden is especially revealing. A Swedish retiree with an average salary of $10,000 received more than 130 percent of that salary as pension, while the same person in the United States would get 60 percent. A Swedish retiree making $200,000 would get less than 33 percent, roughly one-quarter of the percentage of a Swede with $10,000. An American retiring with $200,000 gets 23 percent, more than one-third of the percentage of an American retiring with $10,000. Also, while American pension benefits increase with income, although less than proportionally, in Sweden, the United Kingdom, and Germany they reach an absolute limit at $50,000 of the base salary for the first two countries and $100,000 for the latter.

So, the American poor retirees get proportionally less than the poor retirees in the comparison countries. The American rich in some cases get comparatively more, given the same overall share of the pension systems in various countries. Note that in France where the rich retirees also get a lot, part of the pension benefits come from voluntary contributions to individual accounts required by law.

The German public pension system is not especially generous toward the poor, compared to other European countries. The German system is the prototype of a Bismarck-type social security system, in which benefits are more closely linked to contribution paid and work performance. This type of system is usually contrasted with a Beveridgean-type system, in which pensions are more linked to "needs." Obviously, within the latter system, as we discussed above, the degree of redistribution implied by the structure of pensions can vary substantially.

Conde Ruiz and Profeta (2002) discuss the political economy of Bismarckian versus Beveridgean systems. They note that even though the Beveridgean systems may redistribute more in the specific sense that as a proportion of working salary the poor get more than the rich, the Beveridgean systems (U.K. and U.S. in particular) are smaller, that is total contributions are lower than in Bismarckian systems. So, in Beveridgean systems the rich may not get much in terms of public pensions, but they are also taxed less for social security and can use more profitable private pension systems. Therefore, as Conde Ruiz and Profeta (2002) show, the preferred social security system by the rich is a small Beveridgean type that redistributes to the poor as little as possible, which is a pretty good characterization of the U.S. system.[7]

A different way of looking at the rich–poor redistribution implied by pension systems is to consider income inequality among the elderly and compare it to that among the young, an approach followed, for instance, by Heinrich (2000) for all E.U. countries.[8] Suppose that pensions did not exist. Then the retirees' income would be given by the return on their accumulated wealth. In this case, one would expect more inequality among the retirees than among working age individuals, since wealth distribution is more unequal than income distribution. Heinrich (2000) shows that it turns out that the distribution of income among retirees is not that different than that of the working age population. In fact, in many countries the distribution of income of the old is actually less unequal than that of the young. This suggests that pension systems play a role in reducing income inequality among retirees.

Disney and Whitehouse (2002) review studies comparing poverty among the elderly internationally. For our purposes, the most interesting finding is that with the exception of Greece, the United States

---

[7] In the model by Conde Ruiz and Profeta (2002) the rich would prefer no social security system at all, but in a majority voting equilibrium the rich would favor a small Beveridgean system versus a large Bismarckian one. The poor would prefer a Beveridgean system as long as it redistributes enough; the middle class would prefer a Bismarckian one.

[8] Disney and Whitehouse (2002) provide an excellent survey.

has the highest inequality among the elderly relative to all the other OECD countries. As Disney and Whitehouse (2002) note

the differences amongst countries are very large. For instance in the Unites States . . . the richest pensioners have incomes more than five times larger than the poorer pensioners while the ratio is 2.5 or less in several European countries and Australia. The Nordic countries have especially equal distribution of income amongst the elderly, with Sweden and Denmark showing the two lowest levels of inequality.

Income inequality among the elderly can be the result of two things: The inequality of accumulated earnings and the structure of pensions. Some of the inequality of the earning years is projected into retirement but the pension systems have a strong equalizing role. So, for instance, the United States has a more unequal distribution of income relative to continental Europe for two reasons: It has a more unequal distribution of wealth accumulated during working years, and the U.S. public pension system is less targeted toward reducing inequality than European systems. Note that especially for poor retirees, pensions are a very large fraction of total income after retirement, close to 100 percent in many cases. Therefore, the effect of the pension system on the distribution of income among the elderly is predominant, especially on the lower half of the income ladder.

2.4. Evidence from the Luxembourg income study

The Luxembourg income study is a study of the incomes over time of a representative sample of individuals in several OECD countries. It is widely used in both academic and policy circles.

2.4.1. Transfers

Tables 2.5 and 2.6 show the amount of transfers received by different quartiles of the income distribution in the countries upon which we focus: The United States, France, Germany, Sweden, and the United Kingdom. The first figure refers to a family of four (two adults two children), the second one refers to a family of two adults, no children. These observations are for 1995.

Table 2.5. Mean Social Transfers for Four-person Households (No Member Above 65) with Two Children, According to Pre-tax Income Distribution (as % of Mean Pre-tax Household Income)

	Obs.	Gini	All households			1st quartile			2nd quartile			3rd quartile			4th quartile		
			(1)	(2)	(3)	(1)	(2)	(3)	(1)	(2)	(3)	(1)	(2)	(3)	(1)	(2)	(3)
United States	4,945	0.84	3.8	0.8	0.5	11.1	2.6	0.7	2.7	0.6	0.6	1.2	0.2	0.4	1.1	0.0	0.4
France	1,259	0.45	18.6	0.4	4.0	33.1	0.3	9.5	17.1	0.3	2.9	12.9	0.7	1.5	10.9	0.3	1.6
Germany	687	0.51	10.6	0.2	1.7	23.0	0.6	4.9	9.4	0.1	1.3	7.1	0.0	0.6	4.9	0.0	0.4
Sweden	1,740	0.45	49.0	1.9	11.0	94.8	4.5	27.4	43.8	1.9	8.2	26.2	0.4	3.7	23.7	0.4	2.0
United Kingdom	738	0.46	12.4	0.1	0.2	26.7	0.3	0.6	9.0	0.0	0.2	7.3	0.0	0.1	6.6	0.0	0.2

Notes: (1) Mean total social transfers, including social retirement benefits and unemployment compensation; (2) Mean social retirement benefits; (3) Mean unemployment compensation.

Source: Authors' calculations based on data from the Luxembourg Income Study, Wave IV.

Table 2.6. Mean Social Transfers for All Households, According to Pre-tax Income Distribution (as % of Mean Pre-tax Household Income)

	Obs.	Gini	All households			1st quartile			2nd quartile			3rd quartile			4th quartile		
			(1)	(2)	(3)	(1)	(2)	(3)	(1)	(2)	(3)	(1)	(2)	(3)	(1)	(2)	(3)
United States	50,320	0.74	11.7	7.0	0.3	24.2	15.6	0.2	15.2	7.2	0.4	5.9	3.0	0.4	4.6	2.3	0.3
France	11,294	0.60	41.3	29.0	3.5	64.9	53.4	2.8	55.9	40.7	4.5	24.7	11.3	3.7	15.3	6.4	3.1
Germany	5,841	0.65	25.1	16.9	1.4	50.4	38.0	1.4	20.5	12.2	2.6	8.5	3.1	1.2	6.2	2.3	0.7
Sweden	16,260	0.50	44.5	22.3	6.7	61.2	31.3	8.1	58.1	36.2	8.7	29.8	10.0	6.1	19.1	5.0	2.6
United Kingdom	6,797	0.54	18.9	7.4	0.2	36.1	10.7	0.2	23.4	13.1	0.2	10.0	4.0	0.3	6.2	1.9	0.1

Notes: (1) mean total social transfers, including social retirement benefits and unemployment compensation; (2) mean social retirement benefits; (3) mean unemployment compensation.

Source: Authors' calculations based on data from the Luxembourg Income Study, Wave IV.

Note that we are computing the family income (regardless of whether one or two persons of the family work) with the average pre-tax income of a single person working. The figures show that a Swedish family in the first quartile of the income distribution of pre-tax income receives about 95 percent of the average pre-tax income; a French family receives about 33 percent, a German family about 23 percent, a British family about 26 percent, and an American family about 11 percent. A breakdown of various components of transfers shows that the Swedish number is "off the chart" due to a large value for unemployment compensation in families with one member working and the other one receiving unemployment subsidy. Note that in the mid-nineties unemployment was rapidly growing in Sweden and, in fact, the generous programs of unemployment compensation created a significant strain on the fiscal balance.

Table 2.6 shows the case of a four-person household with no dependent children. Note in this case the very high value for France, about 65 percent, even higher than Sweden (about 61 percent). In France, the particularly large value is due to a very generous pension system and provision for early retirement. Families without dependent children in fact include older couples with grown up children who take early retirement in their late fifties. Encouraging early retirement is often a way to circumvent constraints on layoffs. Even in this case, the U.S. poor in the first quartile receive less than their counterparts in the other countries.

2.4.2. Pensions

Table 2.7 shows the amount received by a single retiree as a percentage of the average pre-tax income of the average worker. Once again, the United States has the lowest social security payment for the poorest quartile, about 20.5 percent of average income. Sweden has about 63 percent, France 45 percent, Germany 44, and the United Kingdom about 32 percent.

Table 2.7. Mean Social Transfers for One-person Households (Age Above 65), According to Pre-tax Income Distribution (as % of Mean Pre-tax Household Income)

	Obs.	Gini	All households			1st quartile			2nd quartile			3rd quartile			4th quartile		
			(1)	(2)	(3)	(1)	(2)	(3)	(1)	(2)	(3)	(1)	(2)	(3)	(1)	(2)	(3)
United States	4,837	0.31	24.0	19.3	0.0	20.5	16.3	0.0	24.1	18.7	0.0	24.7	20.8	0.0	26.8	21.2	0.1
France	1,137	0.30	60.9	58.6	0.0	45.2	42.0	0.0	49.9	47.0	0.0	64.2	62.0	0.0	84.8	83.9	0.0
Germany	493	0.25	45.8	37.2	0.0	43.9	35.1	0.0	45.6	36.9	0.0	44.3	36.7	0.0	49.4	40.0	0.0
Sweden	2,268	0.16	64.3	52.2	0.0	63.1	37.6	0.0	62.6	47.3	0.0	64.8	58.4	0.0	66.5	64.0	0.2
United Kingdom	881	0.16	25.8	20.0	0.0	32.0	19.2	0.0	26.7	20.0	0.0	22.7	20.2	0.0	21.4	20.6	0.0

Notes: (1) Mean total social transfers, including social retirement benefits and unemployment compensation; (2) Mean social retirement benefits; (3) Mean unemployment compensation.

Source: Authors' calculations based on data from the Luxembourg Income Study, Wave IV.

2.5. Fiscal revenues

Fiscal systems in OECD countries tend to be rather complex and differ in many parameters. Perhaps the same argument used for pension systems applies here. Some (or much of) the complexity is unnecessary and it is used to make it easier to introduce favors for special constituencies in the tax code. Calls for simplification of the tax system are common in many countries on both sides of the Atlantic.

For our purposes, the multidimensional nature of fiscal systems makes it hard to come up with a synthetic number that compares how much the rich pay relative to the poor in different countries. In a recent discussion of this issue Wagstaff et al. (1999) argued that even with respect to the income tax, "next to nothing" is known about the effect of personal income tax in equalizing the after tax distribution of income. On top of this, the progressivity of income tax brackets is only one aspect of the question. How capital accumulation is taxed, the structure of value added taxes on different goods, and the share of different forms of taxation are some of the other parameters. An appropriate measure of the taxation of capital for one country is often the subject of an entire research paper. Here we can only scratch the surface.

First of all, total tax revenues in the United States are smaller than in European countries, as can be gathered from Table 2.8; leaving aside deficits which come and go, spending approximately equals revenues. If the United States had the same degree of progressivity as European countries, and keeping as given that the U.S. tax levels are lower, less redistribution is obtained in the United States through the tax system. Thus, in order to reverse this ranking, the tax code in the United States would have to be much more progressive than in Europe, which is not the case.

Table 2.8 also summarizes the composition of government revenue in Europe and the United States. The most striking differences are in social security contributions and taxes on goods and services. Note, however, that there are important differences in the structure of taxation even within Europe.[9]

---

[9] In fact, the harmonization of tax structures across members is a hotly debated issue within the European Union.

Table 2.8. Composition of General Government Revenue (as % of GDP) in 2000

Country	Tax revenue							Nontax revenue[b]
	Total	Direct taxes			Social security contributions[a]	Property income	Goods and services	
		Total	Households	Businesses				
United States	31.0	15.1	12.4	2.8	7.1	1.0	7.7	6.0
Continental Europe[c]	46.7	15.9	12.5	3.8	15.1	1.7	14.1	5.0
France	47.4	12.2	9.4	2.9	19.1	0.6	15.5	4.3
Germany	44.4	12.5	10.7	1.7	19.3	0.5	12.0	9.1
Sweden	56.3	22.2	19.1	3.1	16.4	3.2	14.5	5.9
United Kingdom	38.7	16.6	12.9	3.7	7.8	0.5	13.8	3.3

Notes:

[a] Includes other current transfers.

[b] Data are for 1997.

[c] Simple average for Austria, Belgium, Denmark, Finland, France, Germany, Greece, Italy, Netherlands, Norway, Portugal, Spain, and Sweden.

Source: Authors' calculations based on data from OECD Economic Outlook Database (No. 71, Vol. 2002) and OECD Revenue Statistics (Vol. 2002).

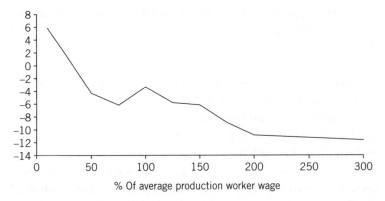

Fig. 2.2. Difference in Marginal Tax Rates, in %, Between the U.S. and EU15 (Excluding Denmark). The Difference Equals the U.S. Marginal Tax Rate Minus the Unweighted Average European Marginal Rate for Each Income Class

Our concern here is with the tax burden of the rich relative to that of the poor. A simple attempt is made in Fig. 2.2, which plots the difference between assembled data on different income tax brackets in the United States versus a European average.[10] Thus, for a given level of income, a positive value in the figure implies that the marginal tax rate in the United States exceeds the European average, and a negative value indicates the opposite. The figures show that marginal tax rates in the United States are higher than in Europe for low levels of income (up to about 50 percent of the average worker's wage) and lower for higher levels of income. Also, the difference between the United States and Europe becomes larger in absolute value as income rises. In short, the income tax system is more progressive in Europe than in the United States.[11]

---

[10] Note that these calculations were performed before the tax cut implemented by the George W. Bush administration, which has made the tax code even less progressive in the United States.

[11] In other countries with federal systems, such as Germany, the structure of taxation also entails automatic redistribution from richer to poorer regions. This is not so, or at least not to the same extent, across United States. Some geographical redistribution does, however, occur within school districts in the United States. See Oates (1999) and the references cited therein.

Wagstaff et al. (1999) examine personal income tax in several OECD countries and ask the question whether this tax can reverse the ranking of countries in terms of pre- and post-tax inequality. That is, take the United States with a relatively unequal pre-tax distribution of income. Does the United States have more progressive income taxes than other countries so that the after tax distribution of income in the United States is actually less unequal than the comparable distribution in other countries? The answer is no. These authors show that with the exception of France and Italy, countries do not switch rank when comparing pre-income tax to post-income tax distribution of income. So, the United States has a more unequal distribution of income than continental European countries, both pre- and post-taxes. In fact, the United States has a personal income tax which is among the least progressive, based upon several indexes of progressivity.

2.6. The regulatory environment

2.6.1. Labor market regulation

Labor regulations such as those that set a minimum wage may keep real wages higher than they would be otherwise.[12] Table 2.9 summarizes the available data on minimum wages in Europe and the United States. The data are from several different sources, but all tell a very similar story. In the European Union, the minimum wage is 53 percent of the average wage, against 39 percent in the United States. In France, the minimum wage is around 65 percent of the average manufacturing wage, compared with 36 percent in the United States.

Table 2.10 reports various other measures of labor market regulation, using data assembled by Stephen Nickell and Richard Layard.[13] Although a fair amount of variation is observed within Europe, on all measures the United States scores lower than the

---

[12] One may argue, correctly, that in many cases labor regulations end up redistributing in favor of the unionized or otherwise "protected" segment of the labor force, at the expense of other workers.

[13] Nickell and Layard (1999); Nickell (1997).

Table 2.9. Minimum Wages in the United States and Europe

	Ratio of minimum to average wage (Percentages)	Ratio to mean hourly pay in manufacturing (Percentages)	Ratio to mean hourly pay in manufacturing (Percentages)	Ratio to mean hourly pay in manufacturing (Percentages)
Source	OECD Jobs Study 1994[a]	OECD[b]	Eurostat[c]	Summary index[d]
Period/year	1991–4	end-1997	2001	1991–2001
France	0.50	0.68	0.63	0.63
Germany	0.55	—	—	0.55
Sweden	0.52	—	—	0.52
United Kingdom	0.40		0.44	0.44
European Union	0.53	0.56	0.53	0.55
United States	0.39	0.36	0.34	0.34

Notes:

[a] Reported from Nickell and Layard (1999), using OECD Jobs Study (1994). European Union average: Austria, Belgium, Germany, Finland, France, Germany, Ireland, Italy, Netherlands, Portugal, Spain, Sweden, United Kingdom.

[b] Employment Outlook, 1999. European Union average: Belgium, France, Greece, Luxembourg, Netherlands, Portugal, Spain.

[c] European Union average: Belgium, France, Greece, Ireland, Luxembourg, Netherlands, Portugal, Spain, United Kingdom.

[d] This index reports the most recent measure.

Table 2.10. Labor Markets in the United States and in Europe

Country	Labor standards 1985–93[b]	Employment protection 1990[c]	Minimum annual leave (weeks) 1992	Benefit replacement ratio (%) 1989–94	Benefit duration (years) 1989–94
France	6	14	5	57	3
Germany	6	15	3	63	4
Sweden	7	13	5	80	1.2
United Kingdom	0	7	0	38	4
European Union[a]	4.8	13.5	3.8	58.7	2.6
United States	0	1	0	50	0.5

Note:

[a] Austria, Belgium, Denmark, Finland, France, Germany, Ireland, Italy, Netherlands, Portugal, Spain, Sweden, and United Kingdom.

[b] Index that combines several measures of labor market regulation and ranges from 0 to 10 with 10 the maximum.

[c] Measure the strength of legal restrictions on hiring and firing and ranges from 0 to 20 with 20 the maximum.

Source: Nickell and Layard (1999) and Nickell (1997).

European average. The first column of the table reports an index compiled by the OECD that combines several aspects of legislation designed to protect workers in the workplace (see Appendix). The minimum score (representing the least protection) is 0 and the maximum is 10. The second column reports an index of employment protection (that is, restrictions on the ability of enterprises to terminate employees), with 20 indicating the strictest protection. On the first measure, the United States has a score of 0, and on the second, a score of 1. The next three columns report measures of minimum annual leave and the level and duration of unemployment compensation. On all three measures, the U.S. score is below that of the European Union as a whole and below that of any of the individual European countries listed (except that the U.K. level of unemployment compensation is lower).

Scores on these measures for a group of non-European, non-U.S. OECD countries (Australia, Canada, Japan, and New Zealand; data not shown) lie somewhere in between those of the United States and continental Europe. Overall, however, the United States and Europe appear to be polar extremes.

Labor market regulation does not necessarily benefit the very poor. In fact, a large literature, which we cannot even begin to review, suggests that the insiders, that is, union members in large industries, have benefited from labor market regulations, while the outsiders, often poorer than insiders, are disadvantaged. One can also argue that these regulations create or at least prolong unemployment, which may be also associated with increasing inequality. Certainly, the rhetoric of European Unions in support of labor market regulation suggests that they defend the underprovided workers against the business community, but this may just be precisely, rhetoric. There is in fact an increasing awareness in Europe that these labor market regulations, perhaps originally introduced with a sincere aim of protecting the disadvantaged, have produced more harm than good. For our purposes, one may argue that labor market regulations tend to redistribute in favor of labor, but not necessarily in favor of the poorest and least protected part of the labor force.

2.6.2. Goods market regulation

The regulation of goods markets such as entry barriers, price controls, vertical integration, and public ownership has complex distributional consequences, as not all benefits flow from the rich to the poor. In fact, as noted by Joskow and Rose (1989) after an extensive survey of the literature, our understanding of the distributional consequences of several aspects of regulatory policy is very limited. The traditional view of regulation holds that regulation is necessary to correct for market imperfection, such as natural monopolies. This is only part of the story. Another important part is given by the "public choice" approach (Becker 1983) in which regulators react to lobbying efforts, and the resulting regulation has very little to do with efficiency. Recent results by Djankov et al. (2002) on the regulation of entry are consistent with a view that regulation is imposed by government to extract rents.

Many aspects of regulation protect insiders versus outsiders (see Blanchard and Giavazzi 2003, for a recent formalization); therefore, the distributional consequences in a rich–poor dimension are unclear. Some aspects of regulation, such as public ownership, price controls, etc. are, at least in the intention of the regulators, designed to protect less-well-off consumers and provide some services at under market cost. An example is public transportation, used proportionally more by the poor, in which prices are below average costs and deficits of this sector are covered by taxes (paid disproportionately by the rich). Regulation of other utilities has a motivation of ensuring equal prices for all consumers regardless of their location.

In any event, the U.S. economy has always been much less regulated than European economies (with the exception of the United Kingdom). In addition, the recent wave of deregulation and regulatory reform started much earlier in the United States and has gone much farther. Nicoletti, Scarpetta, and Boyland (2001) have constructed the largest available data set of detailed information about regulation in OECD countries. This data set includes twenty-one OECD countries (Australia, Austria, Belgium, Canada, Switzerland, Germany, Denmark, Spain, Finland, France, Portugal, the United Kingdom, Greece, Ireland, Italy, Japan, the Netherlands, Norway,

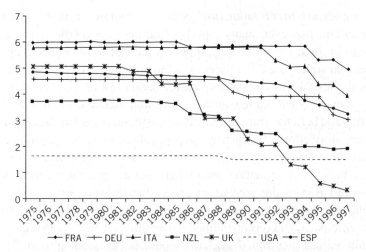

Fig. 2.3. Public Ownership in Selected Countries During 1975–97

Sweden, the United States, and New Zealand), seven sectors (airlines, road freight, railways, telecommunications, post, electricity, and gas) and five regulation dimensions (barriers to entry, vertical integration, price controls, market structure, and public ownership).[14]

Figure 2.3 plots an aggregate measure of this index for selected countries between 1975 and 1997 in the horizontal and vertical axis respectively.[15] The United States and to a lesser extent the United Kingdom are the least regulated countries both at the beginning and at the end of the sample. Countries like France, Italy, and Greece are among the most regulated both at the beginning and at the end.

2.6.3. Regulation: Summing up

The U.S. economy is much less regulated than European economies, both in the labor and in the goods markets. Whether or not this

[14] These data are also used in Alesina et al. (2002) who establish a string negative effect of regulation on private investment. Their interpretation is that deregulation opens up profit opportunities for new entrants.

[15] This figure is reproduced from Alesina et al. (2002). Since not all data for every sector and every year are available for every country, this figure aggregates the seven sectors into three, utilities, communications, and transportation.

complex web of regulations makes the very poor better off is an open question. However, many aspects of European regulations are, at least in the minds of the legislators, an attempt to protect workers, and, in some cases, the users of public utilities. The ideology that underlies this heavy emphasis on regulation in Europe is the view that markets left alone would produce undesirable distributions of costs and benefits; thus, in a sense, a redistributive goal underlies the regulatory efforts. In practice, the political economy of regulation is such that over-protected groups and minorities often reap many of the benefits of regulation even when they are not the weakest or poorest part of the population. Heavy beneficiaries often include old and unionized workers, over their younger and less-unionized counterparts, and certain industries over others. Thus, not all regulation redistributes from the rich to the poor, but the ideology underlying regulation is one that sees a need to correct with legislation the allocation of resources determined by unregulated markets.

2.7. Charity as a private form of redistribution

The preceding evidence makes it clear that European countries provide more public welfare than the United States. But Americans engage in more private provision of welfare (i.e. charity) than Europeans. We use the World Values Survey to calculate the share of adults in each of several European countries who are members of charitable organizations. Although membership in charitable organizations is an imperfect measure of the time contribution to charity (it does not measure the intensity of involvement), it is one of the best measures available. In the United States, 11 percent of respondents say that they participated in a charitable group over the last year; the average for European countries in the survey is 4 percent. The European country with the highest proportion of membership in private charities is the Netherlands, with almost 9 percent of respondents saying that they participate. At the opposite end of the spectrum is Denmark, where 2 percent of individuals claim to have participated in these activities.

The U.K. National Council for Volunteer Organizations and the not-for-profit group United for a Fair Economy document that charitable contributions in the United States totaled $190 billion in 2000, or $691 a person. This compares with reported contributions per capita of $141 in the United Kingdom and $57 for Europe as a whole. Notably, a large fraction of American donors make charitable contributions even though they take only the standard deduction on their income taxes.[16] This means that for many Americans, contributions are not being driven only by the tax deductibility of charitable donations. In any case, in many countries in Europe charitable contributions are also partially deductible. Skocpol, Ganz, and Hunson (2000) document the national coverage of the many U.S. volunteer groups who provide a rich variety of forms of assistance.[17] In general, in fact, Americans show a remarkable tendency to participate in a variety of social entities and social groups, as documented and studied by Alesina and La Ferrara (2000). According to the General Social Survey, a staggering 71 percent of Americans are members of at least one social organization.[18]

These results suggest, but hardly prove, two implications. First, public provision of welfare (in Europe) in part crowds out private charity. As argued by Glaeser and Shleifer (2001), if government transfers to particular individuals fall as private donations rise, these transfers will reduce the incentive for private charity. Secondly, Europe's more generous provision of welfare does not stem from a greater innate endowment of altruism in Europe. In fact, it may be the case that Americans prefer private charity to public welfare because the former may be better targeted to the "deserving poor." That is, Americans (more so than Europeans) may feel that the

---

[16] The tax code in the United States allows the tax payer to choose the standard deduction in a fixed amount or to itemize deductions. Only by itemizing deductions (for health expenses, charity, etc.) can one deduct the full amount for charitable contributions.

[17] Putman (2000) argues that civic voluntarism has declined in the Untied States; we do not address this decline here. We focus on the differences across countries, not over time.

[18] The General Social Survey is a widely used survey conducted on a large random sample of Americans.

generic poor do not deserve public support, but certain poor people reached by certain charities may be more deserving. These considerations are especially relevant when in Chapter 7 we return to the question of moral attitudes toward poverty on both sides of the Atlantic.

2.8. Has it worked?

There is no doubt that European countries make a much larger effort to protect the poor and redistribute from rich to poor than the United States. Is this redistributive effort in Europe successful? What are its economic costs?

These are *not* the questions we ask here. A comparison of the relative efficacy of the various systems is beyond our scope except in one sense. If, despite all the effort, income inequality were actually lower in the U.S. than in Europe, then we might conclude that the United States actually redistributes *more* despite having a smaller welfare state simply because the U.S. welfare state is much more efficient. This is not the case; income inequality both before and especially after taxes is higher in the United States. Despite various shortcomings of the welfare state in Europe, it certainly has achieved a certain degree of equalization of income. However, at what cost and whether the efficiency loss is worth this cost, is a very politically charged issue.

Tanzi and Schuknecht (2000) argue in a recent study of the growth of government that averages of several key social indicators such as health measures, life expectancy, and educational achievement are not that different between countries with a large government like in continental Europe and countries with a small government like in the United States. On the other hand, a large body of research has shown that after-tax income inequality is lower in countries with larger governments and, in particular, in countries with higher social spending.[19] Comparing inequality and poverty rates across countries is extremely difficult. However, it is quite clear that after-tax income inequality is relatively low in the Nordic countries, intermediate in

---

[19] See, for instance, Atkinson (1995).

central and southern Europe, higher in the United Kingdom, and higher still in the United States.[20]

When one compares the distribution of disposable income across population deciles in the United States and Europe, a striking and interesting difference is the much lower proportion of income accruing to the lowest decile in the United States. That is, the greater inequality in the United States does not stem from the top decile being particularly wealthy relative to the median, so much as from the bottom decile being particularly poor. For instance, in the 1980s the average income among the lowest decile was about one-third of the median in the United States, compared with more than 55 percent in many European countries, including France, and more than 60 percent in several Nordic countries.[21] Another way of looking at this is to compute the fraction of the population with incomes below 50 percent of the median. (Many European countries use this as a definition of the poverty line.) Depending on the criteria used, this fraction was around 17–18 percent in the United States in the 1980s, against values of 5–8 percent in Sweden and Germany.[22] In the 1990s, income inequality increased sharply in the United Kingdom and somewhat less sharply in the United States. In the continental European countries, changes in income inequality in the last decade were smaller. It would appear that, because of a smaller emphasis on policies that redistribute toward the poor, the bottom decile of the income ladder in the United States is less well off than the bottom decile in European countries. The American poor are really poor.

It should be clear, however, that this inverse relationship between inequality and the size of government is not monotonic. That is, certain countries are much more successful than others in reducing inequality for a given amount of social spending: The welfare state in different countries has had different degrees of success in reaching the truly needy. One problem is that, in certain countries (Italy being a perfect example), welfare spending is too biased in favor of pensions (see Boeri and Perotti 2002).

---

[20] This picture emerges, for instance, from the detailed studies by Atkinson (1995).
[21] Atkinson (1995: 49–51). [22] Atkinson (1995: 90).

The discussion of the economic costs of the welfare state is an extremely complex and ideologically charged area of research, and it is not our goal here. Assar Lindbeck provides an excellent and exhaustive discussion of this issue for Sweden.[23] His conclusion is that in the long run the trade-off between redistribution and growth is rather steep. In 1970, before the explosion of its welfare state, Sweden had an income per capita equivalent to 115 percent of that in the average OECD country—the fourth highest of all. By 1995, however, Sweden's income per capita was only 95 percent of the OECD average, and Sweden had fallen to sixteenth place. Lindbeck argues that the effect of the welfare state is very subtle and may take generations to show up, but then it is difficult to change. According to him, excessive welfare spending affects social norms, attitudes toward work and leisure, and creates a culture of dependency.

One may wonder whether the trade-off is so steep at levels of social protection less extreme than Sweden's. Also, other countries with extended welfare states have not done as poorly as Sweden. In addition, certain aspects of redistributive policies, such as a well-functioning public education system, may foster human capital accumulation. A related issue is the cost in terms of employment formation and growth of labor protection. In one of the most recent and balanced studies, Blanchard and Wolfers (2000) show how heavy labor regulation may make unemployment spells caused by economic shocks much longer. Nicoletti and Scarpetta (2002) find that good market regulation decrease productivity growth in OECD economies. Bassanini and Ernst (2002) find a negative effect of regulation on R&D. Alesina, Ardagna, Nicoletti, and Schiantarelli (2005) show that several aspects of goods market regulation negatively affect private investment.

2.9. Conclusions

European countries have adopted a wide range of policies that are meant to redistribute income from the rich to the poor. In the United

___

[23] Lindbeck (1997).

States, this effort is more limited. While certain categories (say, single mothers or the old) are not forgotten by the American legislator, if one were to be born poor, one would choose to be born in Europe, especially if risk averse.

Not all government activities are designed to redistribute from the rich to the poor, but certain public policies end up creating unintended redistributive flows, which are not well targeted. Distortions, mistargeting, and the growth of overprotected minorities (public employees, certain retirees, and union members) are common even in relatively well functioning welfare states. Despite all these caveats, it is clear that the poor are better treated in Europe than in the United States.

This different policy stand is not a recent phenomenon. From the very beginning of the development of the modern welfare state, the United States has adopted a much more limited interventionist stance on redistributive policies. Why? This is the question to which we turn in the remainder of this book.

Appendix: Data sources

Revenue and expenditure tables, including historical data and figures

All reported measures are for general government. Historical data are provided by both Tanzi and Schuknecht (2000) for the 1870–1960 period and the OECD Economic Outlook Database for the 1960–98 period. Current data are extracted from the OECD Economic Outlook Database, the Revenue Statistics Database, and the Social Expenditure Database.

OECD Economic Outlook Database (No. 71, Vol. 2002, Release 01), June 2002.

OECD Revenue Statistics (Vol. 2002).

OECD Social Expenditure Database 1980–1998 (3rd edn.), 2001.

Social protection programs

The comparative figures and descriptions of social security systems in Germany, Sweden, and the United States were provided by publications from the German and U.S. Social Security administrations, and by comparative charts published by both the U.S. Social Security Administration and the MISSOC, an E.U. administration gathering information on the social security systems of the E.U. member countries. We report figures on family benefits, healthcare, sickness benefits, unemployment benefits, disability benefits, and social assistance. Information on old age and survivors' pensions was also available but left aside for the purpose of the chapter.

Federal Ministry of Labour and Social Affairs, Germany, Social Security at a Glance, 2001.

MISSOC (Mutual Information System on Social Protection in the E.U. Member States and the EEA), Social Security and Social Integration, Comparative Tables on Social Protection in the Member States, 2000.

Social Security Administration, Office of Research, Evaluation, and Statistics, Social Security Programs in the United States, July 1997.

Social Security Administration, Office of Research, Evaluation, and Statistics, Social Security Programs Throughout the World, 1999.

Evidence from the Luxembourg Income Study

All charts are based on data from Wave IV of the Luxembourg Income Study. The national surveys were conducted in 1994 for France and Germany, 1995 for Sweden and the United Kingdom, and 1997 for the United States. Mean pre-tax household income is the sum of wages, salaries, income derived from self-employment, property income, private pensions, and public sector pensions. We define total social transfers as the sum of social retirement and veterans' benefits, unemployment compensation, child or family allowances, sick pay and accident pay, disability payments, maternity payments, all other forms of social insurance, means-tested cash benefits, and near-cash benefits.

Minimum wages table

The second and third columns of Table 2.9 report measures of minimum wages for countries that have national or statutory minimum wages. The first column, reported from Nickell and Layard (1999), adds minimum wages for Germany and Sweden, which have sectoral minimum wages, but no minimum wage policy.

Eurostat, Minimum Wages in the European Union, 2001.

OECD, Employment Outlook, 2000.

OECD, Main Economic Indicators, April 2001.

Tax rates figure: Refer to Figure 2.2

The figure is based on comparative data published by the OECD. For each country, the tax rate schedule is translated in terms of average production worker earnings. Only central government taxes are taken into account; regional or local taxes, as well as social security contributions, are omitted.

OECD, Taxing Wages, 2001.

Labor market chart: Refer to Table 2.10

The reported rigidity indices are all from Nickell (1997) and Nickell and Layard (1999), and are interpreted as follows:

1. Labor standards: index produced by the OECD (OECD Employment Outlook 1994, and extended by Nickell and Layard 1999) and referring to the strength of the legislation on five different aspects of the labor markets (working hours, fixed-term contracts, employment protection, minimum wages, and employees' representation rights). Each country is scored from 0 (no legislation) to 2 (strict legislation) for each measure. Maximum score: 10.
2. Employment protection: OECD index (OECD Jobs Study 1994) referring to the legal framework concerning hiring and firing. Maximum value: 20, being the value attributed to the strictest legal provisions.

3. Minimum annual leave: (OECD Jobs Study 1994), in addition to public holidays.
4. Benefit replacement ratio: (U.S. Social Security Administration, Social Security Programs Throughout the World, 1999), share of income replaced by unemployment benefits.
5. Benefit duration: same sources.

Nickell (1997), Nickell and Layard (1999).

Table 2.4: Construction

Assumptions

1. Pensions calculated for a single male who retired at the minimum retirement age in the country under consideration.
2. Worker had pension coverage/enrollment in all his working years.

France

Pension = (Public Flat Rate Pension = 41,196 FF in 1994) + (.5*(no. of quarters of coverage)) + (Contribution Pension from AGIRC/ARRCO)

1. No. of working years = 44 years = 176 quarters.
2. Pension rate = .5 because no. of years of coverage > 37.5 years.
3. Contribution Pension = (total no. of points accumulated by retirement) * (value of a point in retirement year).

   No. of points = value of annual contributions (6–8% of income)/reference wage.

   In 1993, the following numbers apply for ARRCO and AGIRC:

	ARRCO	AGIRC
Contractual contribution rate (% of gross wages)	5	13
Reference Wage (FF)	21.18	19.69
Value of a point (FF)	2.24	2.36

Germany

Pension = (Pensionable Earnings Points) * (RAF) * (AR = current pension value) − (Contributions to Health and Nursing Insurance)

1. Retirement age = 65 years.
2. No. of working years = 44 years.
3. For calculation of pensionable earnings points = Σ (individual earnings in year i) / (average earnings for year i) where i = each year of participation in the scheme. Max. pensionable earnings is DM 102,000 (West Germany) and DM 86,000 (East Germany).
4. Income for all pensionable income years = Wage in Average Annual Wage Column subject to upper limit in 3.
5. Average Wage for each pensionable income year = Average Monthly Earnings of Full Time Employees in Industry and Services in 1995 = 2,426 DM per month.
6. Current pension value in 1998 used. DM 47.65 for West Germany and DM 40.87 for East Germany.
7. Contributions to Health and Nursing Insurance = contribution rate determined each year by the Ministry of Health and Welfare. For 1999, about 5.32% (E), 6.39% (W). Calculated from data in "The German Pension System – Status Quo and Reform Options" by Bert Rürup.

Sweden

Pension = (Basic Pension = \$4,710.72 per year in 1995) + ATP

1. Retirement age = 65 years.
2. Number of working years = 44 years.
3. Basic Amount (BA) = SEK 34,986 = \$4,907 per year in 1995.
4. ATP = 60%(Average Points, max = 6.5)*(max (N/30, 1))*BA Average Points = (pension rights income)$_i$/(BA $_i$) i = year.
5. Pension rights income = income recorded in the tax return including all social insurance.
6. N = no. of years person has recorded a pension rights income > 0
7. ATP was not low, so no Special Supplement.

United Kingdom

Pension = (Basic Pension in 1996 = £61.15 per week) + SERPS

1. Retirement age = 65 years.
2. Number of working years = 44 years.

3. SERPS = 25% (average income over the best 20 years of working life).
4. Average income over the best 20 years of working life = Wage in Average Annual Wage Column.
5. No minimum income guarantee pension taken into account because pension > minimum income guarantee pension.

United States

Pension = (PIA (Primary Insurance Amount) applied to AIME = 0.9(first \$426) + 0.32(next \$2141) + 0.15(amount of income > \$2567)) + SSI

1. Retirement age = 65 years.
2. Number of working years = 44 years.
3. Assets < \$2000 (excluding essentials life insurance, burial plots, homes etc.).
4. SSI in 1995: First \$20.00 of OASDI is excluded.
   (i) For an individual with only OASDI income = \$512 − (OASDI monthly income − 20).
   (ii) For an individual with monthly earnings = \$512 − (512 − 20 − 65)/2.
5. AIME (Average Indexed Monthly Earning) = 1.0*(average monthly earning for the 35 best years).

Dave is
HETERO
sexual

Chapter 3

Economic Explanations

3.1. Introduction

We begin our search for answers by examining what we call "economic" explanations of the U.S.–Europe difference in redistributive policies. Clearly, the labeling of different explanations as, say, economic in this chapter and political in the following two is somewhat arbitrary. Redistribution of income by means of taxes, transfers, and other means is a policy measure, and therefore is a result of the politico-economic process. Our labeling is an expositional device meant to indicate that in this chapter we focus on explanations in which institutional features are kept at a minimum and the weight of the explanation is on economic variables. Other groupings are possible but we find this one especially useful for our purposes.

One of the most widely cited explanations for differences in redistributive efforts is the degree of pre-tax income inequality, due to the influential work by Romer (1975) and Meltzer and Richards (1981) which has recently received renewed attention. According to this view, the more unequal is the pre-tax distribution of income, the higher is the demand and the political pressure for redistribution.[1]

---

[1] See Peltzman (1980) for a contrasting view.

In fact, more inequality in these models means that more individuals are below the average income and should vote in favor of taxing those above average. Therefore, this approach implies that there is more redistribution in Europe because the pre-tax distribution of income is more unequal in Europe than in the United States. As we will see this is *not* the case. However, this simple model is useful because it sets the stage to discuss other important points, such as the role of income mobility.

Redistributive policies tend to be long lasting, so when an individual evaluates his net gain from such policies he takes into account not only his current position in the income ladder but also his future position. That is, an individual evaluates his preferences for redistribution not only based upon his current income but also in terms of his lifetime income potential. Therefore, the degree of income mobility (up and down) of various individuals affects their preferences for redistributive schemes. In other words, the degree and nature of income mobility in society is related to the aggregate preference for redistribution. Benabou and Ok (2001) show how to modify the basic Meltzer and Richards model by taking into consideration income mobility and future income prospects, an issue taken up empirically by Alesina and La Ferrara (2005) among others.

A related explanation concerns the degree of income uncertainty. The more uncertain the path of one's future income, given risk aversion, the more one would favor redistributive schemes to be protected in case of misfortune. Rodrik (1998) and Cameron (1978) argue that openness to the world economy increases income uncertainty and therefore requires larger redistributive schemes. Thus, openness to trade and terms of trade shocks would explain, according to this author, the cross-country differences in the amount of redistribution.

Finally, redistributive schemes require the collection of tax revenues. The more costlier it is in terms of economic distortions to collect taxes, the more economically costlier are redistributive schemes. Becker and Mulligan (2003) argue that differences in the degree of efficacy of alternative tax systems explain differing levels of taxation. The more efficient the tax system, the more revenue raised by the government.

In the end, we conclude that one cannot explain much of the difference in the degree of redistribution across countries based upon any or all of the above explanations. Without going more deeply into politics, comparative institutional analysis, the sociological aspect of race relations, and behavioral variables, one cannot make much progress in answering the question that we are studying.

3.2. The pre-tax distribution of income

3.2.1. The Romer/Meltzer–Richards model

The celebrated model by Romer (1975) and Meltzer and Richards (1981) analyzes a very simple redistributive scheme. The tax instrument is a proportional income tax in a model where different individuals have different abilities, and thus income, and choose to work different amounts. All the tax revenues are redistributed lump sum (i.e. in equal amount) to everyone. Therefore, by assumption, everybody gets the same transfer, which is equal to total tax revenues divided by the number of people in the population: This amount equals the taxes paid by the voter with average income.

In order to understand the workings of the model, consider the median voter, which is the voter with fifty percent of the others above and below him on the ability and income ladders. In all real world distributions, the median voter is poorer than the average voter, namely the voter with average income and paying the average tax. Since the median voter is poorer than the voter paying the average tax, he will favor a positive tax rate. In fact, median voter transfers are equal to the average tax paid by the average voter. Since the taxes paid by the median voter are lower, he receives a positive net transfer (i.e. transfers minus taxes paid are greater than zero). All the voters poorer than the median would like at least the tax rate desired by the median voter, in fact they would prefer an even higher one.

By the celebrated "median voter theorem" with the one-person, one-vote rule, the policy that is adopted is the one most preferred by the median voter, that is, the policy with a positive tax rate and positive transfers. In addition, the poorer the median voter is relative to the average-income voter, the larger the tax rate preferred by the median, because the difference between the tax paid by the median and the transfer received is larger.[2]

The implication of this model is that the lower the income of the median voter relative to the income of the average voter, the higher the level of taxation and redistribution. Obviously the model is a drastic simplification of a more complex reality, but it has a very clear and suggestive message: In a democracy, the larger the fraction of the voters who are very poor relative to average, the stronger the support for redistributive policies.

The evidence. The implication of the model described above for our question is that in Europe, there is more redistribution because pre-tax income inequality is higher in Europe than in the United States. So, the question is: Is pre-tax income inequality in the United States lower than in Europe? The answer is a resounding no.

A commonly used source on before-tax income inequality is the database compiled by Deininger and Squire (1996). A standard measure of distribution of income is the Gini coefficient, a measure increasing in inequality. The Gini coefficient measured on pre-tax income for the United States is 38.5, whereas the average for European countries is 29.1, which means that Europe has lower before-tax inequality. The United Kingdom has the most income inequality in the European sample, but its Gini coefficient is 32.3, still lower than the U.S. value. In the United States, the top 20 percent of income earners take home 43.5 percent of before-tax dollars. In Europe on average, the top quintile earns 37.1 percent of before-tax income, and in no European country does the top quintile earn more than 41 percent. It seems clear that the United States has more before-tax inequality than Europe and a more skewed income distribution.

More generally, a recent vast literature has studied whether in a large sample of countries this relationship between pre-tax income inequality and redistribution holds. The most detailed

---

[2] The model assumes realistically that there are some costs (i.e. distortions) in raising tax rates. Otherwise, the median would always expropriate from the average voter and set the tax rate equal to 1. Also, the median will never choose a tax rate above the top of the Laffer curve (i.e. a tax rate that is so high that reducing it increases revenues).

empirical study in this area is the one by Perotti (1996). He considers several measures of redistributive efforts in a cross-section of countries and relates them to a measure of inequality and finds little relationship between the two. Also, an indirect way of testing this proposition is to argue that inequality should lead to more redistribution in more democratic countries, since the mechanism linking inequality and redistribution is based upon voting. Again, the results on this point are inconclusive.[3]

3.2.2. Discussion

There are three possible explanations for the apparent failure of before-tax inequality, as measured by the Gini coefficient, to lead to more redistribution.

First, in countries with greater income inequality, the poor may not have enough political influence and hence may not be able to extract much redistribution from the rich. That is, such countries may de facto lack a one-person, one-vote rule, which underlies the models' results, but instead have something closer to a de facto one-dollar, one-vote rule. We devote much space below to a discussion of the political determinants of redistribution, and the political power of the poor is a critical factor.

Second, different countries may use different means to redistribute income, so in cross-country regressions focusing on one instrument at a time, this complexity may be lost. This is a serious consideration for large cross-country studies, but it does not seem to be of much concern for us since looking at just about any measure of redistributive effort, the United States does less than Europe.

Third, the measured before-tax Gini coefficient is a poor indicator of before-tax inequality, because a host of other policies (in addition to the tax system) affect inequality in the United States. More

---

[3] Alesina and Rodrik (1994) and Persson and Tabellini (1994) among others have argued that more inequality leads to lower growth based on this tax transfer mechanism. However, they present only indirect evidence linking inequality to growth. Perotti (1996) and Barro (2000) show that the relationship between inequality and growth holds only for poorer countries and does not apply to OECD economies.

generally, although these numbers are before-tax, redistribution may nonetheless have taken place in many ways before earnings occur at all (e.g. through education). Indeed, lower before-tax income inequality may be yet another example of the effects of European redistribution. This last objection does not seem particularly strong. Other measures of income inequality are correlated with the Gini index. Also casual evidence on minimum wages and executive compensation discussed above suggests that it is very unlikely to find any reasonable measure of income inequality according to which the United States is less unequal than continental Europe.

The bottom line is that as an explanation of the United States versus Europe comparison, the income inequality argument fails. Whether or not this theory does better for other countries outside the OECD group remains to be seen, but this approach does not help us much.

3.3. Social mobility and income uncertainty

3.3.1. Prospects of upward mobility: Theory

Consider, again, a voter in the Romer/Meltzer–Richards model discussed above. Also, note that the redistributive "stance" of any given country is relatively invariant in the short to medium run. Therefore, the preferences of the voter should take into account his future income prospects and their future position on the income ladder. That is, one person may be poor today, but still opposes redistributive schemes if he feels that soon in the future he will be rich. On the other hand, somebody wealthy today may favor redistributive policies if he expects to be poor tomorrow. In fact, Alesina and La Ferrara (2005) using U.S. data find considerable support for the effect of future income prospects on individual preferences for redistribution, as measured by answers to survey questions. Holding current income constant, aversion to redistributive policies is increasing with expected future income and expected position in the income ladder.[4]

---

[4] See Alesina and La Ferrara (2005) also for a summary of previous results related to these points.

But, what do these effects on individual preferences imply for the determination of aggregate social preferences for redistribution in this model? For a given level of income of the median and average voter, the more favorable the upper-income prospects of the median voter, the lower the social demand for redistribution. That is, the more likely it is that the lower middle class will close the gap, the lower the demand for government intervention in redistributive matters.

Obviously, the median voter can, in general, move up or down and risk aversion tends to make the median voter more concerned with downward movements. Benabou and Ok (2001) show that under certain conditions on expected income prospects, even a risk averse median voter who can move both up and down will be less favorable to redistribution when the social mobility of income of voters close to the median is larger.

The implication of this argument for our question is that one reason why the United States has less redistribution than Europe is that in the United States the median voter (say the middle class) has a higher chance of moving up in life and is less risk averse.

3.3.2. Prospect of upward mobility: Evidence

A discussion of the evidence for these arguments has to distinguish between beliefs about income mobility and actual measures of mobility.

Let us start with the former. There is very little doubt that Americans believe that their society is much more mobile than Europe, and that a hard-working individual can make it on his own. According to the World Value Survey, 71 percent of Americans versus 40 percent of Europeans believe that the poor have a good chance of escaping poverty. This question does not capture precisely what the model needs, which is a measure of the perceived mobility of the median voter; the question is vague and refers to "the poor," but nevertheless it suggests that Europeans much more than Americans think that the poor are "stuck" in their position, and therefore need help from the government.

In fact, a closely related consideration has to do not with mobility per se but with a view about the role of individual effort. As we discuss in Chapter 6, Americans believe much more so than

Europeans that individual effort determines income rather than luck. So, according to the American value system, the poor are less deserving, because to a large extent, it is their "fault" if they are poor. Alesina and La Ferrara (2005) present strong evidence on this point. They find two results: (a) Americans who believe that social competition is "fair," that is, individual effort determines success and opportunities are relatively equal, do not favor redistribution, and vice versa; (b) Americans who believe that social competition is fair view social mobility as a good substitute for redistributive policies.

The bottom line is that Americans feel that their society offers more chances for everybody to become rich, and those who do not take the chance are lazy and do not deserve much support. Europeans believe that the income ladder is very sticky and is determined by preconditions and luck, so the poor are to a large extent unlucky, and for this reason deserve help. What one means by "luck" may also be different across the two sides of the Atlantic. Imagine someone born with a very high intelligence (say IQ). Americans may believe that the individual is entitled to be rewarded for this innate ability. Europeans may consider being born intelligent simply lucky and therefore may consider it fair to redistribute away from intelligent and therefore wealthy individuals.

Let us now turn to actual, measured social mobility. How do these beliefs about different levels of social mobility correspond to harder evidence on the difference in the degree of income mobility in the United States and Europe? Our bottom line is that either Europeans underestimate the amount of mobility in society or Americans overestimate it, but measured differences in mobility are much lower than the size of these differences in opinions across the two sides of the Atlantic.

There are certainly some stylized facts which seem to lend some credence to the view that America is a much more mobile society. After all, America's five richest men include three software entrepreneurs: Gates and Allen (at Microsoft), Ellison (at Oracle), Warren Buffett, and Jim Walton. Only the last of these five (also the poorest) inherited his wealth and he inherited it from the legendary, self-made Sam Walton of Wal-Mart. By contrast, the richest private citizen in England is Gerald Grosvenor, the Duke of Westminster, whose wealth comes from his family's centuries-old holdings of central London real estate. The Queen is another prominent English billionaire. However, the richest private (i.e. excluding the royal family) woman in England is J. K. Rowling, and she was on welfare before beginning her Harry Potter series. Indeed, even a cursory glance at the Forbes list of richest Europeans shows that European billionaires are often (usually) self-made. Silvio Berlusconi is a prominent example. The existence of a few salient aristocrats is not hard evidence that Europe has less economic opportunity than the United States. While there is certainly a widespread belief that European society is more immobile (as shown by the opinion data discussed above), there may not be any truth to this view.

Statistical evidence on income mobility suggests that the similarities between the United States and Europe are more striking than the differences. The empirical literature on income mobility is filled with controversy (see Fields and Ok 1999 for an extensive survey). Furthermore, there seem to be substantial differences across European countries. Gottschalk and Spolaore (2002) compare income mobility in the United States and Germany. They look at a transition matrix across income quintiles in the two countries that examines where people in various income quintiles in 1984 ended up in 1993. In terms of observed mobility these authors find very small differences between the United States and Germany. The middle class in the United States seems only very slightly more upwardly mobile than its counterpart in Germany. They find that 10 percent and 11 percent of Americans in the middle quintiles moved to the top quintile between 1984 and 1999. In the same period 21 percent of Germans and 23 percent of Americans in the middle quintile moved up to the second quintile. Almost the same percentage (about 31 percent) stayed in the middle quintile. They find that middle income Europeans were slightly more likely to become poor over the nine-year period. About 12 percent of Americans in the middle quintile dropped down to the bottom quintile; 16 percent of Europeans in the middle quintile dropped that far. But, in fact, the poor appear to be far more trapped in the United States than in Europe. About 60 percent of the bottom quintile of the population stay in that class nine years later in the United States, whereas only 46.3 percent of the bottom quintile in

Germany stay in that group. So overall, the American middle class seems more upwardly mobile than the German middle class, but the differences seem small. However, these authors note that these differences underestimate the effect of potential as opposed to observed mobility between the two countries. In other words, if a country displays low observed mobility of the poor, it may mean that there are no opportunities for the poor, or that the opportunities are there but the poor do not take advantage of them.

Checchi, Ichino, and Rustichini (1999) compare measures of inter-generational mobility between the United States and Italy and conclude that there is indeed more mobility in the United States. They do not directly work with income, but instead look at an individual's predicted income based on his occupation. Overall, they find greater income mobility in the United States than in Italy. For example, 11 percent of Italian fathers who have occupations in the middle of the income distribution (i.e. are in either the second or third quartile of the occupation distribution) end up with sons at the top end of the income distribution (i.e. in the top quartile of the occupation distribution). However, in the United States, 14 percent of comparably defined middle income parents have children who belong to the top occupation quartile. The Italy/U.S. comparisons suggest that there is at least some truth to America's reputation as a land of opportunity. Still, to us these differences seem far too small to explain the massive differences in opinions about opportunity in the United States.

Moreover, when we turn to the poor, the United States is actually less mobile than Italy, just as it was less mobile than Germany. In Italy, only 21 percent of fathers who are in the bottom quartile of occupation distribution have children who are also in that bottom quartile. In the United States, 25 percent of fathers who are in the bottom quartile have children who are also in that quartile. While there are still profound limits on our measurement of income mobility across countries, the data that currently exist do not suggest that the United States is unusually mobile or that the poor in the United States are particularly likely to leave poverty. Instead, the data seem to suggest that the U.S.–Europe differences are small and, if anything, the poor in the United States are more likely to stay poor than the poor in Germany and Italy.

A refined version of this hypothesis is that while current levels of mobility between the United States and Europe are the same, in the past, when the foundations of the Welfare State were put in place in Europe, the United States was very different. According to this view, in the nineteenth century, the United States was a land of opportunity and Europe was a place of stiflingly static immobility. For this view, to explain current differences in beliefs, and current differences in welfare systems, it would need to be true that these one-time differences got embedded in national ideologies or institutions. As such, current differences in the level of redistribution reflect these nineteenth-century economic patterns.

Some historical evidence seems to support the notion that mobility rates were much higher in the United States than in Europe. When Alexis De Tocqueville wrote about the United States in the 1830s, he was clearly astounded by the level of mobility and economic opportunity for the young in the United States: "wealth circulates with astounding rapidity, and experience shows that it is rare to find two succeeding generations in the full enjoyment of it" (Tocqueville 1959: 53).

But the hard evidence that does exist suggests that Tocqueville overstates American mobility. For example, Pessen (1974) looks at the origins of the Northeast urban elites during the time of Tocqueville and finds that over 90 percent came from well-off families. Gregory and Neu (1974) and Miller (1974) confirm this view for the later nineteenth century. Indeed, most available evidence supports the view that nineteenth-century America was no more and possibly less mobile than twentieth-century America. For example, Grusky (1986) finds rising mobility through the nineteenth and early twentieth centuries. Thernstrom (1973) using a very detailed set of data on working class families in Boston between 1880 and 1960 finds that about 40 percent of their children rise out of the working class and that this number is basically constant over the time period.

For our purposes, the question becomes whether or not the nineteenth-century United States was more mobile than Europe, and on this question the data are shaky but appear to support somewhat higher levels of American mobility. Kaelble (1985) summarizes a wide range of studies (including Thernstrom) on social mobility in the United States and Europe in the nineteenth century. Given the absence of income data (and the difficulty of comparability across places), the best measures of upward mobility are the share of working class parents who have non-working class children. The definitions of working class are based on occupational measures and are certainly quite imperfect. But, these are the only data available which can give us some sense about whether Tocqueville's characterization of U.S. mobility is accurate or just another element of the American myth. Unpublished work by Long and Ferrie (2002) also finds considerably more upward mobility in the U.S. than in the U.K. during the mid-nineteenth century.

Kaelble presents later data on upward mobility (out of the working class) for four U.S. cities in the nineteenth century—Boston (Thernstrom's data) in 1890 and 1910, Poughkeepsie in 1880, Indianapolis in 1910, and Hamilton in 1850 and 1860, The mobility rates for these data samples are 41 percent for Boston (in both time periods), 26 percent for Poughkeepsie, 21 percent for Indianapolis, and 5 percent and 14 percent for Hamilton in 1850 and 1860, respectively. This comparison further supports the idea that mobility rates rose over the nineteenth century, but of course, this might have to do with the sample of cities rather than the years. An unweighted average of the data for the four cities shows an average mobility rate of 23.5 percent.

The data for most European cities appear to be somewhat lower. For example, data from London (two studies) show an average 16.5 percent rate of upward mobility. The only Austrian city in Kaelble's sample (Graz) has an upward mobility rate of 10 percent. There are three pieces of evidence from France (Toulouse in two different years and Marseilles) and together these cities show an upward mobility rate of 10 percent. Sweden and Denmark have higher rates: 27 percent and 21 percent, respectively. There is also a much richer set of German cities, which show mobility rates clustered between 14 and 16 percent.

The United States was somewhat more mobile, at least in comparison to the non-Scandinavian countries, but the differences are not overwhelming, especially given the problems with the data. One would hardly expect an 8 percent gap in upward mobility rates (between the United States and Germany) to produce such massive differences in beliefs about the determinants of income and such massive differences in redistribution. Moreover, the data within Europe do not seem to suggest a pattern where less mobility is associated with a stronger welfare state. The higher mobility levels of Denmark and Sweden (relative to Germany and France) suggests that if high historical mobility deters welfare, then Scandinavia should be a bastion of laissez-faire policies. As such, we are left with the view that neither past nor present realities of mobility and opportunity can actually explain the differences between European and American attitudes.

One final possible explanation is that Americans are less risk averse than Europeans and therefore are less worried about downward mobility. We are not aware of good measures of cross-country degrees of risk aversion, but casual evidence suggest that it may indeed be the case that Americans are more risk-taking. To begin with, the United States is a country of immigrants. It stands to reason that those who left their countries of origin in search of fortune to escape poverty were the most risk-taking of the lot. Casual evidence also suggests that business failure is associated with fewer stigmas in the United States than in Europe. Perhaps this suggests that Americans view failure as a possibility in a risky environment. But then, the question is why Americans are less risk averse, if indeed they are. Answering these questions brings us back to historical, sociological, and behavioral questions which we address later.

3.3.3. *Prospects of upward mobility: Assessment*

Is the United States a society which is more mobile, and in particular is the American "median voter," that is the middle class, more likely to do well in the future than its European counterpart? Given the available evidence, the answer seems to be perhaps yes, but the magnitude of this effect is unclear, probably quite small. What is clear is that Americans are convinced that their country offers equal opportunities and anybody can make it, if he tries hard enough. Or, at least, many more Americans think in that way than Europeans. Differences in perceptions seem much larger than objective measures of differences on the two sides of the Atlantic. Note that this can imply that Americans overestimate how mobile their society is (the interpretation favored by the European left), or that Europeans underestimate social mobility in general and in Europe in particular (the interpretation favored by the American free-marketeers). But, where do these different perceptions come from? This can be explained in two ways. One is that objective measures do not measure differences between the two societies well. The other, much more plausible, is that the difference is attitudinal. That is, Americans are more likely to believe that the mere fact of being poor is proof of lack of effort and laziness, much more so than Europeans are prone to do. Note that an American who feels that way may argue that actual upward mobility of the poor does not measure availability of opportunities but measures only those opportunities taken. So, if the poor are truly lazy they will not take advantage of the opportunity offered to them. We return to this issue below in detail. There is, however, another more subtle point. Measured income mobility may not be a correct measure of how much effort matters, relative to luck, family connection, etc. That is, measured mobility could be very high even in a society where only pure luck determines income. All you need is a very high variability of "luck." The converse is true for a society where individual effort determines income.

3.3.4. Variability of income and openness

Suppose that you live in a particularly unstable economy and you cannot be perfectly sure of how these aggregate economic shocks will affect your position on the income ladder. If you are risk averse, you will favor larger government intervention to stabilize income. Risk aversion implies that the more unstable the economy, the more demand there is for a stabilizing role of the government using transfer mechanisms. Rodrik (1998), following a suggestion by Cameron (1978), has focused on shocks to an economy due to its degree of openness. He begins by arguing that more open economies are more unstable. In fact, whether or not trade and financial integration increases income variability is far from obvious. For instance, openness to world financial markets may allow for better insurance against economic shocks induced by terms of trade variability. The Rodrik–Cameron argument is that open economies should have larger governments, in particular larger redistributive programs, to alleviate the effect of income variability induced by openness.

In support of this view, Rodrik presents the following evidence. In a sample of OECD countries, he notes a strong correlation between

Fig. 3.1. Transfers/GDP versus (Imports + Exports)/GDP for OECD Countries

the degree of openness and the size of transfer over GDP, which appears even from a simple plot reproduced in Fig. 3.1. Rodrik also shows that it is not openness per se that influence this relationship but a measure of variability of terms of trade shock weighted by the share of imports plus exports over GDP. When Rodrik extends his analysis to a much larger sample of countries, he finds no relationship between the size of transfers and the openness of the economy or his measure of openness-induced variability. He argues that this is because transfers in developing countries are badly measured, and he shows a correlation between the size of government consumption over GDP and his measures of openness. Based upon this evidence, Rodrik claims support for the theory.

3.3.5. Openness and redistribution: Discussion

The Rodrik–Cameron argument applied to our question would imply that the welfare state is much less developed in the United States simply because the United States is a much more closed (and large) country than all European countries. There is no doubt that, indeed, the United States is a larger and less open economy than any in Europe. However, according to standard macroeconomic measures of

Table 3.1. Economic Variability in the United States and Europe (Standard Deviations)

Series	Sample range	United States	EU15
GDP growth	1960–1997	0.020	0.017
Total manufacturing labor productivity	1980–1996	0.026	0.016
Unemployment rate (1)	1970–2000	0.414	0.220
Competitiveness (2)	1975–1999	0.057	0.046
Terms of trade shocks	1971–1990	0.086	0.088
Terms of trade shocks × openness	1971–1990	1.65	7.01

Notes: (1) coefficients of variation reported; (2) index of relative export price of manufactured goods. European average for 5 countries: France, Germany, Italy, Spain, and United Kingdom.

Source: OECD Compendium (1999), Rodrik (1998).

volatility, the United States is much less stable than the average European economy. Table 3.1 shows that in terms of growth, unemployment, and productivity, the U.S. economy has displayed more volatility than the average of the European countries over the last forty years. The table also reports Rodrik's measure of externally induced volatility, which multiplies an economy's terms of trade volatility by its degree of openness (measured as exports plus imports, divided by GDP).

According to all measures of volatility (except the externally induced one constructed by Rodrik) the U.S. economy is less stable than European countries. This can be interpreted in two ways. First, the U.S. economy may have more variability precisely because transfers are smaller. However, since the U.S. economy is more closed, it should be less in need of a larger government. In other words, if all countries shared the same objectives in terms of the trade-off between government size and business cycle variability, the United States should be more, not less, stable than Europe.[5] Since the United States

[5] Similar considerations apply to Japan, a country that has a small government, is relatively closed (and large), and exhibits more income variability than European countries.

is larger and more closed, it should cost less in terms of taxation to achieve the same level of stabilization.[6] Therefore, if Rodrik's theory is correct, the fact that the United States has experienced greater variability than Europe suggests that Americans and Europeans evaluate very differently the trade-off between government size and cyclical variability.

A broader examination of the evidence, beyond a United States versus Europe comparison, shows that the relationship between openness and redistribution is not robust. To begin with, Milesi-Ferretti, Perotti, and Rostagno (2000) show that after controlling for the nature of the electoral system in a sample of OECD countries Rodrik's result disappears; that is, the nature of the electoral system dominates the effect of openness.

Thus, in OECD countries political determinants of redistribution dominate the effect of openness. We return to political institutions in the next chapter.

As for developing countries, it is not at all clear that transfers are more poorly measured than government consumption, which is the key assumption that Rodrik needs to argue that his empirical results are supportive of the theory. It is certainly the case that disaggregated measures of government spending for poor countries are full of noise and measurement errors, but there is no reason why one component, transfers, should be more poorly measured than others. As for the result on public consumption, Alesina and Wacziarg (1998) argue that the size of the country is a stronger predictor of the size of government consumption than openness. The theory underlying this result has to do with economies of scale in the production of public goods.[7] The fact is that small countries are also more open, so it is often hard to disentangle the effect of the two variables separately.

Our conclusion is that we do not believe that openness is a determinant of the difference between the United States and continental European countries on the question of redistributive policies.

---

[6] An additional measure of income uncertainty could be the extent of long-term unemployment. However, this measure is very likely to be directly affected by labor market regulation and policies.

[7] See Alesina and Spolaore (2003) for an extensive discussion of the role of the size of countries.

3.3.6. *Geographic mobility and income variability*

Several empirical studies show that Americans are much more geographically mobile than Europeans. Blanchard and Katz (1992) showed that Americans react to downturns and economic adversity by moving, while in similar situations Europeans stay put. In fact, mobility in the United States is higher than in any country in Europe and therefore much higher than across Europe as a whole. The implication is that Americans are more willing to follow economic opportunities and react to adverse shocks to their income by moving. Perhaps this is related to the fact that all Americans are originally "movers" in a sense, as the United States is a country of immigrants, an issue to which we devote much space below.

So, while Americans move more to avoid income losses, Europeans are more static and demand more insurance and redistribution from the state. To put it more strongly, the American poor are more willing to move than the European poor, and rely less on the government to improve their fortune. Costs and propensity to move determine the observed degree of geographic mobility. One important determinant of the cost is the degree of efficiency of the housing market and associated real estate credit market. Probably, however, individuals' willingness to move influences observed mobility more than the costs of moving. Individuals' willingness to search for their own "fortune" rather than relying on the government is a matter of behavior and ideology. These attitudinal questions are at the center of our analysis, which follows in the following chapters. There is also an important issue of causality: Are current American movers willing to relocate because safety nets are relatively limited, or vice versa? Presumably, a bit of both, so we need to find more "exogenous" explanations.

3.4. The costs of redistribution

Redistributive policies involve tax distortions. The more inefficient the tax collection system, the more costly it is to implement redistributive schemes, and therefore the smaller the redistribution system.

If one compares the tax collection systems of developing countries to those of developed countries, one can certainly see much value in this argument. Tax collection systems in much of the developing world are inefficient and highly distortionary; these countries rely on inefficient sources of collection of revenues like import duties and property taxes. For instance, much of the fiscal problems of Latin American countries stem from their inability to implement efficient and workable tax collection systems. Latin American government budgets do not properly take into account, the fact that the inefficient revenue side of their budgets does not allow for expensive spending programs. The result has often been budget deficits and macroeconomic instability.

Also, it is certainly the case that the secular increase in the size of government in developed countries has a lot to do with improved technology for tax collection, a point recently emphasized by Becker and Mulligan (2003). However, which came first is unclear: Is it the desire for more spending that stimulated the search for efficient taxes or the "accidental" discovery of more efficient taxes that stimulated spending? While this question has a bit of a "chicken and the egg" nature, it would seem more reasonable that the <u>spending needs of the government stimulate the search for new and more efficient forms of taxation.</u> In fact, in western Europe, the development of more efficient tax systems was due to the fiscal need of rulers engaged in expensive wars, so in that case it was clearly a spending need (wars) that stimulated the search of new forms of taxation. In any event, the question is relatively tangential to our concerns here.

As far as the question addressed in this book, this theory "works" only to the extent that the American system of tax collection is much less efficient than the European one, and only if one believes that it is the efficiency of the tax system that "comes first" and determines the level of spending. In other words, even if one finds that the United States has a much less efficient tax system than Europe, it is not sufficient evidence that this is a "cause" of different redistributive policies and of smaller government in the United States; in fact, the difference in preferences over spending may be the cause of different degrees of efficiency of the tax system at collecting taxes.

Is there any evidence that the fiscal system in the United States is much more inefficient than in continental Europe? Once again, it is worth distinguishing between perception and reality. As for the former, one may argue that Americans are more averse to government spending because they tend to perceive governments as inherently inefficient and are especially sensitive to government waste and inefficiency while Europeans are more tolerant. According to the World Value Survey, 41 percent of Europeans favor greater government ownership in the economy as opposed to 26 percent Americans who express the same opinion. Note that the question asks whether *more* government ownership is desirable, and in European countries government ownership is already higher than in the United States, as we showed in the previous chapter. This difference in opinion may reflect a different perception about government efficiency.

However, Americans do not oppose every form of government spending as inherently inefficient. In fact, the United States spends much more on defense than European governments do. Traditionally, the United States used to spend twice as much as the highest of European countries (roughly 6 percent of GDP versus about 2). Even in recent years, when the share of military spending in the United States fell, it still remains above the European average and no country in Europe spends more than the United States on defense. Also, as shown above, total public investment (partly driven by defense) is actually higher in the United States than in Europe as a share of GDP, as we showed in Chapter 2. Therefore, it does not seem that Americans object to all forms of government activities, but only to a portion of them, especially those having to do with redistribution.

Skocpol (1992) notes that, historically, the administration of the Civil War pension system was perceived (and in part was) corrupt, inefficient, and arbitrary. Partly because of this perception, it did not develop into a universal social security system despite the pressure of social reformers in that direction during the Progressive Era. On the other hand, perceptions of favoritism, injustice, and corruption are widespread in the expensive pension system of Italy, especially in the area of disability pensions, and in the treatment of public servants, but nevertheless pensions remain the single biggest item of the Italian welfare system.[8]

What about hard evidence on the relative efficiency of the tax collection system in the United States versus Europe? To begin with, as we pointed out before, the tax structure of European countries is extremely diverse. Therefore, in order to make the argument that the United States has a more inefficient tax collection system than "Europe," one would need to compare the United States to every European country, since their tax systems are by no means homogenous in Europe.

An indirect way of testing the ability of the tax system to collect revenue is to look at the degree of tax evasion. The 1996 Global Competitiveness report surveyed business leaders about tax compliance in their countries. Using this subjective measure the United States received a score of 4.47 (out of a maximum score for tax compliance of 6). Although there was considerable heterogeneity within Europe, the average compliance was much lower than in the United States: The average index for Europe was 3.5. Alesina and Mare (1992) surveyed the available evidence on measures of the black economy, closely related to tax evasion, and found that the United States and United Kingdom had the lowest amount of black economy among the sample surveyed, which included most European countries.

3.5. Conclusions

Our examination of explanations which we labeled purely "economic" has left us almost completely empty handed. The only useful insight has to do with the idea that higher social mobility in the United States is viewed as a substitute for redistributive policies. However, we noted that perceptions about the extent of social mobility may be not completely consistent with the available hard evidence. Whether the middle class is more upwardly mobile in the United States than in Europe is unclear. Therefore, the effect of

---

[8] See Boeri and Perotti (2002) for an in depth and almost shocking discussion of the inefficiency of the Italian pension system.

social mobility is a combination of the actual features of society and, perhaps more so, of ideological attitudes toward it that explain why the poor are such. Americans believe that the poor can get out of poverty if they just try hard. Europeans believe that the poor are stuck in poverty. Even if Americans do not observe much more upward mobility of the poor than in Europe, they seem to believe that this is not because there are no opportunities for the poor in the United States, but it is because the poor do not try hard enough. We will return in much detail below to the question of the attitudes toward the poor.

A related point concerns risk aversion. Holding everything else constant, more risk aversion should lead to a demand for more social protection and redistribution. It may certainly be the case that Americans are less risk averse than Europeans, but the question is then why, a question to which we return below.

As for other explanations based upon the pre-tax income inequality, openness, and the efficacy of the tax collection system, we rejected them as explanations of the United States versus Europe comparison. Some of them, especially tax collection costs, may explain comparisons between developing and developed countries, but they do not seem to help much in a comparison of Europe and the United States.

Chapter 4

Political Institutions and Redistribution

4.1. Introduction

We now turn to what we label "political" explanations, those that emphasize the state, the political arena, and political institutions. While American political institutions have several peculiarities relative to their European counterparts, the latter are not uniform by any means. The United States has a strict two-party system, but in many ways so does the United Kingdom. The United States has a Presidential system; France has one too, even though the role of the French and American Presidents are quite different. The United States is a federal system, but so are Germany and Switzerland. The United States has a very powerful Supreme Court that often plays a critical role in the law making process, and this is perhaps unique to the United States. Another unique feature of the United States is that socialist or communist parties never played any relevant political role in national elections.

An appealing, although perhaps slightly tautological explanation of the American–European difference in redistributive policy is that socialist parties favor the welfare state, and the lack of a strong socialist party in the United States explains the small welfare state of this country. This explanation begs the question of why the United States never had a strong and effective socialist party, an issue that we address in the next chapter. A related question concerns the different role of labor unions on the two sides of the Atlantic.

A second explanation focuses on the nature of the electoral system; in particular, proportional representation is more likely to produce larger redistributive policies than a majoritarian system or a district system like in the United States. Two reasons justify this hypothesis. First, in a first-past-the-post system of geographically delimited districts the incentives of legislators involve choosing geographically targeted spending programs, often labeled pork barrel programs.[1] On the contrary, in proportional systems with national districts legislators will favor spending programs that are universal and benefit large groups like pensioners, workers, the poor, etc.; that is, transfer programs rather than pork barrel programs. Second, proportional systems tend to produce multiparty systems and allow the representation of many, even relatively small, groups. This creates incentives to find something for everybody in the budget and expand spending programs.[2]

Another important aspect has to do with the degree of decentralization and the federal system of government in the United States, which may interfere with the adoption of federal or even state level redistributive programs. In fact, fiscal decentralization creates obstacles to an excessive role for the central government in fiscal matters, and makes it more difficult to tax the rich localized in some part of the country and redistribute in favor of the poor localized in other parts. In fact, the main argument of those in Europe that oppose decentralization within each country is precisely that decentralization interferes with redistribution.

---

[1] For an influential formal analysis of this system, see Weingast, Shepsle, and Johnsen (1981).

[2] For an early discussion of how multiparty systems increase government spending in OECD countries, see Roubini and Sachs (1989) and Grilli, Masciandaro, and Tabellini (1990). For recent empirical evidence see Persson and Tabellini (2003), and Perotti and Kontopoulos (2002).

Finally, the separation of powers embodied in the American constitution prevented the introduction of radical welfare policies. The Senate at least until the early twentieth century was a non-elected billionaire's club prone to defend private wealth. American courts, especially until World War II, played a key role in vetoing various redistributive measures. American courts have more latitude than European courts in legislative matters, and they have used it, traditionally in defense of property and against government interference and redistribution. More generally, courts in the United States are representative of the way in which the Founding Fathers tried to create checks and balances to avoid an excessive taxation of wealth.

In the remainder of the chapter, we discuss in turn all these explanations, and we conclude that all of them provide very useful insights into our questions. The lack of socialist/communist parties, the electoral systems, the federal structure, checks and balances, and the role of the courts are all critically related to the development (or lack thereof) of an American welfare state. But then the question is: Why have Americans chosen these institutions? After examining in more detail the role of these institutions in this chapter, we tackle that question in the following one.

4.2. Socialist parties and the welfare state

A vast literature in political science, recently well summarized in Huber and Stephens (2001), argues that the presence of socialist political parties in government explains the adoption of a more generous welfare state. The examples of Scandinavian countries, which, except for brief periods, have been governed by socialist-led coalition governments, are a natural example. Several authors (see Huber and Stephens 2001, for a survey) also emphasize how the corporatist nature of labor market institutions and the close interaction between unions and socialist parties have favored consensus building for redistributive policies. Essentially, the idea is that unions may be more willing to reach agreements with business organizations if they know that a socialist-led government will compensate them with generous welfare provisions, and therefore in labor market negotiation; even for the private sector, the government is an important third party. Nothing could be farther from the U.S. system. In the United States, labor unions have always been much less enthusiastic about government intervention in labor disputes and have always seen their role as independent from political parties. American unions have often seen the government as an enemy more than an ally and they had good reasons for this view. The union movement, from its very beginning, fought for its survival against capital and against a state that was seen as a strenuous defender of private property. American labor almost always saw itself as a private organization that wanted to be "left alone". In many ways, the unions were "anti-government" in the sense that they focused on receiving "private" concessions from employers with no hope for government intervention in their favor.[3]

Various statistical studies also show that left-wing parties tend to spend and tax more than right-wing parties, as shown by Alesina, Roubini, and Cohen (1997), Perotti and Kontopoulos (2002), and Persson and Tabellini (2003), among others.[4] Note, however, that in Europe even right-wing parties often have a very hard time in cutting welfare spending even when pressed by budget constraints, as recent experiences have shown.[5] Even when pressed by mounting deficits, right-wing governments have often chosen to raise already-high taxes rather than cut spending for two reasons. One is the vast support for welfare spending in many European countries even among relatively centrist voters, and secondly because once certain programs

[3] Skocpol (1992) notes how instead the women's movement of the late nineteenth century and early twentieth century looked at the state as its counterpart and was struggling for welfare and progressive legislation.

[4] This ideological difference between left and right also characterizes the United States; that is, the Democratic Party is more favorable to domestic spending and welfare programs than the Republican Party. See Hibbs (1987) and Alesina, Roubini, and Cohen (1997) for an extensive discussion of the ideological differences between American parties in macroeconomic policies.

[5] See Alesina, Perotti and Tavares (1998) and Alesina and Ardagna (1999) for an empirical discussion. Alesina and Angeletos (2003) provide a model that explains why it is especially difficult to reduce the size of the welfare state, in a multiple equilibrial model.

are in place it appears particularly costly to cut them back. This is especially the case in proportional systems in which it is easier for every group, category, and lobby to find a voice in the legislature.

Other political scientists (Wilenski 1981, for instance) emphasize the role of Catholic parties as determinants of generous redistributive policies. In Italy, the transformation from a very small-sized government (by European standards) to an average-sized one occurred in the period of the Socialist–Catholic coalition in government. Current opposition to reduction in the size of the welfare state in Italy comes just as much from Catholic as from extreme left parties. Needless to say there is no Catholic party in the United States.

It is certain that the lack of a nationally powerful American Socialist Party has a lot to do with the small scale of the American welfare state. The question of what prevented the development of a communist and socialist party in the United States is an issue which we discuss in the next chapter.

4.3. The electoral system

The effect of electoral institutions on economic policy has received renewed attention in recent years, with many cross-country studies. The typical structure of empirical studies of this nature is that a certain economic variable, say budget deficit, inflation, total government spending, or its composition, etc., is explained by one or more institutional variables of interest, in addition to various economic variables. In technical language, the economic variable of interest is on the left hand side of a regression and the institutional variables are on the right of the equation. This procedure implies that political institutions are taken as exogenous (or at least predetermined) as explanation of the economic variables. In other words, institutional variables are taken as "primitive" and are not themselves explained.

A lively recent literature has investigated theoretically and empirically the relationship between electoral rules and fiscal policy. Particularly relevant for our purposes is the recent work by

Milesi-Ferretti, Perotti, and Rostagno (2002, MFPR) and by Persson and Tabellini (2003, PT). These authors test the hypothesis that in majoritarian systems characterized by geographically based electoral districts in which each district chooses one representative, the elected government favors spending programs that can be geographically targeted. Proportional electoral systems, in contrast, favor spending on universal programs. The clearest example of this is a purely proportional election in a single national district, where geographic targeting would make no sense at all from an electoral perspective.

Electoral systems are very diverse in many dimensions. Very few can be characterized at the two extremes, single-member districts and a single national district with perfect proportionality of votes into seats. In order to test the effect of proportionality on transfer programs, one has to measure the degree of proportionality of electoral systems, which is a very difficult task as we will see below, since electoral rules differ in many different ways, and it is not simple to summarize these multidimensional differences into one index.

It is also difficult to differentiate between spending programs that can be geographically targeted and those that cannot. In theory, the contrast between these two types of programs is clear-cut; in practice, less so. For instance, anyone above a certain age is eligible to receive social security payments, regardless of residence. Thus, in principle, this would seem an example of a universal program with no geographic relevance. However, certain districts may be disproportionately populated by elderly voters, like many districts in Florida for instance. Therefore, a Florida senator may favor increases in social security spending as a "geographically targeted" program.

Both MFPR and PT report results consistent with the hypothesis that transfer payments are higher in proportional electoral systems. The two papers use different measures of transfers, a different sample of countries (that of PT is larger), and a different definition of proportionality. One important observation concerning the dependent variable is that MFPR use OECD data as source for OECD countries and a data set constructed by Gavin and Perotti (1997) for Latin America. All these data refer to the general government; that is, they include both the central and local governments. PT, in contrast, use International Monetary Fund data, which refer to the central government only, which in the case of the United States would be only the Federal Government. They make this choice in order to expand the number of countries they consider. This distinction is especially important if one is comparing the United States with other countries: The United States is a federal system in which the difference between central and general government data is much larger than in most other countries. For the United States, for our purpose, the MFPR data set is more appropriate since we are concerned with an explicit comparison of the United States and Europe, and we care less about expanding the number of developing countries in the sample.

In order to measure proportionality, PT use a variable, obtained from "Interparliamentary Union," that takes the value of 1 if a country has a majoritarian system and 0 otherwise. Since electoral systems differ in many dimensions and to different degrees, a 0–1 classification may miss important differences. However, this measure is available for a large number of countries, and for this reason it is valuable. MFPR construct (for a smaller sample of countries) a more refined variable which can assume any value between 0 and 1. Since we focus on the OECD countries for which this variable is available, we also use it.

MFPR want to capture the share of electoral votes that guarantees a party a parliamentary seat in an electoral district of average size. This variable, labeled *UMS* (for "upper marginal share"), is declining in proportionality, since the higher the *UMS*, the more difficult it is for small parties to gain access to parliament. In a two-party system with a first-past-the-post rule, *UMS* takes a value of 0.5. This value declines with the degree of proportionality of the system. In the empirical work they use a transformed variable called the "standard magnitude" (LSM), where LSM $= 1/(1 - UMS)$.

Table 4.1 presents results we obtained using the data sets kindly provided by the authors. Column (1) reports the MFPR regression on OECD countries. One should expect a positive sign on this variable if transfers are larger in more proportional systems; in fact this variable (in logarithms) has a highly significant positive coefficient. The other controls used by MFPR are insignificant.

Table 4.1. Effect of Political Variables on Social Spending: Cross-country Regressions

	(1) Transfers/ GDP	(2) Transfers/ GDP	(3) Transfers/ GDP	(4) Social spending/ GDP
LSM: log (proportionality)	2.150 (0.656)[a]	1.809 (0.728)[b]	1.021 (0.421)[b]	
GDP/capita	5.151 (3.571)	5.035 (3.558)	1.823 (1.519)	−0.876 (0.980)
Openness		0.043 (0.040)	0.032 (0.027)	0.009 (0.010)
% 65+	0.753 (0.478)	0.678 (0.481)	1.096 (0.298)[a]	1.315 (0.217)[a]
% pop. 15–64				0.140 (0.138)
Majoritarian regime				−1.526 (0.994)
Presidential regime				−0.207 (1.227)
Caribbean				−0.095 (2.164)
Asia				2.047 (2.691)
Latin America			−0.791 (3.102)	1.042 (1.776)
Constant	−44.885 (34.507)	−44.376 (34.365)	−17.779 (13.751)	−4.597 (9.225)
Observations	20	20	38	60
R-squared	0.58	0.61	0.84	0.82

Note: The table contains cross-country regressions using political variables from PT and MFPR. Log(proportionality) is the MFPR measure of the percentage of a district's vote needed to capture a seat. Openness is (exports + imports)/GDP. Majoritarian refers to a regime in which all seats in a district are awarded to a single party winning a majority or plurality in that district. *T*-statistics in parentheses.

[a] Significant at 1% level.

[b] Significant at 5% level.

Reproduced from Alesina, Glaeser, and Sacerdote (2001).

The regression in column (2) adds a measure of openness (exports plus imports, divided by GDP). This variable is insignificant, suggesting, once again, that openness is not a determinant of the size of the welfare state. In order to explore this issue further, we also explored Rodrik's (1998) specification of openness, which includes a variable representing the interaction of terms-of-trade shocks with openness, but we did not find a significant relationship (results not shown). MFPR report the same result, so measures of proportionality outperform openness in OECD regressions.

Column (3) reports the MFPR result using the entire sample, including Latin America. The proportionality variable is still significant, but the size of the coefficient is much lower and less precisely estimated. (Note that openness is still insignificant.) Figure 4.1(a), which plots transfers as a share of GDP against the measure of proportionality for OECD countries, and 4.1(b), which plots the same for the Latin American countries, shows why: The correlation for the OECD countries is very strong and positive whereas that for the Latin American countries is very weak and negative.

Column (4) in Table 4.1 used the PT data set, which allows us to expand the set of countries. For the sake of comparison, we adopt their specification. In particular, in addition to the majoritarian variable, PT focus on another political variable, namely, whether or not a country has a presidential system. Note that the theory predicts negative coefficients on both these variables, given the way they are defined. Neither, however, is significant in this large sample (nor is the openness variable). If we restrict the sample to the OECD countries, the two political variables come much closer to significance (results not shown), but the MFPR measure of proportionality seems to be more strongly correlated with the dependent variable than do the PT variables. Openness is insignificant in the OECD subsample as well. Once again in this different specification and different data set, political variables outperform openness variables.

The bottom line is that, for OECD countries, a measure of proportionality of the electoral system is highly correlated with the amount of government transfers. This correlation is much weaker or

Fighting Poverty in the US and Europe

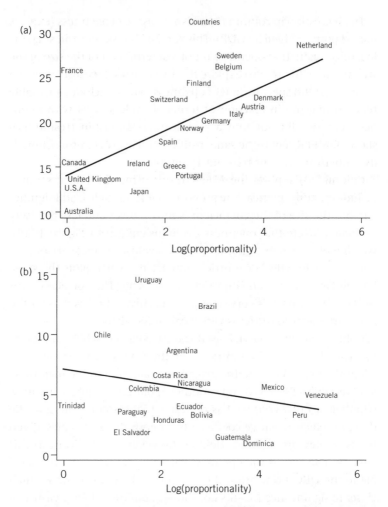

Fig. 4.1. (a) Transfers/GDP versus Log(Proportionality) for OECD Countries; (b) Transfers/GDP versus Log(Proportionality) for non-OECD Countries

(*Source*: Reproduced from Alesina, Glaeser, and Sacerdote 2001.)

nonexistent for developing countries. The openness variable is not significant after one controls for political variables.

An additional feature of proportional representation systems is that they allow for more parties to gain representation, leading to more fragmented legislatures. An extensive literature has shown how deficits tend to be protracted and fiscal adjustments delayed because of political fragmentation.[6] This point is not exactly related to our question, since we are not interested in deficits but in the level of redistribution. However, this argument suggests that it is more difficult in fragmented political system to cut spending programs when needed. To the extent that cuts in welfare spending are needed in the face of budget deficits, fragmented political systems have a more difficult time making these cuts and welfare spending remains insensitive to the needs of tightening the budget.

How much of the difference in the United States versus Europe can we explain with the effects of proportional representation? Consider the value of the coefficients in the two first columns of Table 4.1 that refer to OECD countries. This coefficient is around 2.[7] Let us take this value of 1.9. In the data set the mean value of "social transfers" (SSW) is 14.6 and the mean value of LSM is 2.5. The same values in the United States are 7.0 and 0. If we multiply 1.9 times 2.5 we get an effect of about 4.7 predicted impact of proportionality on transfers as measured by SSW. This is about half of the difference between the United States and the average of Europe. This is an upper bound, since we are not controlling in this regression for other possible determinants of redistribution. Even though much is left to be explained, proportional representation clearly has a large impact.

4.4. The federal system

The United States is a federal nation. All European countries are more centralized than the United States, including Germany, despite its federal arrangements. The vast literature on fiscal federalism

---

[6] For theoretical work on this point see Alesina and Drazen (1991) and Tornell and Velasco (1995). Empirical work by Roubini and Sachs (1989), Perotti and Kontopoulos (2002), among others, show the effect on deficits of coalition governments in OECD countries.

[7] We also repeated the same regression for all countries with per capita income above $15,000 in 1999 (there are eighteen of them) and we obtained a similar coefficient, around 1.9.

points to decentralization as a force that reduces the size of government and the provision of public goods.

The traditional view (Musgrave 1959; Oates 1972) argues that the tax competition between localities should lead to a race toward the bottom in terms of provisions of public goods leading to an inefficiently small size of government. The underlying argument relies on a Tiebout type model in which wealthy individuals move where taxes are lower. Those who instead see government intervention as excessive because of a variety of imperfections in the political arena see fiscal decentralization as a way of constraining the power to tax of the Leviathan (Hayek 1960; Buchanan and Tullock 1962; Brennan and Buchanan 1980). Precisely because of tax competition between localities, taxes are lower in a decentralized system than in a centralized one, and, therefore, tax competition constrains the overtaxing "Leviathan."

These two views are opposite on the nature and efficiency of governments, but agree on the fact that more decentralization implies limits on the government's ability to tax, and therefore to redistribute. The traditional view sees this effect as a problem, because governments are supposed to be benevolent. The public choice approach views this effect as a benefit because it corrects political distortions.

Empirically the relationship between the degree of decentralization and size of government in a cross section of countries is not so clear. One important force leading in the opposite direction (that is toward an increase of the size of government in more decentralized systems) is that decentralization often implies that spending decisions are taken locally while taxes are collected by federal governments. The incentives are clear for local governments: spend more and expect more transfers from higher levels of government. It is a sort of common pool problem: Tax revenues are a common pool, since they are raised nationally, while spending decisions are taken locally.

Enikopolov and Zhuravskaya (2002) have shown how the beneficial effects of decentralization are indeed mediated by various other institutional features and results may vary substantially depending on how decentralization is actually implemented. These authors place, and correctly so, much emphasis on the incentives that local officials face. Interestingly they also show that decentralization without central supervision and control is more likely to be successful in terms of producing good policies and lower government spending at higher levels of development, that is, in OECD countries relative to developing ones.

The American federal system has several incentives in place that reduce the scope for state deficits and redistributive policies. For instance, most states have a balanced budget rule, and most localities cover a good portion of their expenses with local taxation. There are of course transfers from higher to lower levels of government, but in a much less "liberal" way than in less well functioning federal systems.[8] Thus, the incentives for localities and states to spend without a budget constraint (i.e. transferring deficits to higher levels of government) are limited.

If redistributive schemes were totally delegated to the federal government, decentralization would not matter. Many of them in fact are. But in the case of the United States, several public goods and services, which have important redistributive features, are locally provided; think of public schools, to name an example. In fact, the trend of wealthy Americans fleeing to the suburbs to avoid taxation needed to finance inner city schools is well known, and a critical issue in U.S. social policy.

The bottom line is that in the United States, much more so than in Europe, many public programs that have redistributive impacts are taken locally. This has two consequences. Because of tax competition, and mobility, taxes are kept lower. As we discuss above, Americans are more prone and willing than Europeans to move geographically in response to economic incentives. Second, redistributive flows from wealthy localities to poorer ones are avoided, at least as far as locally provided goods are concerned. Far from being a "side effect" of decentralization, reducing the extent of redistribution is one of the main reasons why the United States is so decentralized into thousands of relatively small localities. Obviously, the choice of having a federal system is not "exogenous." In fact, it reflects the desire of the politicians at the federal level who understood that delegating

---

[8] For instance, the relationship between central government and regional and local governments is at the root of many of the fiscal problems in Latin America, including Argentina, Brazil, and recently Colombia.

spending to the states would keep spending down. For example, southern states were particularly keen on having control of spending. The reason has to do with race relations and the race composition of these states with a white majority and a strong minority of relatively poor blacks. We return to the issue of race in much detail below.

Several authors (see Alesina, Baqir, and Hoxby 2004 and the references cited therein) have argued that the desire to avoid white–black redistributions have led to "too many" local governments in the United States. The term "too many" has to be interpreted with reference to a hypothetical number that would maximize economies of scale and efficiency of government. One of the reasons why localities are "too many" is that in the choice of their number, Americans want to reduce the extent of redistribution that the system of government allows for. An additional reason, documented by Alesina et al. (2003), is the desire for racial and ethnic homogeneity. We return to the question of race relations later on.

4.5. Checks and balances

The American Constitution attributes a critical role to various mechanisms of checks and balances. One is the independence of the Courts. The interaction of the President and Congress and the different methods of appointment to the Senate and House are another one.

The American system of government allows for an interaction of Executive and Legislative power in the formation of legislation. Often one party holds a majority in one or both branches of the Legislature and the other party holds the presidency, a situation labeled a "divided government." Alesina and Rosenthal (1995) have argued that divided government delivers policy moderation; that is, a middle-of-the-road stance. In fact, middle-of-the-road voters can "create" divided governments precisely to keep in check excessively extreme policies. One aspect of this moderating effect is the mid-term loss in legislative elections of the party holding the presidency. Often Democratic majorities in Congress had to face a Republican President, making it more difficult to pass welfare legislation. In addition, certain institutions, especially the Senate, were created with an explicit role of protecting property rights, an issue which we discuss in much detail later. Brinkley (1995) eloquently describes the right-wing combination of Republicans and Southern Democrats who repeatedly blocked New Deal legislation after 1938. Indeed, it was also in the Senate that the modern conservative movement, which culminated in Ronald Reagan's presidency, first had its most vocal spokesman in Barry Goldwater.[9]

For much of American history, and at least until World War II, the courts played a major role in rejecting legislation that was perceived as antibusiness. A most notable example was a decision of the Supreme Court in 1894 against the introduction of a federal income tax. It took the sixteenth amendment of the Constitution almost twenty years later to pass the federal income tax in the United States. During the Progressive Era, in the early part of the nineteenth century, the courts were a formidable obstacle to the establishment of a European-style early welfare state, despite the notable efforts of many social reformers. Skocpol (1992) defines the United States as a "court dominated" state and notes that between 1900 and 1920 courts struck down about 300 labor laws (p. 227). Judges "invoked constitutional prohibitions against special, or class legislation" (p. 255).

President F. D. Roosevelt felt that the only way to adopt socially progressive legislation was to engage in a confrontation with the courts, as he did. In 1937, he proposed a reform of the Supreme Court, nicknamed the "court packing plan." This plan would have allowed the President to appoint a new Supreme Court member if any of the sitting members did not retire before six months after his seventieth birthday. With this threat of stripping the Court of some of its independence, he managed to get some legislation passed. As Brinkley (1995) noticed "the Court packing plan was a success . . . the Supreme Court began prudently to change course by upholding New Deal measures that months earlier it seemed prepared to invalidate."

[9] Of course, it was Tip O'Neill's House that put the brakes on the "Reagan Revolution."

Fighting Poverty in the US and Europe

Different legal systems (for example, the French versus the Anglo-Saxon system) attribute different roles to the courts, whose institutional structure also differs.[10] The involvement of the courts in social legislation in the United States has been a constant feature of the U.S. experience, unlike that in countries whose legal tradition is based on the French or the German model. Indeed, the power and independence of the U.S. courts are unique, unmatched even in England, where parliamentary dominance is much more established.

In the United Kingdom, the House of Lords was the closest equivalent to the U.S. Supreme Court until its power was stripped from it in the triumph of parliamentary democracy. In the first decade of the twentieth century, when the Liberals gained office after a very long period of Conservative dominance, social reformers within the government faced a strong challenge from the House of Lords. The latter's rejection of a major 1909 budget which included several pieces of important progressive legislation and welfare provisions created a major political stir and led to a renewed constitutional debate about the power of the upper house. The Lords were especially incensed by an increase in a capital gains tax on land and by a tax on mining concessions used to create a welfare fund for injured and aging miners. A young radical member of the Cabinet, Winston Churchill, was leading the charge against the upper house. In response to the 1909 budget rejection, Churchill drafted a memo proposing a comprehensive reform of the House of Lords modeled a bit on the U.S. Senate. His proposal was ignored, but a long reaching constitutional debate about the role of the upper house was in motion.[11] Bismarck in Germany did not have to worry about these kinds of checks and balances when introducing its proto-welfare state. In fact, the British liberal reformers looked at Germany's welfare provisions as a model to be followed, had they not to fight with the House of Lords. The 1909 crisis signalled, in a sense, the beginning of the end for the House of Lords, whose veto power was severely limited soon after.

---

[10] See Glaeser and Shleifer (2003) for a recent discussion.
[11] See Jenkins (2001) for a discussion of these events.

4.6. Conclusions

In this chapter, we have made some progress in understanding the difference between the United States and Europe. All the political and institutional variables which we have studied provide useful explanatory power: The lack of a strong socialist party; the nature of the electoral system in the United States versus Europe; the nature of the federal Constitution in the United States versus more centralized states in Europe; and the different role of the courts.

But, the role of U.S. courts as well as the House of Lords in the United Kingdom is due to an explicit institutional design, so one cannot take it as an "explanation." In fact, this "explanation" simply begs the question of why the United States chose these kinds of checks and balances and attributed this role to the courts. The same observation applies to the choice of a decentralized fiscal system and to the choice of an electoral system not based on proportionality. Why did Americans choose institutions that were likely to prevent the growth of a redistributive state? Nobody imposed the choice of certain electoral systems or a certain constitution. Nobody prevented changes in the Constitution; a strong socialist party and socialist unions could have emerged from labor conflicts. Therefore, one has to go deeper to explain these institutional choices. This is the task to which we now turn.

Chapter 5

The Origin of Political Institutions

5.1. Introduction

American political institutions, including majoritarianism, federalism, separation of powers, and indirect democracy, can together explain about one-half of the difference in the level of redistribution between the United States and Europe. But why are American political institutions different from European ones? Are institutions innate, exogenous first causes that are themselves the result of historical accident? No. Instead, institutions should be seen as flexible, and ultimately the result of deeper, and perhaps more permanent differences between countries.

To truly understand why Europe and the United States differ so much in their welfare policies, we must delve into the history of these institutions and ask why the United States and Europe have such different institutional arrangements. Even the most cursory historical overview shows that even seemingly permanent institutions have developed steadily. American institutions have been more stable than their European counterparts, but understanding the reality of American continuity and change requires us to substitute history for political myths. American stability has often been over-emphasized in an attempt to confer historical gravitas on current institutional arrangements and to discredit political opponents as proponents of radical change. Two of the greatest proponents of radical change in the twentieth century White House, Franklin Roosevelt (FDR) and Ronald Reagan, both claimed the mantle of continuity. Reagan claimed "to restore the division of governmental responsibilities between the national government and the States that was intended by the Framers of the Constitution" (Reagan 1987). Roosevelt argued that his attempt to pack the Supreme Court was "a way to take an appeal from the Supreme Court to the Constitution itself" and that he wanted "an independent judiciary as proposed by the framers of the Constitution" (Roosevelt 1937).

But many American institutions show as much change as stability. No branch of government even faintly resembles its counterpart in 1789. Over the period from 1800 to 1835, the Supreme Court established itself as a powerful, third branch of government. During the Civil War and the 1960s, power was reallocated between states (particularly southern states) and the federal government. More generally, all branches of government have grown fairly steadily over the entire history of the republic. There were major changes in the rules concerning suffrage as late as the 1960s, when African-Americans in the south were finally allowed to vote in large numbers. America has seen a great deal of institutional change.

It is only in comparison with Europe's massive shifts that American institutions look static. There is no country in continental Europe whose institutions today look remotely like its institutions in 1789. Indeed, as late as 1917, Europe was overwhelmingly ruled by hereditary monarchs. In most cases, those monarchies were only mildly constitutional. As late as 1945, almost all of continental Europe was ruled by totalitarian (or authoritarian) dictatorships. Portugal, Spain, and Greece had dictatorships as late as the 1970s. There are many European institutions which have roots prior to 1945—for example, some legal systems display significant continuity—but the idea that Europe is a continent of stable democracies with durable institutions is somewhat laughable. While James Madison would probably recognize that America still adheres to many aspects of his

Constitution, Louis XIV, Clement von Metternich, and Otto von Bismarck would surely be appalled by the changes in the government of their own countries.

In 2003, American institutions are much less friendly to redistribution than European institutions. But in 1890, most European countries had hereditary monarchies and limited franchises. Before World War I, American institutions were much more oriented toward representing the poor than the institutions of mainland Europe. In order to understand the connection between institutions and the welfare state, we must understand why Europe changed much more than America over the twentieth century. Now, we turn to the history of a small set of institutions to understand this transformation. In this chapter, we will focus on the history of proportional representation, the rise of socialist parties, and the U.S. Supreme Court. These are not the only institutions that matter, but by focussing on them we can glimpse the trends of 20th century institutional change.

5.2. Proportional representation

In the previous chapter, we documented that proportional representation is strongly correlated with more spending on social welfare. But, as we will document, proportional representation is not a centuries-old national institution. It is a twentieth-century phenomenon that comes about as a response to remarkably similar events in different countries. As such, is it not better to think of proportional representation as the effect of deeper political forces than as a first cause? In more technical terms, is proportional representation itself not an endogenous variable?

The importance of this question and the error involved in thinking of institutions as set in stone is particularly well illustrated by the case of France. The French Third Republic was formed in 1871 after the disastrous French defeat at Sedan and the uprising of the Paris Commune. The constitution of the Third Republic initially had no proportional representation. In the first election of the republic, the monarchists triumphed. The same electoral rules held until 1919, when in the aftermath of World War I, France adopted the *scrutin de liste*, which introduced a modest amount of proportional representation.

France returned to single-member districts in 1927. In 1945, France elected the constituent assembly that would write the constitution of the Fourth Republic. Leftists had dominated the resistance movement and leftist vigilantes appear to have been killing probably thousands of right-wing collaborators. As a result, communists and socialists together controlled more than 50 percent of the assembly, and they wrote a constitution with proportional representation. This constitution reliably led to the election of left-wing governments.

In 1958, the crisis over Algeria threatened to engulf France in a civil war. Right-wing leaders in Algeria engineered a revolution. Gaullist sympathizers seized Corsica. Closer to the capital, "there were rumors (not entirely empty) that [the right-wing revolutionaries in] Algiers had set a date for a paratroop attack on Paris, coordinated with an advance on the city by army units in the provinces," (Wright 1995: 410). The Prime Minister (Pflimlin) and the cabinet resigned in favor of de Gaulle, which was both a capitulation to the right and a turn to a strong hand to manage the disorder. de Gaulle crafted a new constitution. His new institutions included a strong executive and no proportional representation. But this majoritarianism was again impermanent. The first socialist president, Francois Mitterand, briefly brought proportional representation back.[1]

In France at least, proportional representation is hardly a permanent feature of the political landscape. It is a weather vane that moves with the power of the left. When the left was strong, after both world wars, proportional representation was instituted. When the army had reestablished its dominance in 1958, proportional representation was eliminated. The French case may be extreme, but it suggests some general features of the history of proportional representation to which we now turn with the goal of understanding why Europe has this system and the United States does not.

Proportional representation is a relatively recent phenomenon. In 1890, no European country had proportional representation, and

---

[1] This change was short-lived. By the time of Mitterand's Presidency, the Socialists were a majority party and could only lose by empowering fringe groups through proportional representation. One can only think that Mitterand's establishment of proportional representation reflected an adherence to longstanding socialist ideals at the expense of clear political advantage.

only Belgium, Finland, Portugal, and Sweden had this institution at the start of World War I. In the rest of Europe, the conversion to proportional representation happened mainly between 1917 and 1920 when Austria, Denmark, France, Germany, Italy, the Netherlands, Norway, and Switzerland all adopted proportional representation. Greece and Spain, adopted proportional representation when they shed their dictators in the 1970s.

The proportional representation movement began in the middle of the nineteenth century. Intellectual credit for the idea is generally shared between an Englishman, Thomas Hare, and a Dane, Carl Andrae. J. S. Mill often shares some credit as a popularizer.[2] There was substantial support for proportional representation in both the United Kingdom and the United States. A number of states, starting with Illinois, adopted proportional representation for their own elections, despite the initial opposition of the courts. In the 1860s and 1870s, Congressman Buckalew urged proportional representation as a means of ensuring the enfranchisement of blacks in the post-bellum south. Horace Greeley supported proportional representation as a means of enfranchising a wider group of minorities. Unsurprisingly, the positive impact that proportional representation would have had on minority representation turned out to be a political weakness for proportional representation, not a strength.

The absence of proportional representation in the United States and the United Kingdom is particularly surprising because the idea first circulated widely in those countries. But, despite the early success of the idea in England and America, and indeed the popularity of proportional representation among many thinkers in both countries proportional representation never came to their national governments, and it gradually lost steam as an idea. During the Progressive Era, when electoral reforms (such as the referendum and the recall) were very much at the fore, proportional representation never became a big rallying cry. Progressives did make major institutional changes, such as eliminating the indirect election of

---

[2] Apparently, Thomas Hill had worked out an early variant in 1819, which was actually implemented by his son Rowland in Australian municipal elections in the 1840s (Tideman and Richardson 2000).

senators, but proportional representation at the national level never came close to passing. Local proportional representation, which had become quite common by the 1930s, was generally rolled back after the war. By the 1950s its detractors emphasized a link between proportional representation and the communist menace (Kolesar 1996).

Proportional representation failed to catch on in the United States in this early period for two reasons. First, the tendency of proportional representation to particularly favor both a large, new immigrant population and African-Americans made it unappealing for the majority of white, native Americans. Barber (1995: 66) argues that "The election of two Communist Party members in New York City in 1945, and of African Americans in Toledo and Cincinnati, figured prominently in repeal campaigns" that eliminated proportional representation. Kolesar (1996) writes:

The Cincinnati Republican organization in 1957 focused its efforts . . . on the more general charge that P.R. fostered "bloc voting." By this they meant voting on racial, ethnic, or religious lines. "Whether by design or by chance this campaign exploited current social tensions in a manner disastrous to P.R.," Forest Frank reported, including "widespread word-of-mouth rumor-mongering to the effect that 'if P.R. is retained, a Negro will be the next mayor.' " In white precincts, P.R. lost by a 2 to 1 margin; voters in black precincts supported its retention by 4 to 1.

As such, the defeat of proportional representation in the United States presents us with an example of the primary theme of our next chapter: American racial divisions acting to limit movements toward a welfare state.

Second, conservative forces within the United States were too powerful to allow a reform of that magnitude. The courts, which were often a bulwark of conservatism in the early twentieth century, struck down proportional representation in California and Michigan. The left-wing uprisings that pushed proportional representation through in many European nations were much less threatening in the United States. The right tarred proportional representation by linking it with both Nazism and Communism and relied on American nationalism to defeat this reform (Kolesar 1996).

But, just as proportional representation disappeared as a potential reform within the United States, it swept continental Europe. The first country to adopt proportional representation on a nationwide level was Belgium in 1899 (Barber 1995: 15). At the start of the decade, the Belgian franchise was among the most restricted in Europe. Indeed, the political dominance of the wealthy in Belgium prior to 1890 led Karl Marx [1869] (1975: 47) to describe that country as "the paradise of the landlord, the capitalist, and the priest." Starting in the 1880s, with the Worker's Revolt of 1886 and culminating in the massive General Strike of 1893, the labor movement was able to force reform. These strikes were devastating. Rosa Luxemborg [1906] (1971: 72), an eyewitness, wrote that "the mass strike is the first natural, impulsive form of every great revolutionary struggle of the proletariat." The 1893 strike led the country to expanded male suffrage in the elections of 1894, and to a significant increase in the power of the social democrats.

Over the next five years, electoral reform continued and the socialists and the Catholic party together produced Europe's first national proportional representation scheme. While ethnic heterogeneity worked against proportional representation in the United States, the Catholic Party seems to have supported proportional representation to ensure that the votes in areas where Catholics were minorities would be counted. The difference between the United States and Belgium appears to come from the fact that in the United States, the minorities were politically (and militarily) weak, while the Catholic groups in Belgium were much stronger (which is consistent with the predictions of the model by Aghion et al. 2002).

Finland was the next European country to adopt nationwide proportional representation in 1906. During this period, Finland was an autonomous part of Russia. The push for constitutional reform came from the Social Democrats who led a national strike in 1905 (which followed the general strike in Russia that started in October). In Finland, the strikers were more effective and essentially forced the Tsar to acquiesce to at least some of their demands, one of which was proportional representation. As in Belgium, proportional representation was a direct result of the power of the left.

Sweden introduced proportional representation in 1907 when it significantly extended the size of the franchise by moving to universal suffrage. Again, demonstrations appear to have been important in creating reform and extending the franchise, but they were considerably less extensive than in Finland or Belgium. Proportional representation in this case was put in by conservative, not socialist, forces (led by Prime Minister Lindmann) which expected to be a minority after the extension of the franchise. Proportional representation could ensure that the old elites could maintain at least some representation in the newly democratic state. In this case, it was the lingering elite, not the nascent worker's movement that pushed through proportional representation. As proportional representation accompanied populist reforms in Sweden, but was meant to reduce their impact, the Swedish example definitely raises the possibility that proportional representation may correlate with the welfare state, not because it caused the welfare, but because it accompanied the power of the labor movement.

Portugal revolted against its monarch, King Manuel II, in 1910 and introduced proportional representation in its 1911 constitution. Although the revolution's success owed much to the support from the armed forces, its leaders were radicals. Proportional representation in Portugal was introduced as a direct result of the ability of the left to mobilize military power and seize control of that relatively small country.

Despite these early movers, in 1914 most of Europe (outside of France) had monarchs and did not have proportional representation. At the end of the war, this would change. Between 1917 and 1920, Austria, Denmark, France, Germany, Italy, Norway, the Netherlands, and Switzerland all adopted some form of proportional representation. Indeed, within western Europe, the only major countries that did not have proportional representation by 1920 were England and Spain. Venizelos of Greece pulled a Mitterand-like flip-flop and first introduced proportional representation in 1926 (when the military dictatorship ended) and then eliminated it in 1928.

The smaller countries that adopted proportional representation during this period—Denmark, the Netherlands, and Switzerland— did so during the war and relatively peacefully. The case of Switzerland mirrors Belgium and Finland. During World War I, Switzerland had hosted a remarkable congregation of leading left-wing revolutionaries, including Lenin, Trotsky, and Zinoviev. During this era, the left grew strong, and in 1918, partially inspired by the Russian Revolution, Swiss socialists led a revolutionary national strike. As the socialists believed (surely correctly) that majoritarianism stymied their electoral chances, they demanded proportional representation. To quell the strike, their demand was met. Again, proportional representation was instituted as a response to the power of the left.

In Denmark and the Netherlands, the move to proportional representation was more gradual and nonviolent. In both cases, proportional representation was instituted during World War I, but constitutional reform was not a response to a general strike. Instead, the move to proportional representation was a peaceful electoral reform. In Denmark, this reform reflected the powerful left-wing combination of the Vestre (Liberals or Radicals) and the Social Democrats, which formed a dominant bloc even prior to proportional representation. The Dutch case is particularly idiosyncratic. Proportional representation (and universal suffrage) emerged from a package deal where the socialists supported the religious parties' demand for public funding of schools in exchange for support for electoral reform. This odd pairing of reforms became the Pacification of 1917.

The adoption of proportional representation in Austria, Italy, and Germany is much closer to the Belgian model: The political (indeed, military) power of the left, which was expressed in revolutions and strikes, led to electoral reform. In these cases, however, there is a slight twist; the left became powerful only because the right, and the army, was enormously weakened by the chaos of World War I.

Before World War I, Germany and Austria were both dominated by the political right and by their hereditary monarchs. From 1848 onward, left-wing agitation was suppressed with the explicit, or more commonly implicit, authority of loyal armed forces. Military defeat, however, left the army disorganized and demoralized. In Germany, after defeat, the Kaiser abdicated and fled to Holland. In 1919, the Spartacists, led by Karl Liebknecht and Rosa Luxemburg (who was a keen observer of the Belgian experience), seized Berlin. Eventually, the more moderate Social Democrats, with the help of right-wing paramilitaries (the Freikorps) and the army, suppressed the revolution. The continuing threat of allied intervention limited the ability of the army to impose a military government, and the army handed the government over to the socialists. The Weimar constitution, and the ensuing electoral law, put into place the proportional representation that had long been a part of the socialist agenda.

The Austrian experience resembles that of Germany. Military defeat was followed by riots, strikes, and the abdication of the last Habsburg (under duress). The Social Democrats then immediately declared a republic and won a plurality (40 percent) in the first elections. The Austrian socialists crafted a constitution, closely modeled on that of Weimar Germany, which included proportional representation. Again, institutional reform reflected the collapse of the military and the right, and the growing power of the socialists.

Italy adopted proportional representation in its electoral law of September 1919. This move reflected Italy's political instability and the increasing power of the unions (who staged strikes on a monthly basis). Even before the reform, the socialists had become the largest single party in Parliament. Moreover, World War I left a large group of armed and disgruntled veterans who were relatively unhappy with the status quo, so revolution was a clear possibility. The electoral reform both reflected the power of the socialists and attempted to head off the possibility of a complete overthrow of the government.

Proportional representation in Austria, Germany, and Italy did not last. Mussolini began to establish a Fascist dictatorship in 1922. Austria and Germany both became dictatorships eleven years later. Proportional representation disappeared along with democratic representation. However, after World War II, proportional representation returned in all three countries. In Austria, this return is not difficult to understand. In 1945, the Austrian Republic returned exactly to the 1920 constitution (as amended in 1929), which was itself loosely modeled on Weimar and which deeply reflected the demands of the labor movement.

In Germany and Italy, the postwar constitutions require somewhat more analysis. In both cases, the war had decimated the secular right.

In both countries, there were essentially two functioning political blocs, which were not tarred by association with Hitler or Mussolini: the Christian Democrats and the left (Social Democrats in Germany and a combination of socialists and communists in Italy). In both countries, constitutional change was managed by Christian Democrat leaders (Adenauer in Germany and De Gasperi in Italy), but these leaders were constrained by both the power of the left and the desire to create some link to the pre-fascist constitutions. In Germany, Adenauer tried to weaken proportional representation by strengthening the majoritarian upper house (the *Landtag*) and by instituting the 5 percent rule, which created a barrier blocking the smallest parties. Nonetheless, the uniform support of the left for proportional representation left it part of the German constitution. In Italy, support for proportional representation came both from the left and from De Gasperi himself, who thought its fractionalizing tendencies would limit dictatorship.

By 1921, the only countries (England and Spain) to have not instituted proportional representation in western Europe were larger countries that had not been invaded during the war, and where civil authority kept control. Ultimately, both Iberian nations used proportional representation as soon as they became democracies in the 1970s. Only England and France would end up without proportional representation systems.

The absence of proportional representation meant that England during the interwar years was led by a sequence of relatively conservative leaders (Bonar Law, Stanley Baldwin, Neville Chamberlain, and even Ramsay MacDonald were far to the right of the continental socialists). Indeed, the lack of proportional representation surely helps us to understand both the small size of the English welfare state relative to the welfare state of continental countries and the moderation of Labour leaders (e.g. Tony Blair).

Why did England not adopt proportional representation? One possibility is that the labor movement only acquired power when Labour became the largest party. There was never a situation when Labour was both a clear minority party and able to create disorder in a way that forced constitutional change. Labour leaders did lead national strikes both before and after World War II, but by the time these strikes occurred, MacDonald had already been Prime Minister and Labour was already one of the two main parties. By that time, there was little to gain in supporting proportional representation, which would only lower the barriers to entry for potential opponents. During earlier periods, when Labour was a minority and would have benefited from proportional representation, the army was too strong to be challenged by national left-wing uprisings. Moreover, England's large size (relative to Belgium and Switzerland) meant that the industrial heartland of the north was too far from London for strikes in those areas to directly impact the nation's political elite.

As we discussed above, France moved to proportional representation in the Fourth Republic. The case of France also suggests that proportional representation comes and goes with the political and military power of the left. Proportional representation came in after the war, when the heavily communist resistance was in power (both politically and militarily). As the right gained strength in the 1950s, proportional representation was eliminated. One can easily see de Gaulle's presidency as the result of an aborted rightist coup, so it is not a stretch to argue that again military strength drove political institutions.

The history of proportional representation illustrates three aspects of constitutional change. First, proportional suffrage has generally been the policy of socialists who thought it would strengthen their hand. Presumably, this belief came about because at the moment of constitutional reform, the socialists were generally a minority party. Perhaps labor unions knew that they could always count on a core of single issue voters, and these voters would confer success in proportional representation systems. As such, proportional representation has tended to reflect the existence of socialist power.

Second, suffrage reform and proportional representation were generally accompanied by a breakdown in law and order. In most cases, these reforms were touched off either by general strikes or actual revolutions. This breakdown in law and order reflects both the growing power of the left to disrupt society and often a breakdown in the power or willingness of the military to defend the status quo. Armies are generally used by leaders for two purposes: Defending against outsiders and repressing internal disorder. When the outsiders have dealt the military crushing blows, the military does not remain able to discipline internal threats. This is certainly the story of the Russian Revolution or the early successes of the Spartacist uprising (which was eventually checked by the right-wing elements that remained in the German army).

Third, as time has passed there has been an increasing tendency of new constitutions (such as the Spanish and Portuguese constitutions) to adopt proportional representation. In these cases, we suspect that adopting proportional representation has more to do with conforming to European norms than anything else. These countries became democracies late and indeed a major force propelling them towards democracy was a desire to integrate with the much wealthier democratic European nations. As integration was a key element of the switch to democracy, it was also natural for them to adopt the dominant form of European democracy: proportional representation.

As such, the political power of socialist and labor groups in the early part of the century are the primary cause of proportional representation in Europe. In country after country, the ability of these groups to call general strikes, or outright revolutions, led to constitutional reform. Now we must ask why these socialist groups were so much more powerful in Europe than in the United States.

5.3. Socialist parties in Europe and the United States

Why did socialist and communist parties flourish in Europe but not in the United States? Why was the labor movement in Europe much more successful than in the United States in imposing institutional changes in its favor? Our analysis will point to three elements of United States exceptionalism: (a) geography, (b) ethnic and racial heterogeneity, and (c) military success. We believe that other factors, such as the tendency of American unions to focus on wages rather than politics, are also important. But we see these other factors as results of these innate elements.

America's vast geographic spread ensured that despite the dramatic local success of many early labor groups in the United States, it was impossible to organize an effective nationwide movement that threatened the entire nation. For example, during the heyday of the movement, labor unions never made significant inroads into the primarily agricultural south. In Europe, small size made it easier to organize national strikes that shocked the entire country. The size of a largely unsettled American continent also allowed for an escape from poverty in the cities of the East through westward migration, searching for individualist "fortune" rather than collective redistribution.[3] This feature of the United States may also have had profound cultural implications that we discuss in the next chapter.

The relative ethnic homogeneity of European countries ensured a unified labor movement, which was able to generate broad sympathy from the population at large. On the contrary, the racial and ethnic fractionalization of the American labor force made up by successive waves of immigrants of different nationality had a profound implication on the strength of the labor movement. Irish workers felt first Irish and then workers; they often saw, say, Italian workers as antagonists more than they saw capital as their enemy. America's ethnic and racial heterogeneity made it easy for antilabor groups to divide the left. Marx and Engels had already perceived this problem as a key reason why a European-style labor movement in the United States was unlikely to take root. Race conflicts between whites and blacks were of course even more marked and remain a critical feature of U.S. history, as we discuss in Chapter 6.

Finally, from 1865, the United States never lost a war on its own soil against a foreign army, let alone a war fought on its territory with the devastating effects of World War I in Europe. The devastation of the Great War increased grievances among the poor. Moreover, the connection between soldiers and workers became a powerful anticapital tool, as we will see below. America's military success meant that the labor movement always faced an organized military with the discipline to fire on marchers. The disorganization of the military in times of military failure (such as in Germany in 1919) or even in military quasi-success (such as in Italy during the same era or France in 1945) made it possible for organized left-wing groups to dominate the country. As we will discuss later, the military power of the American

---

[3] Of course, Russia shares America's vast size, and they became Europe's leading communist nation. There are two explanations for this puzzle. First, Russia's government suffered a shattering defeat during World War I. Second, Russian concentration of political power in Moscow and St. Petersburg made it much more vulnerable to organized revolution.

organized left in some sense reached its apogee in 1863, and if Gettysburg had gone differently, it is hard to tell what would have happened in the north. The south did lose a war on its own soil and had its government completely reorganized as a result. But the terms of this reorganization were dictated by the victorious, Republican north.

5.3.1. The roots of labor movements

Popular labor movements were the stepchildren of the industrial revolution and the move to cities. Effective organization requires density. Throughout most of history, communication (especially somewhat subversive communication) required word-of-mouth discussion and that requires high densities. The city brought large groups of workers together who could discuss their grievances and possible methods of eliminating their problems. Furthermore, urban density helped civilian strikers (or marchers or rioters) resist the organized military. As Napoleon III and Baron Haussmann knew when they widened the streets of Paris in an attempt to reduce the possibility of revolution, narrow city streets make it difficult for cavalry to maneuver and for infantry to keep in formation.

Before the Industrial Revolution, farmers certainly had grievances. Indeed, despite the well-known social problems associated with industrialization, it is at least as likely that the common association of poverty with the Industrial Revolution comes from the fact that industrial workers were better at airing their problems than dispersed farmers, as that these workers were actually worse off than their agricultural forbearers. Preindustrial farmers certainly formed temporary political groups and had peasant revolts, especially when starvation threatened. However, low rural densities and high transportation costs made organization difficult. Furthermore, the overwhelming military advantage that soldiers have in an open field ensured that these revolts were almost always easily suppressed by military forces that were often much smaller than the peasant mobs.

Cities made it possible for workers to meet regularly to exchange ideas and to organize. After all, the cradle of the American Revolution was urban Boston and it was the *sans-culottes* of Paris who were the popular backbone of the French Revolution. Indeed, one view (Moore 1966) is that the mixing of military and civilians in eighteenth-century

Paris ensured exchange between these groups and limited the willingness of the French army to fire on the revolutionaries. As mentioned above, one clear lesson is that sympathy by the army for strikers or revolutionaries tends to be deadly for existing regimes. As urbanization spread in the nineteenth century, there were large numbers of propertyless workers in high-density areas. In all major European countries and the United States, some form of labor movement accompanied industrialization.

Given the strong connection between industrialization and left-wing political groups, it shouldn't surprise us that the first labor movements occurred in England, France, and the United States, where nascent labor movements formed as early as the 1820s and 1830s. Somewhat oddly, in at least two of the countries where socialism first developed, socialism had the least impact.

5.3.2. *The labor movement in England*

In England, trade unions were legally repressed by the Combinations Act until its repeal in 1824. After this point, the labor movement moved in two different directions: Economic (towards unionism) and political (towards a labor party). The lines between these two movements are often blurry and, until the rise of Tony Blair, the trade unions were dominant actors in the British Labour Party. The early history of the trade union movement in Britain included both Owenism, which focused on idealized cooperative communities, and Chartism, with its more practical goal of universal manhood suffrage.

As Acemoglu and Robinson (2000) have argued, there is a strong symbiotic relationship between the expanding power of the labor movement and the expansion of the franchise in the United Kingdom. Violent actions preceded the voting reform acts and were certainly one of the key motivations for these acts. Even if individual politicians pushed voting reform in the hope that the new voters would be loyal to the leaders responsible for giving them the vote, the violent upheavals ensured a common consensus that the highly restricted franchise was ultimately untenable. There was also a belief, which generally proved to be accurate, that by extending the franchise, the labor movement would see that its cheapest and most effective means to power was to win elections rather than to lead uprisings.

While large-scale strikes were a regular tool of the English Labour movement (through the Thatcher era), after the Voting Reform Act of 1867 these strikes never truly threatened revolution. The British labor movement did take the view that it was easier to acquire power through the voting booth than through constitutional upheaval. Two factors ensured that the returns to the labor movement of legal political activity were greater than the returns to massive uprisings. First, the British parliamentary model was much more conducive to organized labor than other systems, such as the American system, would prove to be. Second, British military authority was always sufficiently strong to suppress national strikes. Britain never lost a major war, and its army remained a competent force. Furthermore, the peacetime army tended to be a socially distinct group that was unlikely to develop major sympathies for the labor movement.

The amenability of the British parliamentary system to the labor movement requires more explanation. The relatively small size of parliamentary districts combined with the segregation of workers meant that many districts were naturally dominated by labor. Once universal manhood suffrage became established, it was inevitable that the mining areas of Britain would end up electing labor leaders like Keir Hardie to Parliament. The combination of small districts and the geographic concentration of working men led to a situation like that created by proportional representation where socialist groups were able to get their representatives elected.

As such, from an early date, Parliamentary leaders became highly sympathetic to the wishes of the labor movement. This initially took the form of elite leaders moving to the left. The most conspicuous example is William Gladstone who moved over his very long parliamentary career from being a high Tory with a deep commitment to the esoteric issues surrounding the traditional Church of England to the People's William, who ran for election in the labor-heavy Midlothian district (Edinburgh). Later, elite leaders of the Liberal Party were replaced by leaders with more humble origins (such as Lloyd George) and by leaders from the labor movement itself, such as Ramsay MacDonald and Clement Attlee. Even Winston Churchill in his early days in government was very sympathetic to the grievances of the labor movement.

Additionally, the British parliamentary system did not have strong institutional checks, which would have barred the progress of the labor movement. From 1640 to 1860, there had been steady erosion in the power of the traditional chief executive (the King) and a concentration of power in the lower House of Parliament. This erosion had been accomplished primarily by Whig Grandees, hardly natural supporters of the labor movement; nonetheless, by the time the labor movement began, there was no independent executive to check Parliament. There was, however, the House of Lords. However, as was shown in 1909, the dominance of the lower House over the King could effectively ensure the subservience of the House of Lords. All that the King needed to do was to threaten to pack the House of Lords with a large, new crop of appointed nobles and the House fell into line. As England had a small-district parliament, which faced few external checks, the labor movement found it relatively easy to ride to power within the established constitution and saw no reason to challenge the well-organized military through a more general uprising.

5.3.3. The labor movement in western continental Europe

In the middle nineteenth century, socialist movements began to become strong in Germany, France, and the Low Countries, where workers organized and formed labor unions and working class political movements. As discussed above, in these countries socialist parties were able to rewrite their constitutions in a way that entrenched their political power. The history of socialist success in continental Europe highlights the ability of labor uprisings to force constitutional change. In smaller countries, these uprisings were effective because the seats of power were so close to the masses of industrial workers. In larger countries, labor uprisings only became successful when the regular army became too disorganized to be used against marching workers. Thus, there are two factors that led to socialist dominance in Europe: Density and military defeat (or at least disorganization).

Belgium provides an example of how powerful a labor uprising can be in a small, industrial country. The Belgian Workers Party was founded in 1885, and as discussed above, its early struggle focused primarily on achieving a broader franchise. In its early history, this socialist party primarily used strikes and other uprisings to force electoral reform. Starting in Liège and then spreading throughout Belgium, laborers rioted and demanded change. Eventually, the strikes were suppressed by the army, but these suppressions were bloody and costly. Ultimately, the conservative authorities were convinced that electoral reform was better than continued violence, and these uprisings led to an extension of the franchise in 1893, proportional representation in 1899, and ultimately universal male suffrage in 1913.

Why were these assaults so successful? While Belgium's army was not disorganized, it was small and less socially isolated from the population than the armies of England and the United States. Belgium had its classic Walloon–Fleming divide, but its small size ensured social proximity between soldiers and rioters. Social links between soldiers and strikers makes repression more difficult. Furthermore, Belgium's small size ensured that riots in Liège were going to be felt in Brussels. It was the first continental country to industrialize and it had large pockets of industrial areas. Finally, by 1913, the German threat meant that the government chief, Broqueville, preferred concession to chaos. In a sense, Belgium was the ideal spot for a workers' uprising and we should not be surprised that it was the first country in Europe to adopt proportional representation in response to workers' riots.

The extended franchise and proportional representation was the basis for socialist electoral success in the 1920s and 1930s. The first major socialist successes occurred in the 1925 election, when socialists joined the Catholic–Socialist governing coalition. But despite these early successes, the interwar years were marked by relatively conservative control. The first socialist Prime Minister (Spaak) led the country for less than a year beginning in May 1938. Belgian socialists only fully achieved power in the immediate postwar period under Van Acker, where they governed during the period of royal exile, and again during the 1954–8 period. Socialist authority during the postwar period was helped by the strong communist presence in the resistance, and the collaboration between right-wing politicians and the Nazis. Since the 1960s, Belgian politics has generally been divided among liberals (the right), Catholic parties, and socialists, and proportional representation has ensured that the socialists often have enough power to keep the welfare state strong.

The socialist movement in Germany achieved impressive electoral results, but little real power. The Wilhelmine constitution kept an astonishingly large degree of power in the hands of the monarch who personally selected the Chancellor. As such, the electoral success of Social Democrats before World War I translated into little real authority. Furthermore, before 1917, Germany's army was both superbly organized and socially distinct from the general population. As Ritchie (1998) discusses, the Prussian kings were acutely aware of the danger of revolution and kept their soldiers separate to ensure their willingness to attack the general population. As a result, until 1918 Prussian soldiers repeatedly showed themselves willing to fire on civilians. Furthermore, Germany's large size meant that workers uprising in industrial areas were unlikely to upset the Kaiser or his core support group of Prussian Junkers. Even after the brief revolutionary successes of 1848, the Prussian military ultimately found it relatively easy to reestablish its supremacy.

As a result of Germany's large size and military power, until the end of the World War I German institutions were in place that ensured the relative impotence of the left. Until World War I, Germany was a conservative state with a fairly weak labor movement. This situation changed radically in 1918. Four years of fighting under terrible conditions finally led to military collapse. The traditional military leadership was unable to retain control of the country, in part because they ultimately lost control of the military itself. After the British broke through the German lines on August 8, the military high command, in an attempt to mollify the allies, proclaimed a constitutional monarchy and installed Prince Max of Baden (a relatively liberal aristocrat) as Chancellor, still leaving the Social Democrats marginalized.

But in 1918, Berlin exploded in the Spartacist uprising. Led by Karl Liebknecht, this left-wing (indeed communist) uprising took control of the capital and it seemed briefly that Germany would go the way of Russia. Liebknecht was particularly violent, but he was not particularly popular. Both Ebert and Scheidemann were socialist leaders with far more popular support and far more legitimacy. Ebert broke from the revolution and struck a bargain with the remaining leaders of the German military. The generals agreed to accept his government and repress the revolution, and Ebert agreed to keep Hindenburg at the head of the army. The paramilitary right-wing Freikorps (many of whom later provided the muscle for the Nazis), as well as the regular army, ended the Spartacist uprising and handed power over to Ebert. At this point, they were not ready to create their own right-wing regime (that would have to wait until the 1930s).

Why did the army hand the government over to the Social Democrats? Why did the generals not just end the uprising and impose a military dictatorship? In fact, Ebert's presidency sprung from his own sources of military strength. First, he had his own supporters, the soldiers' and workers' councils (which had been established in imitation of comparable revolutionary councils in Russia), and his own socialist volunteer corps (led by Gustav Noske). Second, he had the shadowy presence of the victorious allies who appeared quite willing to intervene to stop the establishment of German military dictatorship. Ebert's internal and external supporters gave him the military clout to induce the military to hand him the reins of power.

In February 1919, Ebert opened a national assembly in Weimar that wrote a new constitution designed to support socialist aspirations. Institutions were remolded to reflect the new military reality. The Weimar constitution featured proportional representation and relatively few checks, such as the House of Lords or the U.S. Supreme Court, on the power of elected legislators. Only the strength of the office of the Presidency, which would first be held by Ebert himself, offered balance to the legislature. Furthermore, the constitution enshrined certain long-desired workers' aims such as the right to collectively bargain and the eight-hour day. Pro-socialist institutions eventually came to Germany, but only in the wake of a disastrous military defeat and a successful, but brief, workers' revolution. Indeed, the socialist inspired institutions led to significant socialist success during the 1920s.

Of course, by 1933, using a combination of legal and extralegal means, the German right reasserted its power. Hindenburg was elected President after Ebert, and he was able to use that one major check on socialist power to push his own right-wing agenda.

Furthermore, during the Weimar era (at least during the Hindenburg era) the army used its muscle to suppress left-wing military power. The Nazis' armed supporters generally acted with impunity. As soon as the right had reestablished its military dominance, the pro-socialist institutions vanished and were replaced by the repressive Nazi regime.

But while Hitler destroyed the pro-socialist institutions, he did not eliminate social service spending. After all, the Nazis were National *Socialists*. The "unalterable" twenty-five-point Program of the National Socialist party established in 1920 included: "all unearned income, and all income that does not arise from work, be abolished" (point 11), "profit-sharing in large industries" (point 14), "a generous increase in old-age pensions" (point 15), and "the enactment of a law to expropriate the owners without compensation of any land needed for the common purpose" (point 17). Indeed, Hitler was a much more aggressive redistributor than FDR. Hitler was unfettered by constitutional constraints and engaged in redistribution (often through public works programs) both to build popular support and to increase the power of the state.

In the aftermath of World War II and the reforms of the 1949 constitution, Germany came to be dominated by the Christian Democrats (initially under Adenauer, then under Kohl) and the Social Democrats. The Christian Democrats, however, were initially far from right wing. The Christian Social Union (their coalition partner) called for nationalization of key industries. Adenauer promulgated the co-determination law, which gave labor unions seats on company boards. Even though the Social Democrats would have to wait until 1969 for their own Chancellor, key objectives of the labor movement, including the welfare state, were being implemented by the Christian Democrats. No doubt much of this was the result of the strength of the socialist opposition and a desire to ensure reelection.

Like Germany, pre-World War I Italy had institutions that were less friendly to socialism than those in the United States and Britain. The Italian monarchs retained more control than their English counterparts and suffrage was restricted until World War I. A relatively elite group of nationalist, classically liberal politicians dominated Italian politics during this time period. Their dominance was ensured through institutions that limited suffrage and kept control over the executive branch in the hands of the king. Violent uprisings were suppressed by the army, and martial law was declared in several major cities in the 1890s. Still, despite the failure of armed uprisings, the socialists were gaining power. In 1903, they were invited to join the cabinet, but they strategically declined.

However, at the end of World War I, while Italy was victorious, its army returned dispirited and in disarray. Many soldiers were sympathetic to socialist aims, and the left had made large inroads into the conscripted army. Riots and strikes at the end of the war could not be met with overwhelming military force and the country moved towards compromise with the left, rather than repression. The result was constitutional reform that left Italy with a constitution that was less pro-labor than that of Weimar, but certainly with fewer checks against socialist power. Universal male suffrage was adopted in 1918; proportional representation was established in 1919. These changes meant that following the 1919 elections, the socialist party became the largest party in parliament, with 34 percent of the seats. The Populari, a left-wing Catholic party, also elected more than 100 deputies.

The period between 1919 and 1922 saw the first socialist Prime Minister (Bonomi) and an increasing quantity of both right-wing and left-wing inspired disorder. D'Annunzio's nationalist group captured Fiume in 1919 and labor unions called a general strike. Uprisings occurred throughout Italy. Indeed, at this point, it seemed perfectly possible that Italy would follow Russia into communism. Instead, the authorities supported Mussolini and his blackshirted thugs who specialized in unregulated violence, often against the labor movement. Under Mussolini, the electoral reforms of 1918–19 became dead letters as the country became a dictatorship. Like Hitler, Mussolini certainly was sympathetic to many aspects of socialism, and during the Fascist regime, social spending expanded (although surely less than what it would have under a socialist government).

After World War II, the Italian constitution returned to proportional representation. The left had generally been extremely strong and in many elections, the communists were the largest single party.

Communist opposition to Mussolini provided one source of their legitimacy. Indeed, the political power of the left is reflected in the fact that even many members of the supposedly right-wing Christian Democratic Party, such as Prime Minister Fanfani, strongly supported the welfare state. The destruction of the right in 1945 and the postwar constitution created the basis of left-wing political power.

While sustained left-wing power did not occur in Italy until the period after 1953, France is a pioneer of left-wing power. In 1789, 1830, 1848, 1871, and 1945, left-wing groups gained some form of military ascendancy, at least over Paris, and the centralized nature of French society (a legacy of Philip Augustus and Louis XIV) meant that control over Paris generally implied control over the rest of the country (notwithstanding the counter-revolutionaries in the Vendée). In each of those years, left-wing groups were able to take control of the government and to craft new institutions thought to be more conducive to left-wing power. In 1830 and 1945, these changes were relatively moderate. In 1789, 1848, and 1871, the changes were revolutionary in every sense.

Despite the remarkable revolutionary success of the French left, the left has governed France for only relatively brief periods. Generally, left-wing revolutionary success has not led to permanent left-wing institutions. The first revolution was followed by Bonapartism. The revolution of 1830 led to the bourgeois monarchy of Louis Philippe. The 1848 revolution led to the second Bonaparte and the 1871 Paris commune was replaced by the relatively sedate Third Republic. Left-wing institutions enacted in 1945 lasted for only thirteen years when they were replaced by de Gaulle's Fifth Republic, which has elected only one socialist president in forty-five years.

France's first socialist party, the French Workers' Party, was founded in 1880, but a socialist government was not elected until 1936. In that year, Leon Blum and the Popular Front started a short-lived socialist government. After the war, the 1944–58 period saw a significant number of socialist governments and again the socialists returned to power under Mitterand. Indeed, looking at election results one might be tempted to conclude that the history of the French left is a story of failure and impotence.

This conclusion would, however, severely understate the impact of the left on French politics. While the right has steadily won Presidential elections since 1958, like the Christian Democrats in Germany and Italy, they adopted policies that were in many respects close to those of the socialists. Nationalized industries, heavy regulation, and the welfare state have been accepted by both parties. The policies of Giscard D'Estaing or Jacques Chirac are much closer to the policies of Francois Mitterand than to the policies of Margaret Thatcher or Ronald Reagan. While the socialists have been relatively unsuccessful at winning Presidential elections, they have been quite successful at moving French politics to the left and ensuring the establishment of the welfare state.

Indeed, the socialists have never been as weak as Presidential election results make them seem. By 1936, socialists had managed to make themselves a powerful presence. In the 1944–58 period, the left was dominant and it used that period to entrench nationalization and the welfare state. During the Fifth Republic, right-wing victories have often been narrow, and often socialists have controlled the legislature. In 1958, the left lost the presidency, but labor unions remained able to influence elections. De Gaulle's Presidency was a victory for French nationalism, not laissez-faire. The continuing power of the labor movement makes it doubtful that de Gaulle could have maintained his popularity if he had tried to roll back the welfare state, and his successors, Geroges Pompidou and Valerie Giscard d'Esating had more lassaif faire views but the latter was electorally defeated.

The office of the presidency, and the formal structure of French politics, has had a right-wing orientation since 1958, but this orientation has enabled the right to win elections, not to eliminate the French welfare state. The strong power of labor unions, which continue to be able to paralyze the economy with strikes, combined with the entrenched bureaucracy, which has a strong stake in seeing the welfare state continue, ensures that the shift to the left, begun under Blum and extended during the Fourth Republic, remains to this day.

5.3.4. The labor movement in the United States

Finally, we turn to the United States and ask why the American left was so much less successful than its European counterparts. Unlike the British Labour party, the American left was never able to achieve success within the existing American institutions. Unlike the socialist parties on the continent, the American left was never able to force a major change in the constitution. Both of these failures need to be explained.

The early labor movement in the United States resembled that of the United Kingdom, but if anything it was more violent. After the brief vogue of Owenism in the 1820s and 1830s, the American labor movement moved towards aggressive strike and riot activity that regularly turned bloody. For example, "at the peak of [pre-Civil War] labor activity in 1853–54, more than 400 union strikes were recorded in the largest American states" (Wilentz 1990: 115). These strikes were both economic and political. Extremist rhetoric called for an end to both wages and to the "wage system."

The labor movement in the United States really gathered steam after the Civil War. The decades after the Civil War witnessed the rise of the first national labor movement—the Knights of Labor. The late nineteenth century saw large-scale labor violence throughout the country. Railroad strikes were particularly bloody and Chicago's 1883 Haymarket Street riot is now commemorated throughout the world (outside of the United States) on May 1 as a day of the labor movement. The American labor movement of the nineteenth century was strong and often committed to violent confrontation with authorities.

Over the twentieth century, the labor movement met as much failure as success, and completely failed to develop (or co-opt) a major political party. One reason for this failure was American racial and ethnic fragmentation. Many labor unions were originally segregated. As the numbers of African-Americans in northern cities increased, original policies of exclusion were replaced by separate (and unequal) unions for blacks. This racial divide provided an important tool for management, which could use African-Americans as strikebreakers, which was done on many occasions such as the 1919 steel strike (Spero and Harris 1931). Over time, unions, especially industrial unions (as opposed to craft unions, see Ashenfelter 1972), came to include minorities. But during the period of initial union growth, when unions in Europe were becoming dominant political actors, racial divisions within the United States served to split the labor movement.

In political battles, racial animosities often tended to hurt political groups that tried to represent the interests of labor. The Populist Party, the first American party dedicated to redistribution between rich and poor, was defeated in the south by southern conservatives playing on the racial hatred of the region, a topic that we revisit later. The American Socialist Party was one heir to the populists, and Eugene Debs (the socialists' perennial standard bearer) had initially supported populist icon and Democratic candidate William Jennings Bryan. Debs, and the Socialists, were often depicted as representing foreign ethnics and other treacherous enemies of the republic. Indeed, Debs was put in jail for his opposition to World War I, and ran for president in 1920 (receiving almost one million votes) from a jail cell. During and after World War I, socialism was attacked as practiced by "hyphenated-Americans." At the height of the Red Scare, traditional ethnic divides were exploited to build terror of the supposedly burgeoning Bolshevik threat. Later, candidates who purported to represent the working man, such as Democrat Alfred Smith (who later became a conservative critic of FDR) were similarly attacked for their ethnicity or Catholicism.

While racial fragmentation was certainly extremely important in explaining the relative weakness of America's labor movement, American political institutions were at least as important. One major reason that socialism failed to develop within existing American institutions is because these institutions were "rigged" against socialism, or any comparable minority movement. The American constitution has at least three major institutions, which worked against socialist parties: The Presidency, the Senate, and the Supreme Court.

Winning the presidency requires a majority of electoral votes and this means winning a plurality across a wide geographic area. This majoritarian system not only makes it hard for new parties to get started but specifically over-represents low density, non-industrial states. American presidential candidates have always been close to the middle of the political spectrum, and it was hard for a nascent socialist movement to have any influence on these elections.

The majoritarian and anti-industrial nature of the Senate is even more extreme. The Senate was specifically set up as a check against having too much democracy in the United States. Until the twentieth century, senators were indirectly elected and the corruption in this process generally meant that the Senate became a "millionaire's club." The fact that getting elected was expensive and that the Senate allowed huge opportunities for financial gain (through the modern era as Caro's (2002) *Master of the Senate* makes plain) meant that the few men who were not rich when they were elected became rich afterwards. Such men were unlikely to have much sympathy for the labor movement.

In addition, the Senate disproportionately represents non-industrial areas of the country. The agricultural regions of the south dominated the Senate through the 1960s. The non-industrial west also has had unusual influence. By giving power to politicians from low density areas, the Senate has served as a check on the goals of the labor movement. Nowhere is this more obvious than in the 1930s, where despite the huge popularity of FDR and the New Deal, a coalition of conservative Republicans and Southern Democrats acted to stymie progressive legislation after 1937 (see Brinkley 1995).

One could easily argue that the nineteenth century House of Lords was inherently as anti-redistributionist as the Senate. However, the House of Lords was inherently much weaker than the Senate, because it was ultimately dependent upon the King, who was himself ultimately beholden to Parliament (at least after 1689). Since the King could appoint new lords anytime he wanted, he could completely remake the composition of the House of Lords on a whim. Thus, through its control of the King, the House of Commons was able to dictate terms to the upper chamber and in the first decade of the twentieth century, it used this power to force the House of Lords to eliminate almost all of its authority. The Lords' remaining veto rights were effectively wiped away during the first postwar Labour administration. The unwritten English constitution had separation of powers, but it did not ensure the strength of this separation to the same degree as the written American Constitution did. As such, while the Senate was surely more democratic and progressive than the House of Lords, it was also much more independent and that is what finally counted. While the House of Lords was eliminated as a political force in 1908, the Senate continued as a general check on executive action and in particular as a center of conservative activity.

The courts have been the third bulwark of American conservatism throughout much of U.S. history. The courts are generally protected from popular sentiments and the strength of the Stare Decisis doctrine means that precedent has power. The enormous importance given to precedent ensures a generally conservative bent to the court. Furthermore, the lawyers of the courts (with certain prominent counterexamples) have often been inherently unsympathetic towards the demands of labor.

For example, antitrust acts, meant to strike at monopolies, were understood by the courts to make labor unions illegal. Labor market regulations, which enforced minimum hours or required some limits on working conditions, were seen as violations of the freedom to contract. The Lochner court, which struck down labor regulations, is not a bizarre aberration; it is the norm. It is the liberal Warren and Burgher courts that are much rarer, and even these courts were modest in their support for the goals of organized labor.

These institutions help us to understand why the labor movement might be weak, but as we mentioned above, in 1900, many European countries had institutions that were at least as hostile to the labor movement and to socialism as the institutions of the United States. However, as we discussed above in continental Europe, the labor movement was able to force changes in those institutions. Now we discuss why the labor movement failed to force changes in the institutions of the United States.

5.3.5. The failure of the U.S. left

The single most spectacular uprising in the history of the United States labor movement was the New York City draft riot in 1863. While the draft may not seem like a labor issue, the leadership of this riot came from the labor movement (particularly, the longshoreman's union) and the initial tactics (such as marching while beating copper pots) were borrowed from the labor movement. The rioters were "workers from the city's railroads, machine shops, shipyards and iron foundries, together with building and street laborers working for uptown contractors" (Burrows and Wallace 1999: 888); in other words, workers from the industries that had been centers of trade union activity before the war.

This riot remains the deadliest in U.S. history (at least 105 people died) and it was specifically targeted at stopping the extension of the draft. Over three days, rioters were able to dominate New York City. Two things stopped this riot from toppling Lincoln's government. First, it was in New York, not Washington, and this spatial separation reduced its impact. Second, five Union Army regiments marched north after their victory at Gettysburg. One can easily imagine if the Battle of Gettysburg had been lost that these soldiers would have been far less willing to violently suppress rioters calling for peace. In that case, the riot would not have just forced a relatively minor change in draft administration (the draft was handed over to the infinitely corruptible William Marcy Tweed), but would surely have led to far-reaching reforms.

As such, the riot's failure again highlights the importance of military strength, but there is a second lesson embedded in the history. Ethnic divisions among the rioters had opened up after the first day. While the core of the riot was Irish, Germans had originally joined in, but by the end of the riot, there were a number of Germans who joined with the authorities to patrol their own neighborhoods. As early as the 1860s in the United States, conflicts between ethnicities were detracting from the political power of a laborers' uprising.

In the nineteenth and early twentieth centuries, there were a large number of violent labor uprisings in the United States. Indeed, as mentioned earlier, the international workers' holiday of May 1 commemorates the Chicago Haymarket riot of 1886. The riot began as a nationwide strike for the eight-hour day. The peaceful strike turned into a riot when the police attempted to disburse the crowd. A bomb was thrown and seven policemen died. Ultimately, the riot was ruthlessly suppressed and seven men were sentenced to death (four would eventually hang).

The Homestead strike of 1892 is another example of the bloody labor wars fought in the United States during the nineteenth century. In this incident, an army of 300 Pinkerton detectives and the Pennsylvania State Militia supported Andrew Carnegie in his attempt to disperse workers striking for higher wages. The Pullman Strike, centered in Chicago in 1894, also turned bloody. Using legal backing from the Interstate Commerce Act and the Sherman Anti-Trust Act, railroad officials managed to get a federal court injunction against the strikers. President Grover Cleveland (a Democrat thought to be sympathetic to employers) sent in federal troops to break the strike. Mayhem ensued, but eventually the overpowering strength of the U.S. military broke the strike.

The labor strikes against Carnegie Steel and Pullman Railroad cars are notable both for the tremendous military power used to suppress the strike and also for distance between the strike and Washington. While strikes in Liège at around the same time influenced all of Belgium, Homestead was primarily a local affair and was handled by the Governor of Pennsylvania, not the President of the United States. These strikes were handled with the full might of the U.S. army directed by government officials who lived and worked hundreds of miles from the strikers. Furthermore, the highly professional, geographically isolated nature of the American military ensured that the soldiers could be counted upon to fight against the strikers.

Protestors got closer to Washington in 1894 and 1932. In 1894, Jacob Coxey led an industrial army to Washington to protest the lack of government response to the recession of 1893. The "army" ultimately numbered only 500 and was easily dispersed by the U.S. army. Almost forty years later, at the height of the Depression, the Bonus Expeditionary Force, a band of ex-veterans, marched on Washington demanding early payment of their veteran's pensions as a response to the Depression. This group numbered almost 15,000 and represented a more serious risk to the capital.

Far from showing sympathy to the marchers, Douglas MacArthur (aided by Dwight Eisenhower and George Patton) turned the full might of the military on them. Gas and bayonets were used to dispel the marchers, and while the elected President demanded moderation, the professional soldiers engaged in a devastating chase destroying the march. While the peacetime army was never large (prior to 1945), as they showed in 1932 (and earlier in their dispersal of Coxey's march), they were certainly up to the task of protecting Washington against left-wing uprisings.

American labor uprisings were as large and as violent as those in Europe. Indeed, labor uprisings brought chaos to New York in 1863 and Chicago in 1886. Two factors limited the ability of these uprisings to force constitutional changes. First, America's great distances have made it difficult for strikers in industrial areas to impact Washington, D.C. Second, even when marchers came to Washington, the military proved itself able and willing to maintain order.

American military strength, and the corresponding weakness of European militaries, must be understood as the result of American geography and military success. Over the past 200 years, every major country in mainland Europe has been successfully invaded. Particularly, unsuccessful wars have tended to leave the military weak and unable or unwilling to fight revolution, and defeats have often toppled governments. The empire of Napoleon III was ended at Sedan. The German empire that defeated him was destroyed as Germany was defeated in 1918. World War I was a great ender of empires, as Russia, Austria, and Germany (and Turkey) all lost their autocratic dynasties in that maelstrom. The carnage from that war led to a collapse of republican rule in Italy. World War II ended the Fourth Republic and the fascist regimes that had grown up during the war. By and large, the institutions of continental Europe (with the exception of France and Norway) were formed in 1945 after World War II had destroyed the older regimes. Conversely, America has never lost a major war and has never faced a foreign invasion. As such, its military proved able to keep its dominance against domestic disturbances.

5.4. The American Supreme Court

We end this chapter by considering the curious institution of the American courts. Nowhere is this third branch of government as removed from the political process and as strong as in the United States. While the U.S. judiciary was originally modeled after that of England, the English judiciary has ended up being far less independent and far less powerful than its American counterpart.

In the United States, judges are generally appointed (although some are elected) and they are often explicitly protected from electoral pressure. This is particularly obvious among those judges, such as the Justices of the Supreme Court, who have life tenure. They are generally chosen from the set of successful lawyers. They are also bound by rules of precedent and it is understood that they are allowed to ignore the legislature if they feel that legislation goes against the vague principles of the 200-year-old Constitution. European judges, by contrast, are generally part of the Civil Service. They are often much less independent and much more likely to be influenced by the political process. They are not bound by rules of precedent, and are not usually allowed to reject current legislation on grounds of constitutionality.

The power and independence of the courts in America has often made them a check on the welfare state. They have ruled that labor unions are illegal. They have ruled that legislation interfering with the workplace violates the freedom to contract. They decided that the income tax was unconstitutional. In the 1930s, conservative Supreme Court judges struck down a wide swath of New Deal legislation. While there have certainly been liberal episodes during the history of the court, much more commonly they have been a force of reaction acting to limit popular, progressive movements. The strong attachment of most lawyers to property rights almost ensures that the courts would be fighting against redistribution, not spearheading socialism.

It may seem natural to take the Supreme Court as a constitutional given, but this would be a mistake. The strong American Supreme Court was not established in 1789. It did not become a reality until the middle of John Marshall's first term and even as late as the 1830s, President Andrew Jackson would ignore the Supreme Court and declare "Marshall has ruled, now let him enforce it." John Marshall, more than anyone else, established the Supreme Court as an independent powerful entity. He turned the lackluster, inactive Court of the 1790s into a true third branch of government.

Surely, the most important single case in the evolution of the Court was *Marbury v. Madison*. The details of the case are worth remembering. Marbury was a relatively minor official (a Washington Justice of the Peace) who had been appointed in the waning hours of the Adams administration (like Marshall himself). Indeed, Marshall had been the Secretary of State responsible for the appointment. James Madison, the new Secretary of State under Jefferson, had refused to deliver his commission, and Marbury sued.

The right for Marbury to go to the Supreme Court was established by the Federalist Judiciary Act of 1789. The act conferred explicit powers in this area to the Supreme Court. However, it was possible (and only slightly possible) that this act itself went against Article III of the Constitution. In principle, the Supreme Court could have gone in many different directions. As Marshall himself essentially appointed Marbury, it must have been tempting for Marshall to rule in his favor.

But he didn't, and in this self-denying proposition, he established the right of judicial review of legislation. Marshall declared that while Marbury (on moral grounds) deserved his appointment, the Supreme Court did not have jurisdiction. Not only did he turn against his employee, but he also seemed to even be denying powers to the Court. However, he argued that the Supreme Court did not have jurisdiction because the Judiciary Act of 1789 itself violated the Constitution. As the Supreme Court was the ultimate judge of the law of the land, Marshall argued that the Court had the obligation to decide when the Constitution superseded certain acts of legislation. This ruling essentially established the Supreme Court's claim to judicial review (Simon 2002).

Marshall put Jefferson on the horns of a dilemma. Jefferson could accept the ruling and get what he had wanted—the right to deny Marbury his commission. However, by doing so, he would have to accept Marshall's right to review all future legislation. He could have rejected the ruling, and said that the Supreme Court was forced to accept Congress's laws, but in that case, Marbury would have had to be given his commission and the Supreme Court would have maintained the continued right to intervene in cases of this kind. Unsurprisingly, just as Marshall was forever patient, working over decades to establish a powerful court, Jefferson was impatient and took the poisoned chalice. He accepted the ruling and the principle of judicial review. While Jefferson himself was a strong advocate of democracy unfettered by federalist justices, he could not turn down the easy victory.

While the triumph of the Supreme Court owes much to Marshall's genius, it also owes much to the powers that were backing him up. Marshall was on the moderate side of the Federalist Party. If that party split entirely from Jefferson, the possibility of New England secession was certainly out there. If Jefferson had run roughshod over the Court, there was certainly a chance that the Union would have dissolved. Marshall's power came in part from his regional political and military support—the Supreme Court had to be respected because it was in part the representative of the nationally weak, but regionally strong, Federalists.

Throughout the past 200 years, the Supreme Court has acted entrepreneurially to build its power base. It is an independent check on the elected officials, but one that never strays too far from the support of at least some significant portion of Americans. If the popularly elected officials want to ignore the Supreme Court, then they lose the cover of legality and ultimately face the possibility of insurrection. Thus, even the Court's power comes in part from military strength and from a continued ability to rally some significant group of Americans to their side.

5.5. Conclusion

This section has emphasized the extreme mutability of political institutions. Proportional representation and independent courts are not etched in stone; they are the result of underlying forces. Indeed, the history of the past 200 years suggests that the institutions that support the European welfare state are ultimately the result of the military and political success of labor movements in Europe. Conversely, in the United States, older institutions that are less favorable to the labor movement have been left in place because labor uprisings were ultimately suppressed by the national government.

Indeed, there is a general relationship between the age of institutions and their unfriendliness to the welfare state, shown in Fig. 5.1. This figure shows the relationship between the share of GDP that

Fighting Poverty in the US and Europe

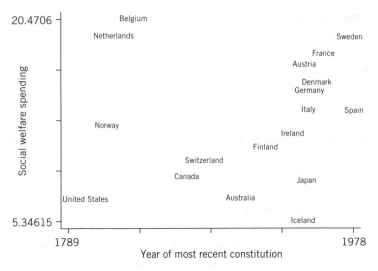

Fig. 5.1. Constitutional Change and Spending on Welfare

is being spent on social services and the year of the most recent constitution.

The Low Countries (Belgium and the Netherlands) are the big outliers on this graph—as they appear to have older institutions and much social welfare spending. The previous discussion casts doubts on their classification as countries with older institutions. As we have argued, both countries experienced massive constitutional changes around the turn of the last century. If these countries are excluded, the correlation between social spending and year of most recent constitution is statistically significant and the correlation coefficient is over 50 percent.

The reason for the permanence of American institutions is American success in suppressing attempts to force change through violence. America's counter-revolutionary success itself is the result of its large size and its isolation. No modern country that was defeated on its own soil has survived with its institutions unchanged. The United States is among the few countries that has not been successfully invaded.

The second factor that strengthened the U.S. militarily was its vast size. Labor uprisings in distant mining towns could not impact

130

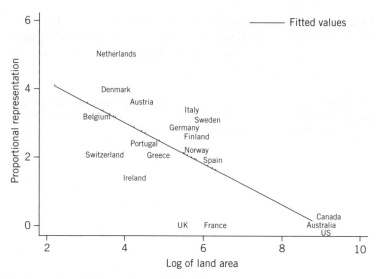

Fig. 5.2. Land Area and Proportional Representation

Washington. As Fig. 5.2 illustrates, this is a general phenomenon. This figure shows the relationship between proportional representation and country size (a similar graph should be shown for density) for the countries of western Europe and the former British colonies that are primarily made up of western Europeans. Countries that are bigger are less likely to have proportional representation—smaller countries are more likely to have proportional representation.

The remarkable evolution in European institutions nuances the claims of authors like Douglass North and Acemoglu et al. (2000), who see long-run growth as being a function of European institutions. While we agree with their view that institutions, especially those that protect property, are central to growth, we have doubts about the view that good institutions in developing countries are the legacy of longstanding European institutions. What exactly were the institutions of Habsburg Spain that were all that conducive to growth? It seems just as likely that a more permanent presence of Spaniards in the seventeenth century Americas would have led to more spectacular *auto-da-fes*. Indeed, the data suggest that settler mortality is largely irrelevant except in countries that adopted the

131

English common law institutions that appear to protect property.[4] As we try to understand the role of institutions in economic growth and the welfare state, we must understand that institutions are quite flexible and ultimately reflect deeper forces.

---

[4] If we exclude countries with an English legal origin from the sample, then there is no significant relationship between historical settler mortality and income in 1998, once location in Africa is taken into account.

Chapter 6

Race and Redistribution

6.1. Introduction

In the previous two chapters, we argued that about 50 percent of the gap in welfare spending between the United States and Europe can be explained by differences between American and European political institutions, such as American majoritarianism (versus proportional representation) American federalism and separation of powers (versus European centralization). These institutions are themselves in part the legacy of the military and political power of the European left which was able to dominate small, industrialized countries during peacetime and the larger countries in the aftermath of debilitating wars. These institutions are also the legacy of American racial fragmentation and European homogeneity. In this chapter, we argue that racial heterogeneity, both directly and indirectly through political institutions, can explain the bulk of the unexplained portion of the gap between the United States and Europe in welfare spending.

A large literature has documented racial and ethnic antipathies, and a smaller literature has compellingly linked these feelings with hostility to welfare. The literature documenting prejudice, discrimination, and ethnic hate is vast. Classics include DuBois (1903) on race relations in the United States, Allport (1954) on the psychology of racial prejudice, Becker (1957) on the economics of discrimination, Taeuber and Taeuber (1965) on housing market segregation, and many others. The literature linking racial or ethnic divisions with low levels of redistribution is smaller, but also impressive. Lipset and Marks (2000) review the early literature and point out that Karl Marx, Friedrich Engels, and Werner Sombart all thought that ethnic divisions posed a challenge for socialism in the United States. More recently, Gilens (1999) has written an entire volume on the role that racial stereotypes play in forming Americans' opinions on welfare. Luttmer (2001) shows that people are less likely to support welfare within the United States if they live near welfare recipients of another race. Indeed, no single individual characteristic predicts support for welfare more than race. Regardless of income, African-Americans are far more likely to support redistribution than whites (see Alesina and LaFerrara 2005).

The welfare-specific literature and the general literature on racial discrimination fit together nicely. The larger literature on prejudice documents that people are more likely to be hostile to people who are different, that is toward people who are defined as members of an out-group along some salient dimension. As such, when there are significant numbers of minorities among the poor, then the majority population can be roused against transferring money to people who are different from themselves. Another way of thinking about racial or ethnic divisions is that the proponents of the welfare state generally attempt to draw distinctions between economic classes. Racial, religious, and ethnic divisions distract from those distinctions and reduce the ability to forge a common class-based identity.

At the state level, we show that welfare payments are less generous in American states that have a higher proportion of minorities. At the country level, we document a pervasive connection between fractionalization and the degree of social welfare spending—countries with greater racial division spend less on welfare. Using our estimates of the impact of racial fractionalization on welfare spending, we conclude that about 50 percent of the gap between the United States and Europe may be due to racial fractionalization.

This evidence squares well with the historical record. Within the United States, racial politics played a role in two important episodes when redistributive politics were blocked by the American right. In the 1890s, at the same time the socialists were gaining ground in Europe, the first American party emerged which actively fought for redistribution from rich to poor: The Populists. The Populists were particularly strong in the impoverished South, but in that region, the conservative forces were able to use race hatred regularly to defeat Populist politicians. Martin Luther King himself, citing C. Vann Woodward, argued that the rise of segregation in the South in the 1890s "was really a political stratagem employed by the emerging Bourbon [right-wing Democrat] interests to keep the Southern masses divided" (McFeely 2002 in Afterword to Woodward [1955] 2002: 231–2). Elite southern senators elected on the basis of racist politics would serve as a bulwark against the New Deal in the late 1930s. More recently, Republican victories have been based on support from Sunbelt states. The critical switch of those states from being solidly Democratic (from 1876 to 1960) to being strongly Republican occurred in 1964, when southerners deserted Lyndon Johnson because of the Civil Rights Act.

Of course, racial or ethnic divisions do not always block redistribution. When a racial minority is particularly rich, then it is hardly natural to fight the welfare state by exploiting racial hostility. For example, Fleming–Walloon hostility, which is intense, has not historically blocked the Belgian welfare state because the smaller group (the Walloons) also tended to be richer. Recently, the Flemings have become the richer group, and we expect rising Fleming wealth to be associated with a decreasing willingness of Flemings to accept state welfare transfers to poorer Walloons. The American situation is ideal for using race-baiting to fight redistribution. Blacks are particularly poor and socially segregated. As such, they are vulnerable and conveniently provide the opponents of welfare with a means of making welfare seem an extravagant transfer to a despised race.

There are two possible explanations for why racial divisions matter. One simpler view argues that members of one racial or ethnic group naturally dislike members of other groups (Becker 1957 provides an early economic exposition). According to the classic altruism models of Trivers (1971) and others, people are less likely to be altruistic to those with whom they share fewer genes. This view suggests that taxpayers will automatically be more supportive of welfare when payments go to people who physically and socially resemble themselves. Unfortunately, this view offers little reason for optimism about racial attitudes.

A slightly more nuanced view, which we favor, is that racial hatred is endogenous and often created by entrepreneurial politicians. Political entrepreneurs will naturally vilify particular ethnic groups when their policies are likely to hurt those groups. This enables voters to feel better about supporting the politician. According to this view, human beings are genetically endowed with an ability to hate, but the targets of their hatred are situational and can be readily manipulated. This view gives us somewhat more hope that changing political situations can lead to improvements in race relations. But, it also makes us aware that the introduction of minorities, such as the new immigration into Europe, creates a potential for entrepreneurial politicians to create hatred in order to gain support.

In the next section, we turn to the cross-country evidence on the connection between heterogeneity and spending on social welfare. In Section 6.3, we turn to the evidence within the United States. In Section 6.4, we discuss the historical record in both the United States and Europe. In Section 6.5, we present our view of how and why hatred is formed.

6.2. International evidence on the importance of heterogeneity

We begin our discussion of the international evidence on heterogeneity and transfers by discussing the measurement and levels of heterogeneity in the United States and Europe. We then discuss the empirical connection between transfers and racial fractionalization.

6.2.1. Heterogeneity in the United States and Europe

Historically, groups have divided by language, religion, culture, or place of origin. By almost any measure, many European countries, especially those that are small, are remarkably homogeneous. Even today, despite all of the political discourse surrounding recent immigrants, over 90 percent of the residents of these countries are ethnic Swedes, ethnic Dutch, or ethnic Germans. Historically, the degree of ethnic similarity has been even higher. In some countries, this ethnic homogeneity is supported by remarkable religious homogeneity as well. For example, 92 percent of Swedes and 95 percent of Danes are Lutherans.

By contrast, the United States is now and has always been diverse. In the United States as a whole, 75.1 percent of the population classify themselves as white. Of the rest, 12.3 percent classify themselves as African-Americans, 3.6 percent as Asians, and 5.5 percent as two or more races. About 12.5 percent of the population (of all races) classify themselves as Latinos and 10.7 percent of the population speak Spanish at home. Within the white population, there is also a striking ethnic diversity. Only 34.8 percent of the population describes themselves as having English, Irish, or German ancestry (the three biggest ethnic groups); 5.6 percent of the United States has primarily Italian ancestry and 3.2 percent describe themselves as having Polish ancestry.

These national figures mask the even greater heterogeneity within many states; after all, in many cases it is state government—not national government—that sets the level of redistribution. For example, in Mississippi, 36 percent of the population is black. In Louisiana, 32 percent of the population is black. In America's largest state, California, 32 percent of the population is Latino.

There are many ways of measuring diversity, but one particularly natural means of doing so is the fractionalization index (Mauro 1995; Alesina et al. 1999, 2000; Alesina and La Ferrara 2000). This index measures the probability that two people, drawn at random from the population, will be from different groups (racial, ethnic, or religious). Formally, this index is defined as

Ethnic Fractionalization

$$= 1 - \sum_{\text{races or ethnicities}} \left(\frac{\text{Population in Race or Ethnicity}}{\text{Total Population}} \right)^2 \qquad (1)$$

The measure can be calculated for ethnic, racial, religious, or linguistic groups. These measures take on a value from 0 to 1, where 0 refers to countries that are perfectly homogeneous and 1 refers to countries that are completely split between an infinite number of tiny groups. Values of 0.1 or lower of this index indicate extremely high levels of homogeneity. A value this low can only be achieved if at least 95 percent of the population belongs to one group.

To use this measure, we need to define different races or ethnicities. A traditional definition has involved linguistic differences, hence the index of ethnolinguistic fractionalization from the Atlas Narodov Mira (1964), which has been used by a number of authors (following Mauro 1995; Easterly and Levine 1997). Of course, when applied to our data this index will show that Belgium is extremely diverse and the United States much less so. It misses any diversity that occurs within a single linguistic group and therefore misses all of American racial heterogeneity.

Other measures have tended to use alternative definitions of race or ethnicity. For example, Alesina et al. (1999) used the ethnic and racial divisions in the U.S. census. Following this work, Alesina et al. (2002) have produced ethnic, linguistic, and religious fractionalization values for more than 160 countries. This work has attempted to use comparable racial and ethnic division measures across the world so that comparisons are sensible. We supplement this work by using measures based exclusively on race.

The values of different racial ethnic, linguistic, and religious heterogeneity measures for the United States and a number of European countries are shown in Table 6.1. Racial definitions are based on the 1990 U.S. Census. As the table shows, there is heterogeneity among some dimensions within western Europe. Looking across every dimension, Portugal is the most homogeneous country in the sample (and one of the most homogeneous in the world). Apart from religious heterogeneity, which in these cases is somewhat artificial because it represents the sizable presence of people who report having no religion, the Scandinavian countries, Austria, and Italy are all quite homogeneous along all three dimensions. Among these nations, the maximum value of any fractionalization measure (apart from religion) is 0.2 (for linguistic heterogeneity in Sweden), which

Table 6.1. Fractionalization Indices

Nation	Racial fractionalization[a]	Ethnic fractionalization[b]	Linguistic fractionalization[b]	Religious fractionalization[b]
Austria	0.03	0.11	0.15	0.41
Belgium	0.05	0.56	0.54	0.21
Denmark	0.02	0.08	0.10	0.23
France	0.10	0.10	0.12	0.40
Germany	0.06	0.17	0.16	0.66
Italy	0.02	0.11	0.11	0.30
Netherlands	0.11	0.11	0.51	0.72
Norway	0.06	0.06	0.07	0.20
Portugal	0.05	0.05	0.02	0.14
Spain	0.03	0.42	0.41	0.45
Sweden	0.05	0.06	0.20	0.23
Switzerland	0.05	0.53	0.54	0.61
United Kingdom	0.10	0.12	0.05	0.69
United States	0.49	0.49	0.25	0.82

Notes:
[a] From authors' calculations.
[b] From Alesina et al. (2002).

still means that about 90 percent of the population belongs to the dominant ethnicity. Furthermore, while all of these countries display religious heterogeneity, the active churchgoers in the population tend to belong to a single denomination.

Germany is also quite a homogeneous place and is marked only by genuine religious heterogeneity between Catholics and Protestants. Even France and England are still generally homogeneous. The Netherlands is more linguistically diverse. Only Belgium, Spain, and Switzerland display large levels of different forms of linguistic and ethnic heterogeneity. Belgium is deeply split between Flemings and Walloons. Switzerland has an ethnic heterogeneity measure that is higher than that of the United States, reflecting the strong division between the German, French, and Italian Swiss.

However, no European country has racial division which is comparable to that of the United States. Moreover, the United States also has a very high level of linguistic fractionalization and religious fractionalization. We suspect that racial divisions prove particularly important both because they are salient and because different races often have significantly different incomes which are themselves the legacy of slavery, colonialism, and wildly different levels of development across continents.

6.2.2. Heterogeneity and transfers

The most natural test of the importance of redistribution is to look at whether countries with greater amounts of ethnic division have lower levels of redistribution as a share of GDP. Just as in the previous chapters, our primary measure of redistribution will be the ratio of total social spending to GDP. Our primary dependent variable is the level of racial fractionalization.

Figure 6.1 shows the basic relationship between racial fractionalization and social spending as a share of GDP. The connection is quite striking. The overall correlation between racial heterogeneity and redistribution is −66 percent. Among the sixteen countries with racial fractionalization that is greater than 40 percent, the mean share of GDP that is being spent on social services averages 2.42 percent. The maximum share of GDP being spent on social services in this group is 7.19 percent (Brazil) and the United States has the second most

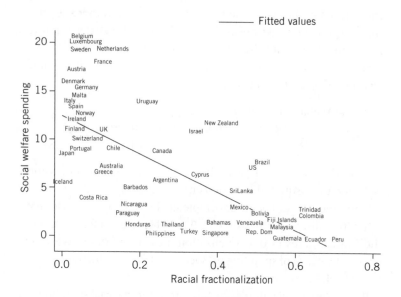

Fig. 6.1. Racial Fractionalization and Social Welfare Spending

generous system in this group, spending 6.96 percent of GDP on social services.

The group of racially homogeneous countries are completely different. There are seventeen countries with values of racial fractionalization that are less than 10 percent. Among these countries, the average level of social spending (as a share of GDP) equals 12.87 percent. The minimum level of spending in this group (Costa Rica at 3.72 percent) is still 1.5 times the average level of spending in the set of ethnically diverse countries. Another way of putting this relationship is that there are eight countries which spend more than 14 percent of GDP on social services, the maximum value of ethnic fractionalization in those countries is 10.53 percent—less than one-fourth of America's racial fractionalization.

In order to test whether this relationship is spurious and the result of a connection between poverty and racial fractionalization (which does exist), we can look only at richer countries. Among countries with GDP per capita greater than $15,000, we find that the correlation between the racial fractionalization index is greater than 50 percent (and statistically significant at the 99 percent level). Alternatively, we can use a bivariate regression, which looks at the relationship between social welfare spending and racial fractionalization holding GDP constant:

Social Welfare Spending
$$= -10.5*\text{Racial Fractionalization} + 0.36*\text{GDP} + 5 \quad (2)$$
$$(3.2) \qquad\qquad\qquad (0.08) \qquad (1.8)$$

Standard errors are in parentheses. The number of observations is 52 and the r-squared is 63 percent. The meaning of this is that if a country moves from being as completely homogeneous as Denmark (a fractionalization measure of 0.02) to being as heterogeneous as the United States (a fractionalization measure of 0.49), we should expect the share of spending on social welfare (as a fraction of GDP) to fall by 4.7 percent.

Racial fractionalization is the best predictor of social spending, but other forms of division are also negatively correlated with the degree of redistribution. For example, the correlation between ethnic fractionalization and redistribution is 43 percent, which is lower than the correlation with racial fractionalization, but still quite impressive.

The correlation between ethnolinguistic fractionalization and social spending as a share of GDP is 41 percent. As Fig. 6.2 shows, the weakness of linguistic fractionalization as an explanatory variable is due to Belgium, which is linguistically diverse (Flemings and Walloons), but still has a generous welfare state.

As we discuss later, ethnic politics are certainly quite potent in Belgium. However, the income differences between Flemings and Walloons are too similar for this to be the basis of opposition to the welfare state. Currently, the level of unemployment is much higher among the Walloons than among the Flemings, but the relative wealth of Flanders has not been a permanent feature of the Belgian economic landscape. Indeed, industrialization began among the Walloons and it really was not until the 1970s that the Flemings began to pull ahead economically. One view is that the relative economic similarities of the two groups (throughout much of history) means that the welfare state does not represent large scale

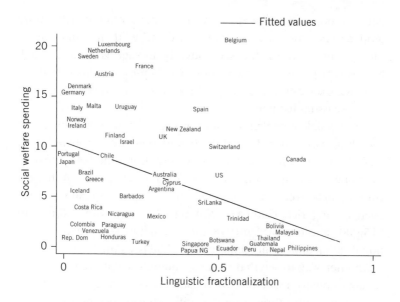

Fig. 6.2. **Linguistic Fractionalization and Social Welfare Spending**

redistribution between the groups and as a result racial hatred is not an effective means of fighting redistribution.

By contrast, the extreme poverty of blacks in the United States makes it inevitable that redistribution to the poorest Americans will lead to racial redistribution. After all, in the United States the poverty rate among non-Hispanic whites is 7.7 percent. The poverty rate among blacks is 23.6 percent. While non-Hispanic whites make up 70.7 percent of the U.S. population, they only make up 46 percent of the poor. In metropolitan areas, less than 40 percent of the poor are non-Hispanic whites. Thus, while a super-majority of American voters are non-Hispanic whites, a majority of the poor are minorities. The relative concentration of minorities among the poor is not recent, and throughout American history minorities have been over-represented among the most disadvantaged.

These facts make us think that it would be better to measure the racial makeup of the poor rather than the ethnic makeup of society as a whole. We suspect that one of the advantages of the racial

143

data—as opposed to the ethnic data—is that racial minorities have tended to be economically more disadvantaged than ethnic minorities. In many cases, the race–poverty linkage is quite natural, because the presence of racial minorities came about because those races were once enslaved. Hopefully, future work will be able to sort out these issues further.

One possible complaint about our racial fractionalization–social spending connection is that both variables are correlated with income, and it is income that ultimately drives the level of social spending. One way to answer this complaint is to point out that the correlation between racial fragmentation and social spending is high even among rich countries. Among countries with more than $15,000 per capita GDP in 1998, the correlation between racial fractionalization and social spending is −37.88 percent.

Another way to see that social spending is connected with fractionalization even holding GDP constant is to run a regression across our sample of fifty-three countries controlling for income. Regressing social spending as a share of GDP on the logarithm of per capita income and racial fractionalization, we estimate:

$$\frac{\text{Social Spending}}{\text{GDP}}$$
$$= 0.04*\text{Log(Per Capita GDP)} - 0.11*\text{Racial Fractionalization} - 0.26$$
$$(0.008) \qquad\qquad\qquad (0.03) \qquad\qquad\qquad\qquad (0.08)$$

Standard errors are in parentheses. The number of observations equals 55 and the r-squared is 61 percent.

As this regression makes clear, there is certainly a potent relationship between national income and the share of income that is spent on social services. A 100 percent increase in per capita GDP is associated with a 2.77 percent increase in the share of GDP being spent on social services. Indeed, controlling the logarithm of GDP causes the coefficient on racial fractionalization to drop by almost 50 percent. However, even with this control the impact of racial fractionalization remains quite strong. A 10 percent increase in the level of racial fractionalization is associated with a 1.4 percent drop in the share of spending on social services.

In Alesina et al. (2001), we repeat this regression controlling for a wider range of country-level characteristics, such as demographics (the share of the population between 15 and 64), political system (having a majoritarian regime), and geographic area dummies. The main geographic effects are that Caribbean and Latin American countries tend to have less redistribution. With a wide set of these country controls, the coefficient on racial fractionalization remains significant but falls to 0.075. The geographic area dummies are the most important for reducing the size of the racial fractionalization index and without those dummy variables, the coefficient is hard to push below 0.09.

How much of the gap between Europe and the United States can be explained by racial fractionalization? Our data include all of the current members of the European Union except for Luxembourg. Across these countries, the average share of spending on social services is 14.27 percent; the average level of racial fractionalization is 0.057. In our data, the United States spends 6.96 percent of GDP on social services and its racial fractionalization is 0.49.

The gap in racial fractionalization between the United States and Europe is 0.433, which according to our regression implies that America's racial fractionalization predicts that the United States will spend 4.8 percent less on social services. The overall gap in social spending between the United States and Europe is 7.31 percent percentage points. Thus, the gap in racial fractionalization can in principle explain almost two-thirds of the gap in social spending between the United States and Europe. Even given a more conservative estimate of the effect of racial fractionalization (perhaps a coefficient of 0.075), racial fractionalization can still explain about 43 percent of the U.S.–Europe gap in spending (3.2%).

While the international evidence certainly does not explain why racial fractionalization reduces social spending, it documents a strong correlation. It also helps us to understand how much of the U.S.– Europe differences can be explained by higher levels of racial fractionalization within the United States. In the rest of the chapter, we will look at the other evidence suggesting that there is an important link between fractionalization and spending on welfare. However, our best estimate of the overall impact of race is based on this international evidence. We believe that about one-half of the U.S.–Europe gap can be explained by European homogeneity. As such, American racial heterogeneity stands, along with political institutions, as one of the two critical factors explaining the absence of a welfare state in America.

6.3. Evidence within the United States

We now turn to evidence of racial heterogeneity's effect on redistribution within the United States, for which we have two primary sources of information. First, there are hard data on the level of welfare benefits and the share of the population that is African-American. Welfare benefits are chosen at the state level, and, as such, by comparing states with larger and smaller African-American populations, we can test whether racial heterogeneity reduces generosity. Second, Luttmer (2001) and Alesina and La Ferrara (2005) use survey data on attitudes towards welfare, which can then be linked to race and proximity to members of different races. We begin with state welfare spending.

6.3.1 Welfare spending and racial composition of states

To avoid the complications that come from welfare reform in the 1990s, we will focus on the level of Aid to Families with Dependent Children (AFDC) across states in 1990.[1] The AFDC program is arguably the largest welfare program in the country and certainly the largest program providing income targeted towards the poor. The AFDC program began as a piece of New Deal legislation, under Title IV of the 1935 Social Security Act. During the history of the program, states have always had the freedom to set the level of AFDC payments (initially up to a cap). Federal involvement was limited to restrictions on the rules concerning eligibility

---

[1] In the 1990s, there was a substantial attempt in the United States to "end welfare as we know it" which led to a substantial decrease in the size of the welfare system. Thus, data from the beginning of the decade are somewhat more representative of the entire postwar period.

and funding. During the early days of the program, the national government compensated states for one-third of their spending. Since 1965, the national government has paid for at least 50 percent of the program. As such, states have a strong incentive to increase the level of payment, since at least one-half of their spending is paid for by the country as a whole.

Despite this strong incentive for generous welfare payments, there is wide heterogeneity in the level of payments across states. For example, in 1990, Alaska's maximum AFDC payment was over $800 per family per month. California was the second most generous state in that year with a maximum benefit of close to $700 per month. In the same year, the maximum AFDC benefits in Alabama and Mississippi were below $150 per family per month. Obviously, there is a great deal of variation across states to be explained.

Even the most cursory look at these payments shows a connection with race. The raw correlation between percent black and maximum AFDC payment is 49 percent, and this relationship is shown in Fig. 6.3. While there is a substantial amount of cross-state variation even among states with few blacks, there can be little doubt that the

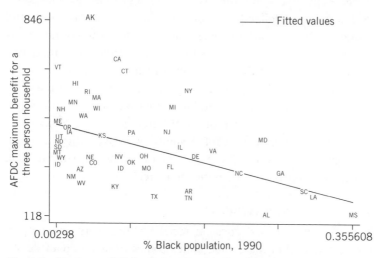

Fig. 6.3. Maximum AFDC Benefits and Percent Black Across U.S. States

states with large numbers of blacks are much less generous than the states with fewer African-Americans.

Just as in the case of the cross-country evidence, an obvious confound is per capita income. As the states with more minorities are generally poorer, it may be that low AFDC benefits just reflect poverty, not racial fragmentation. To address this concern, we ran a regression connecting state maximum welfare benefits with the share of the state that is black. This regression estimates:

Maximum AFDC Payment
$$= -232 - 758*\text{Percent Black} + 0.016*\text{Median Family Income}$$
$$\quad\ (90)\ (139) \qquad\qquad\quad (0.002) \qquad\qquad\qquad\qquad (3)$$

Standard errors are in parentheses. There are fifty observations and the r-squared is 67 percent. This simple two-factor model does a pretty good job of explaining the cross-state variation in the level of maximum AFDC payments. The coefficient on median income tells us that if annual state median income rises by a dollar, the level of maximum AFDC benefits rises by 20 cents per month. The coefficient on percent black means that if the percent black in the state rises from 0 to 20 percent, the monthly benefits are predicted to decline by $151.

The coefficient on percent black suggests that as the percent black increases by 20 percent, the expected level of AFDC payments will decline by $138 dollars. This quantity is large both statistically and economically. The racially mixed states in the south are much less generous than their more homogeneous northern counterparts, even controlling for the overall level of income in the state. We will explore the history of racial antagonism in the south and its relationship with welfare later, but the hard data seem to confirm the continuing importance of racial heterogeneity as a barrier to redistribution within the United States. Moreover, the data seem to suggest that the racially homogeneous areas of America look much more like Europe than the mixed regions of America.

6.3.2. Attitudinal survey evidence

A second piece of evidence on racial heterogeneity and support for welfare within the United States comes from survey evidence. There is a large literature documenting the connection between racial attitudes and support for welfare (Sidanius et al. 1996; Virtanen and Huddy 1998) and this literature has argued that while racism and antipathy towards welfare may always have been linked, in its most modern incarnation, the "new racism" is particularly political and targets its dislike towards African-Americans who are receiving government support. Most recently, Gilens (1999) has methodically examined the connection between stated attitudes towards welfare and attitudes towards race. He concludes that "racial stereotypes play a central role in generating opposition to welfare in America" (1999: 3). We agree, and we believe that survey evidence can usefully supplement the cross-state evidence to show the connection between race and redistribution.

The National Opinion Research Center's General Social Survey (GSS) has asked respondents for opinions about redistribution since 1972. The survey question asks about welfare in the following fashion:

We are faced with many problems in this country, none of which can be solved easily or inexpensively. I'm going to name some of these problems and for each one I'd like you to tell me whether you think we're spending too much money on it, too little money, or about the right amount.

Poverty is listed as one of the nation's problems and we, like many previous researchers (Gilens 1999; Luttmer 2001) take people's answers to this question to reflect their views about welfare. Obviously, there are problems with this interpretation. The answer to this question depends on the current level of government spending, and as such, using this question to compare attitudes towards welfare in the United States and, say, Sweden, may be highly misleading. However, within the United States, the question is likely to help us understand what determines the level of support for welfare.

Luttmer (2001) provides a helpful confirmation of the value of this question. He first uses the GSS to estimate the determinants of support for redistribution using a regression with twenty individual level characteristics. Using block group level information from the census and his estimated regression coefficient, he estimates a predicted level of support for welfare. To check whether this predicted support maps into voting on welfare, Luttmer (2001) looks at votes for California's Proposition 165, which mandated cuts in welfare spending and whether block groups that are predicted to support less spending on the poor actually voted for the proposition. He found an extremely high correlation between the survey-based measure and actually voting against welfare. The *t*-statistic of his measure is over 100. The correlation coefficient between the survey-based predicted support measure and voting for the proposition is 64 percent. This tells us that the GSS survey question yields results which map quite well into observed voting behavior.

As many researchers have already noted (see Luttmer 2001; Alesina and La Ferrara 2005), the race of the respondent is an important determinant of people's answer to this puzzle. In regressions reported in Table 6.2, we find that race is by far the most important determinant of support for redistribution. In that paper, we coded answering too little as "1," about right as "0.5," and too much as "0." Holding income, education, gender, martial status, and urban residence constant, we found a coefficient of 0.26 on race. The *t*-statistic on this variable was 25, which made it by far the most statistically significant coefficient in the regression. Even holding income and education constant, whites were much more hostile to redistribution than blacks.

Among whites, we also found that racially oriented variables predicted the level of support for pro-poverty spending. Whites who think that blacks are lazy are less likely to support more spending on poverty. Whites who have had a black over to dinner are more likely to support spending on poverty. These effects were not overwhelmingly large, but we did control for the same wide array of individual characteristics.

In Fig. 6.4, we show the correlation between the average response to this question at the state level and the percent black in the state. There is a −46 percent correlation between percent black in the state and survey support for welfare. This highly significant correlation further supports our view that racial fractionalization tends to limit support for redistribution.

In a much more comprehensive study on attitudes towards welfare and race, Gilens (1999) documents a striking pattern of connection between hostility to blacks and hostility to welfare.

Table 6.2. Effect of Race and Beliefs About Race

	(1) Support for increased welfare	(2) Support for increased welfare	(3) Support for increased welfare	(4) Support for increased welfare
Black	0.232 (28.55)**			
Income	−0.020 (19.78)**	−0.019 (17.19)**	−0.022 (5.36)**	−0.018 (13.54)**
Female	0.007 (1.35)	0.009 (1.67)	0.032 (1.94)	0.010 (1.39)
Married	−0.033 (5.82)**	−0.038 (6.19)**	−0.016 (0.91)	−0.036 (4.58)**
Number of children	0.006 (3.96)**	0.006 (3.38)**	0.010 (1.77)	0.007 (3.04)**
Education				
Less than HS	0.042 (5.84)**	0.042 (5.56)**	−0.010 (0.38)	0.048 (5.08)**
Some college	−0.002 (0.28)	−0.002 (0.28)	−0.005 (0.21)	0.003 (0.26)
College graduate	0.031 (3.62)**	0.030 (3.40)**	0.029 (1.16)	0.025 (2.22)*
Graduate level	0.106 (8.76)**	0.107 (8.65)**	0.080 (2.47)*	0.133 (8.20)**

Table 6.2. (Continued)

	(1) Support for increased welfare	(2) Support for increased welfare	(3) Support for increased welfare	(4) Support for increased welfare
Log city size	0.010	0.010	0.011	0.010
	(7.77)**	(7.21)**	(2.61)**	(5.90)**
Percent black in state		−0.044		
		(1.14)		
Believe that blacks are lazy			−0.030	
			(4.27)**	
Black person home for dinner recent years				0.043
				(5.38)**
Constant	0.403	0.395	0.597	0.362
	(31.59)**	(27.32)**	(9.85)**	(21.18)**
Observations	20848	18157	1921	11048
r-squared	0.10	0.04	0.04	0.05

Note: This table uses data from the GSS. The dependent variable is a scale (normalized 0–1) for how much the respondent supports increased spending on welfare. The three possible responses are that the United States is currently spending too much, about right, or too little on welfare. Column (1) shows the race effect on support for welfare. Columns (2)–(4) limit the sample to whites and show the connection between support for welfare spending and percent black in own state, the belief that black people are lazy, and whether or not the person has had a black person over for dinner.

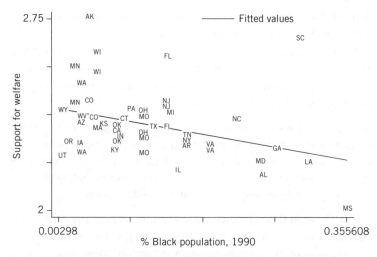

Fig. 6.4. Percent Black and Support for Welfare Across U.S. States

Luttmer (2001) represents the most comprehensive examination of race and support for welfare. This chapter examines the support for welfare as a function of proximity to poor people of different races using the GSS question on support for spending for the poor described above. Using tract level data from the census, Luttmer calculates an exposure index, which measures the extent to which respondents live close to welfare recipients of different races. The main variation occurs across metropolitan areas and his identification is based on the fact that in some cities, non-welfare recipients live further away from welfare recipients than in other cities.

He finds that proximity to welfare recipients of one's own race increases the level of support for redistribution, but proximity to welfare recipients of another race decreases support for redistribution. This can also be seen as implying that as the share of nearby welfare recipients who are from another race rises, support for welfare falls. Together, these results suggest that race matters. People are inclined to support welfare if they live close to recipients of their own race, with whom they presumably identify. However, proximity to recipients of another race just increases antipathy. We believe that this is some of the strongest evidence suggesting that distaste for welfare is linked to the race of welfare recipients.

Alesina and La Ferrara (2005) use a different question concerning individual attitude. The question asks whether the respondent believes that the government should redistribute from the rich to the poor. The exact question is the following:

Some people think that the Government in Washington ought to reduce the income differences between the rich and the poor, perhaps by raising the taxes of wealthy families or by giving income assistance to the poor. Others think that the Government should not concern itself with reducing this income difference between the rich and the poor.

The question then gives a scale that captures how the respondent classifies himself between these two extremes. These authors find that the race of the respondent is an extremely strong determinant of preferences for redistribution. Whites are much more likely than blacks to feel that the Government should stay out of distributional matters even after controlling for the income of the respondent. Clearly the poor feel that the government should redistribute, but the Black poor feel this much more strongly than the white poor. The effect of race is much larger than other effects capturing individual characteristics, like gender, employment status and experience, or education.

In summary, the evidence of attitudinal surveys is loud and clear: Race relations are a critical element of individual preferences toward welfare, redistribution, and the fight against poverty.

6.4. The historical record

As our final piece of evidence, we turn to the historical record. In the United States, there are two key episodes that display the power of racial politics to distract from class-based redistribution. The first episode is the defeat of the southern Populists. During the 1890s, southern elites used hatred and fear of blacks to undercut America's first class-based party—the Populists. The legacy of this victory included a steady stream of conservative southern Democrats who blocked left-wing policies at both the state and national levels.

The second episode occurs between 1960 and 1980 when the New Deal Consensus was unmade by the rise of Sun Belt Republicanism. We end this section by discussing race and redistribution in Europe.

6.4.1. Race and the defeat of the Populists

As a political issue, large-scale income redistribution only comes alive in the nineteenth century, and in the United States, only in the late nineteenth century. Before this time period, governments lacked the ability to raise large amounts of income based taxes and to administer large-scale welfare programs. Also, before this time period, the poorer members of society lacked the political clout to make their interests important politically. However, as governmental competence and the political organization of the poor increased over the 1800s, large-scale redistribution became an important topic.

In the United States, as in many other countries, a determined pro-redistribution party emerged from an economic recession. In the 1870s, real farm incomes were stagnant as an agricultural recession made farm life even harder for millions of small farmers, despite the remarkable wealth created in some sectors of the Gilded Age economy. Of course, rural poverty was not new, but by the 1870s, the rise in rural poverty was accompanied with an increased ability of the central government to change the country. During the Civil War, the national government had shown a remarkable ability and willingness to remake American society. Between 1861 and 1865, the federal government had transformed itself from an abstract entity that was practically irrelevant to the lives of most Americans into a leviathan whose policies touched every worker and firm. Government spending as a share of GDP rose from about 2 percent in 1860 to over 10 percent during the war. Even though government spending then returned to its antebellum level, the federal government had shown its strength by freeing the slaves. It may have been natural to ask the government to fight poverty as well.

Nowhere was the power of the government to redistribute income more evident than in its monetary policy. In 1861, facing a severe run on the dollar, Secretary of the Treasury, Salmon P. Chase suspended the conversion of dollars for gold. The value of the dollar fell rapidly relative to gold. Chase then issued greenbacks, or unconvertible currency, which by law had to be treated as legal tender. This inflation helped pay for the war, but it also led to a widespread redistribution between lenders and borrowers. Creditors who had lent money in hard currency in 1860 were suddenly owed debts in greenbacks, which were worth a fraction of the original loan.

This massive transfer of income led to inevitable legal wrangling and the Supreme Court itself in 1870 (led by the same Salmon P. Chase) now declared that the Legal Tender Act of 1862 was unconstitutional. In the Supreme Court's view, the U.S. government did not have the power to redistribute between private parties through the use of inflation (or deflation for that matter). The court played its traditional role as the arch-defender of private property. The decision did not stand. Within a year, Ulysses S. Grant appointed two new justices to the court and they confirmed the government's power to change the value of money in *Knox v. Lee* and *Parker v. Davis*.

But, while these cases affirmed the government's right to inflate, in the 1870s government policy caused deflation not inflation. In 1873, the government eliminated bimetallism—the use of both silver and gold—and this would be called by the populists the Crime of 1873. Although silver was more valuable than gold at that time, this made little difference to the value of currency. More importantly, in 1875, Grant pushed through the Resumption of Species Act, which would bring the dollar back to the gold standard by 1879. This act meant that individuals who held greenbacks suddenly received a significant windfall as their notes were to be eventually redeemable in gold. The act also meant that the real value of dollar-denominated debts soared. Within a few years of the Supreme Court accepting the government's authority to change the value of the dollar, the government used that power to deflate the currency and significantly change the value of existing debts.

The inflation of the Civil War, the deflation of the 1870s, and the Panic of 1873 (which set off a national recession) set the stage for the Greenback Party and its more important descendent, the Populists. The Greenback Party was formed in 1874 and its key issue was inflation (i.e. more greenbacks). It is remarkable how quickly constitutional authorization of redistribution through inflation produced a party dedicated to exactly that aim. The Greenback Party appealed to poor farmers in the south and west who had dollar-denominated debts that had become increasingly more onerous with the deflation of the 1870s. The Supreme Court had accepted the government's right to inflate in 1871. The Grant administration had used that power to increase the value of the dollar in a move that was seen as supporting relatively wealthy creditors. The Greenbacks wanted to use the power of the government to redistribute towards debtors and their support came primarily from poor, indebted agriculturalists.

The Greenbacks fared badly in the mid-1870s as they failed to capture the Democratic nomination in 1876 (which went to conservative Samuel Tilden) and received less than 100,000 votes in their 1876 third party presidential campaign. In the 1878 election, the Greenbacks fused and formed the Greenback-Labor party which received more than one million votes and elected fourteen representatives to Congress. However, the economic upturn of the late 1870s led Greenback-Labor presidential candidate James Weaver to be soundly defeated in the 1880 Presidential election.

After 1880, the Greenback party dissolved but its supporters gradually formed a more important political movement: The Populists. Throughout the 1880s, farmers' groups, which eventually referred to themselves as the People's Party, had been politically organizing. By 1890, Populists had taken control of the Kansas state legislature and elected their first senator. In 1891, in a fusion of farmers' alliances and the Knights of Labor, the Populist Party was itself formed. This party, even more than the Greenback-Labor party, represented the first major party in U.S. history dedicated to redistribution from rich to poor.

The People's Party platform of 1892 included provisions for a graduated income tax, more generous pensions, public ownership of railroads, and (like the National Socialists) expropriation of land held by foreigners. But their primary focus was on inflation, and the first two demands of their 1892 platform were "free and unlimited coinage of silver and gold at the present legal ratio of 16 to 1" and that "the amount of circulating medium be speedily increased." This monetization of silver would have significantly inflated the currency and would have reduced the real value of existing nominal debts, important to the people with "homes covered with mortgages" whom the Populists saw themselves as representing. As if to underscore their debt to the Greenback Party, they nominated the Greenbacks' old warhorse, James Weaver, in the 1892 election.

Since the Populists' policies were pro-poor and inevitably pro-black, the Populists looked to black votes. C. Vann Woodward (1953) wrote, "More important to the success of Southern Populism than the combination with the West or with labor was the alliance with the Negro" (1953: 254) and as a result, "Populists of other Southern states followed the example of Texas, electing Negroes to their councils and giving them a voice in the party organization" (1953: 256). This alliance between white and black Populists led southern Populist politicians to urge interracial tolerance and to attack racism. Tom Watson, a leading Populist, said "I have no words which can portray my contempt for the white men, Anglo-Saxons, who can knock their knees together, and through their chattering teeth and pale lips admit that they are afraid the Negroes will 'dominate us.'"

However, as Populists' policies aided the blacks and as Populists actively reached out for black support, the enemies of Populism turned to race hatred. C. Vann Woodward [1955] (2002: 79) writes: "Alarmed by the success that the Populists were enjoying with their appeal to the Negro voter, the conservatives themselves raised the cry of 'Negro domination' and white supremacy, and enlisted the Negrophobe elements." Antiblack hysteria was furthered by politicians and the press who sought to use racial antagonism as a means of distracting class-based politics. "In Georgia and elsewhere the propaganda was furthered by a sensational press that played up and headlined current stories of Negro crime, charges of rape and attempted rape, and alleged instances of arrogance. . . Already cowed and intimidated, the race was falsely pictured as stirred up to a mutinous and insurrectionary pitch" (Woodward [1955] 2002: 123). Lynching became a very tangible expression of the rise of race hatred.

The remarkable success of playing the race card is shown by the political events of the 1890s. While Bryan did win the Democratic nomination, he failed in national elections. Gold remained the basis of the national currency. The Populists' opponents, the Southern Bourbon Democrats, skillfully used race to divide the Populists. Barton and Cantrell (1989: 660) wrote, "When a sizable majority of

Texas Populists perceived that they faced a choice between White supremacy and a populist governor in Austin, they chose white supremacy and doomed the people's party to defeat." Tom Watson himself argued that race hatred ("the Negro question") was "the invincible weapon of Bourbon democracy in the South" (from Woodward 1938: 26). And he should know. The right-wing Bourbons defeated him repeatedly in Georgia elections.

Certainly, there were successful southern Populists, but by and large, income redistribution was held to a minimum. Southern politicians generally supported free silver, as the whole region was highly indebted and would benefit significantly from inflation, but other aspects of the Populist agenda were stripped away. Instead of Populism, the south got the system of segregation known as Jim Crow. The state governments embarked on a spree of disenfranchising (and effectively robbing) the former slaves. During the era when the Europeans used the growing power of the state to start building a nascent welfare system, the United States assembled its own apartheid system.

The importance of race in defeating Populism is well illustrated by the differences between the west and the south. While southern farmers were generally the poorest in the country, Populism had a much longer hold over the west than over the south. It was in Kansas that Populists actually took control of the state legislature. Bryan represented Nebraska. Left-wing politics took root under LaFollette in Wisconsin. These relatively homogeneous states were fertile bases for redistributive politicians.

But, the south generally remained in the hands of conservatives who focused politics on race, not redistribution. Key's (1949) classic analysis of southern politics documents the extent to which southern states were regularly run by politicians with only a marginal interest in redistribution. Race became the dominant issue of the south and it crowded out the voices of agricultural reform. To this day, as shown in Fig. 6.3, the southern states are the least generous to their poor, while the western states are among the most generous in their welfare payments.

The legacy of the national battle over Populism continued for decades. Hofstadter (1955) presents the Progressives as the Populists' first heirs. While the Progressives were far more successful than the Populists, they were far less inclined towards redistribution. The Progressive coalition was wide and quite limited in its support for genuine, pro-poor policies. The Populist Party platform looks a great deal like contemporaneous socialist platforms elsewhere (apart from its monomaniacal concern with silver); no one would ever mistake Progressive Presidents Theodore Roosevelt or Woodrow Wilson for socialists.

These presidents were quite limited in their redistributive aims, and quite willing to take advantage of American ethnic politics. Although Roosevelt did create considerable uproar when he entertained Booker T. Washington in the White House, he also allied himself with the racist branch of the southern Republican party. During World War I, he railed against hyphenated-Americans. Wilson's election depended on the Jim Crow south, and he aggressively segregated federal government employees. While Wilson may have represented the high tide of redistribution in national politics before the New Deal, his policies were aimed more at reform than redistribution. He never pursued any action which would have upset the prevailing social order in the American south. Certainly, Progressive regulation entailed redistribution, but the Progressives were surely far less redistributive than a President Bryan would have been.

During the 1920s, the forces of reaction triumphed, and race and ethnic hatred were there to support them. For example, the Republican campaign against Al Smith in 1928 used this New York governor's Irish-Catholic background as a weapon against him throughout the American hinterland. Indeed, 1928 was the first election since Reconstruction when the Republican party won five southern states (Hoover took almost 50 percent of the southern vote). The 1920s also saw the rebirth of the Ku Klux Klan which served as a potent organization against blacks and immigrants. While the first Klan had been a southern organization, primarily opposed to reconstruction, the second Klan had a national following (Jackson 1964). It organized urban and rural citizens against minorities and not incidentally against left-wing politics as well.

It was during the Great Depression that America finally adopted significant redistributive policies. Franklin Roosevelt was elected in

1932 and his New Deal certainly represented a radical break with the past. While Roosevelt enormously expanded the level of redistribution within the national government, race continued to serve as a tool of his opponents. Despite massive popularity and a seemingly huge electoral success in 1936, gradually southern Democrats in the Senate were able to block New Deal programs in alliance with northern Republicans. These senators were able to maintain their independence (and their allegiance to their financial supporters) in part because the race-based one party system in the south gave them a security that no northern politician could match. Ultimately, as Brinkley (1995) details, it was these senators who brought the New Deal to a halt.

6.4.2. The Civil Rights era and the Republican rebirth

While the progression of the New Deal was halted after 1938, it remained firmly in place through the 1960s. The Eisenhower administration accepted the New Deal consensus and made little attempt to undo these generally popular policies. In some senses, Eisenhower was a mirror of Winston Churchill. Both leaders did nothing in the 1950s to reverse the redistribution instituted by previous administrations. During the 1960s, the welfare state in the United States moved forward as Lyndon Johnson used his stunning legislative skills to push his Great Society programs, which were targeted at the poorest Americans.

But, it was in the 1960s that the Republicans shifted to the right. In 1964, for the first time since 1936, they offered a candidate who was "a choice, not an echo" (the title of a popular right-wing book of the period by Phyllis Schlafly). In 1964, Barry Goldwater bucked the traditional Republican establishment, which had made its peace with the welfare state, and won the Republican presidential nomination. While European conservatives like Adenauer, de Gaulle, and Edward Heath all supported their welfare states, the United States produced a politician who was dead set on rolling back redistribution. Moreover, while European opponents of redistribution became marginalized, Goldwater defeated the Republican accomodationists like Nelson Rockefeller and George Romney.

How did the Goldwaterites capture the Republican Party? Goldwater's supporters included several disparate elements in American politics. First, the Goldwater partisans included the extreme anti-communists, the remaining followers of Joseph McCarthy. This group saw Roosevelt, Truman, Eisenhower, and Kennedy as traitors whose supposedly soft stance had lost Eastern Europe, China, and probably America to the international communist menace. Second, Goldwater received backers from the die-hard enemies of the New Deal and the enlarged government. This group felt increasing taxes and regulation to be a huge burden and a sure sign that socialism was coming to American soil. These groups were natural supporters of Goldwater, and his views on both the New Deal and on the Soviet Union naturally fit with the views of these two groups.

But, if Goldwater's support had been limited to these natural supporters he never would have won the Republican nomination, and, in the general election, he would not have received a single electoral vote outside of his home state of Arizona. The force that gave Goldwater the nomination was a third group that saw a solution to their own problems in Goldwater's antigovernment rhetoric: Southerners committed to segregation. Barry Goldwater was an unlikely paladin of Jim Crow. He was a half-Jewish member of the NAACP. It is impossible to find any Goldwater speech even tinged with racist demagoguery. Still, Goldwater was committed to less federal government, and in 1964, to the American south, less government meant an end to the federal assault on Jim Crow.

The federal attack on organized discrimination began during the Truman administration, with the integration of the civilian government and the military in executive orders 9980 and 9981 (both in 1948). This integration and Truman's endorsement of the pro-integration plank in the 1948 Democratic Party platform inspired the revolt of the States' Rights Democrats, or Dixiecrats. This revolt deprived Truman of southern electoral votes and almost managed to put the more conservative Thomas Dewey in the White House. In 1953, the Supreme Court demanded the integration of public schools in *Brown v. Board of Education*, and the federal government had begun "intruding" into the "Southern way of life" in earnest. In 1957, Eisenhower (somewhat reluctantly) sent troops into Little Rock to enforce the Supreme Court's ruling. Also in 1957, the Senate passed the first (relatively weak) Civil Rights Act since Reconstruction. In the 1960s, Kennedy (also reluctantly) sent federal agents south to enforce integration in schools.

Despite all these actions, by 1963 the apartheid system of the American south remained intact. But in 1964, Lyndon Johnson finally broke the Southern Caucus (which had originally propelled him to power) and secured the passage of the monumental Civil Rights Act of 1964 and Voting Rights Act of 1965. These acts, particularly Title VII of the Civil Rights Act, ended the ability of businesses and firms to choose their own customers or workers on the basis of race or religion. These acts were watersheds and they would change southern politics and society forever.

Unsurprisingly, a large number of furious southerners saw the intervention of the federal government as a repeat of the Civil War and Reconstruction, where Yankees used their military power to run roughshod over the "rights of the sovereign states". A steady stream of racist demagogues including Orval Faubus, Gene Talmadge, and most notably George Wallace fueled the sense of transgression. Indeed, it was George Wallace who brought southern racist demagoguery to the national stage. Wallace himself was apparently a strategic, not a convinced, racist. In 1958, he ran as a pro-redistribution racial moderate and lost to John Patterson, the Klan-backed candidate. In his later years, when blacks could vote, he again espoused racial tolerance. But from 1960 to the mid-1970s, Wallace vowed never to be "out-niggered" again and began to dominate Alabama politics with his fervent defense of "segregation today, segregation tomorrow, segregation forever." At his gubernatorial inauguration (1963), he warned of the "liberals" who "seek to persecute the international white minority to the whim of the international colored majority."

In the Democratic primaries, Wallace showed how appealing to racist anger could challenge even a powerful presidential incumbent. For example, in Milwaukee in 1964, Bronco Gruber, Wallace's master of ceremonies, declared that blacks "beat up old ladies eighty-three years old, rape our womenfolk. They mug people. They won't work. They are on relief." (Perlstein 2001: 321). While Wallace never really came close to upsetting Johnson, he did remarkably well, even outside the south in states with growing black minorities (e.g. Wisconsin and Maryland).

It was Goldwater, not Wallace, who would get the votes of the southern racists apoplectic over the Civil Rights Act. Barry Goldwater had voted against the Civil Rights Act, not because he approved of discrimination, but because he disapproved of the expansion of the federal government that the Act required. Goldwater's campaign steadily attacked the increasing size and scope of the national government, which meant that he was opposed to both the welfare state and federally fostered integration. He attracted southerners, even poor southerners who had benefited substantially from federal welfare spending, because of his stance against the Civil Rights Act.

Southern delegates were his base at the Republican convention. He won overwhelming support from the south (and the west) and lost the traditional Republican strongholds of the east. This pattern would be repeated in national elections for the next thirty-eight years. While Goldwater was himself soundly defeated by Lyndon Johnson in the general election, Goldwater was the first Republican to win the south since Reconstruction. Important southern politicians like Strom Thurmond, who were particularly associated with Jim Crow, defected to the Republican party. Goldwater's defeat set the stage for future Republican victories.

Richard Nixon was a transitional figure whose policies were closer to those of Eisenhower than to those of Goldwater, but who followed Goldwater's southern strategy. Like Goldwater, Nixon relied on southern votes to win the Republican nomination. Strom Thurmond helpfully endorsed Nixon and reassured delegates that he would not enforce Johnson's Civil and Voting Rights Acts. Thurmond was a stalwart ally of Nixon's throughout the campaign and helped to win over southern voters. Nixon ran as a law and order candidate promising to end urban unrest, and he spoke of states' rights and the need to limit the growing reach of the federal government. His democratic opponent was Hubert Humphrey, whose electric speech at the 1948 Democratic convention had been the rallying point for civil rights advocates. Like Goldwater, Nixon did not resort to racial demagoguery, but he did not have to. It was obvious that he was running against the Johnson legacy of civil rights and programs that increased transfers to poor African-Americans.

The only thing that stopped Nixon from complete victory in the south in 1968 was the presence of George Wallace, who ran an overtly racist campaign which also attacked welfare. While Wallace had originally supported more redistribution, now his party platform (1968) declared that "welfare rolls and costs soar to astronomical heights" and that "we believe that the private sector of our economy has the will and capability of providing a solution to the problem of poverty much more promptly and efficiently than any or all governmental programs of indiscriminate welfare contributions." Wallace connected welfare payments with recent race riots: "we have spent billions of dollars in the poverty program to give people money and you still have street mobs" (Mayer 2002: 86).

Still, despite Wallace's popularity, enough southern states supported Nixon to give him the presidency. Nixon would not roll back the welfare state. Indeed, Nixon was certainly on the left-side of the modern Republican party. But Nixon did stop the growth of Great Society programs, and he began an era of Republican strength based on southern support that continues today. During the thirty-six years before 1968, there had been only one Republican president and his actions were limited by Democratic legislatures. During the thirty-six years since 1968, there have been five Republican presidents, and often Republican majorities in Congress. This Republican ascendancy, which was built on southern support, has pushed the nation and the Democratic party significantly to the right.

In the thirty-nine years since Ronald Reagan endorsed Goldwater in the 1964 campaign, Republicans have often used racially tinged messages. Ronald Reagan's famous Welfare Queen—a woman who supposedly lived ridiculously well from welfare payments—was based loosely on an African-American woman (Mayer 2002: 154). George H. W. Bush used advertisements about African-American killer Willie Horton, released under Dukakis' furlough program, to discredit his opponent.[2] While George W. Bush has more prominent African-American cabinet members than any previous party, his Solicitor General still fights against affirmative action. Moreover,

---

[2] Interestingly, it was Al Gore who first raised the Willie Horton issue in a primary debate against Dukakis.

despite the fact that the forty-third President has never come close to using racist politics, the strong Republican electoral base in the south is ultimately the result of white anger over the policies of Lyndon Johnson. American history confirms the role that racial divisions have played in limiting the welfare state.

6.4.3. European welfare systems and racial fragmentation

From Adolph Hitler to Joerg Haidar, European demagogues have shown as much willingness to exploit racism as their American equivalents. But European homogeneity has generally left them with much less to work with. Furthermore, since European minorities (at least before the increase in non-European immigration) were not particularly poor, it was less natural to link anti-welfare rhetoric with ethnic hatred.

There are three broad categories of European ethnic politicians. First, there are some politicians who have exploited the genuine ethnic or religious divisions that do exist in Europe. These divisions are rare in most European countries, so these politicians have generally been confined to Belgium, Spain, the multiethnic Balkans, and to a much weaker degree in Italy. Religious divisions have been exploited by politicians in the Netherlands (particularly in the nineteenth century) and Germany (through today). Second, there are the anti-Semitic demagogues, such as Karl Lueger and Adolph Hitler. Anti-Semitism was used steadily against the left. However, as Jews have often been rich, anti-Semitism is less naturally tied to hostility towards redistribution. Finally, there are the modern anti-immigrant politicians, such as Pim Fortuyn and Jean-Marie LePen. These fit the American pattern most closely. If the European welfare state gets rolled back in the near future, it is likely that anti-immigrant rhetoric will be used. We will address these three forms of divisive politics in order.

6.4.4. Exploiting traditional national divisions

The general path of the European nation state has been that a central force has steadily expanded its borders and the reach of its control over its neighbors. The kingdom of England conquered Wales and Ireland. Scotland was also brought in when the Stuarts were crowned, but that country needed to be reconquered in 1715 and 1745. The Kings of France, starting from control over a small area around Paris, gradually established control over all of modern France, acquiring Alsace and Lorraine in the eighteenth century and Nice in the nineteenth century. In Spain, the Castillians gradually married and conquered their way to dominate the Iberian peninsula (including Portugal for a while). The Hohenzollern Kings of Prussia managed to subdue Germany and the Kings of Savoy united Italy. In all of these cases, there were substantial, region-based divisions within the country. Perhaps these regional divisions were not as great as the divide between blacks and whites in the United States, but in many cases, the differences were indeed extraordinary. Echoing American racism, today it is easy to find northern Italians who will tell you that Africa begins at Rome (or Naples). As Weber (1979) documents, even in France, which is now seen as a model of homogeneity, regional differences were extensive even in the late nineteenth century.

For understandable reasons, in every one of these countries, the central leadership undertook a mission of creating a common national identity. In most cases, these campaigns for unity took place in a pre-democratic, or at best quasi-democratic age, when leaders were trying to create loyal citizens. Indoctrination was used "to teach the child that it was his duty to defend the fatherland, to shed his blood or die for the commonweal ('When France is threatened, your duty is to take up arms and fly to her rescue'), to obey the government, to perform military service, to work, learn, pay taxes, and so on" (Weber 1979: 333). These campaigns for homogeneity involved a steady stream of nationalistic literature, songs, symbols, etc. National leaders suppressed regional politicians and regional dialects (e.g. Franco's campaign against Catalan).[3] National leaders built national road networks that increased the degree of interactions between their peoples and used military service as a means of creating cross-regional connections.

---

[3] For more discussion on the role of instilled homogneity in nondemocratic societies with the goal of maintaining large nations and empires , see Alesina and Spolaore (2003).

Perhaps most importantly, they used school systems to create a common national ideology. "The school, notably the village school, compulsory and free, has been credited with the ultimate acculturation process that made the French people French" (Weber 1979: 303). Weber details how the entire education system became oriented towards producing a homogeneous people. He cites regulations meant to eliminate linguistic heterogeneity such as the "need to teach exclusively in French. Regulations to be reviewed in *pays* where Basque, Breton, Flemish, German patois, etc., are spoken" (Weber 1979: 311), and describes the use of a "token of shame to be displayed by the child caught using his native tongue" (Weber 1979: 313). French linguistic homogeneity is not exogenous. It is the result of enormous government effort. Most strikingly, the schools were used to push a powerful nationalist ideology, to induce students to worship "a secular God: the fatherland and its living symbols, the army and the flag" (Weber 1979: 336).

The formation of a national German identity follows a similar path, but is in many respects far more remarkable because the German nation is such a recent phenomenon. German nationalism first rose 200 years ago as an ideological prop for the fight against Napoleon. During the 1815–71 period, nationalism became a common ideology among elites, but regional differences still ran strong. After all, it was hardly in the interests of the Guelphs or Witteslbachs (rulers of Hesse and Bavaria, respectively) to push an ideology that would undermine their claims to their subjects' loyalty. The elimination of regional differences really took off after 1871, when it became a primary goal of the new, national leadership. As Bismarck said, "my highest ambition is to make the Germans into a nation."

Between 1871 and 1945, a succession of nationalist leaders used a variety of weapons to create national homogeneity. The German school system, which was both extremely efficient and remarkably state-controlled, became a mechanism for promoting nationalism both under the Kaisers and under the Nazis. Indeed, Bismarck gave credit for nationalism to primary education: "the seeds planted in our youth have borne fruit and have given us a national political consciousness" (Pflanze 1955: 559). Indeed, after 1889, public education was used against socialism as well (which we will discuss further in the next chapter). The *Kulturkampf*, Bismarck's fight against the church, can be seen as a battle to implement nationalism by eliminating existing religion-based differences within Germany. Germany's extensive transportation infrastructure, its coherent national bureaucracy, and its large army all helped to forge a single German identity. While on the whole this effort was remarkably successful, Adenauer's willingness after World War II to embrace a western Germany, without Prussia, illustrates that even the Germans had problems creating a complete national identity.

England also has a strong national character (generally limited to the traditional kingdom of England), but the decentralized and democratic government of nineteenth-century England was less interested or less able to eliminate the national identities of the Irish, the Scots, or the Welsh. In some areas, Gaelic was still spoken and a strong sense of being different remained. Perhaps the more democratic nature of the English regime prevented the extreme nationalist ideology pushed in France and Germany.

As such, within England, France, and Germany, longstanding divisions have only rarely been exploited by entrepreneurial politicians. In France, these divisions are just too muted. In England, Margaret Thatcher's support did tend to come from the richer south and perhaps there was a regional subtext implicit in her fight against the welfare state. But as national identity is strong in England, if this subtext existed it was certainly quite muted. Germany has a large division along religious lines, and the Christian Democratic party (which is on the right) is particularly based in the Catholic, southern regions of the country. However, the relative economic equality of Catholics and Protestants in Germany means that even if some politicians have exploited regional divisions to get elected, these divisions have rarely provided for a natural attack on the welfare state.

In Spain and Italy, ethnic and regional divisions are much stronger than in the larger, northern countries, mostly because their nationalist governments were much weaker along almost every dimension. In some ways, the recent political history of Italy mirrors that of Germany. Italian nationalism made claims to a mythic past (the Roman Empire instead of the Ottonian empire) and rose as part of the opposition to Napoleon. Italian Unification came late and was followed by more than seventy-five years of nationalist leadership. Like Bismarck, Cavour saw education as the key to creating a national identity. The Casati legislation of 1859 "sought to provide an organic plan for public education in Italy, hoping to create a solid national consciousness" (Coppa 1995: 137).

But while the French and German schools succeeded in producing a national identity, the Italian experience was more mixed. There are several reasons for the weakness of Italian nationalism. First, Italian education was never as centralized as French and German education. During the critical early period of the monarchy, it was left in the hands of the local communes, probably because of a lack of resources on the part of the central government. Second, Italian education was much less widespread than education in the north. As late as 1960, the average Italian had less than five years of formal schooling while the average West German had more than eight. Third, the fight with the church over education was much stronger in Italy and the church engaged in an ideological battle against the Italian nation-state through 1930. The other tools of national unity, transportation infrastructure, a national bureaucracy, and a large well-trained army, were also less prevalent in Italy. Fourth, income differences between northern and southern Italy may have been more extreme even in the late nineteenth century than any comparable differences in Germany.

The end result has been an Italy that has mild degrees of regional heterogeneity, which have only recently been used against the welfare state. Most notably, in the early 1990s, Umberto Bossi and the Northern League attacked welfare and urged the formation of Padania, a separate Northern Italian nation, which would stop the cash flow from north to south. Bossi is currently part of Berlusconi's ruling coalition, so it is clear that this rhetoric has had some success, but as of yet, the legacy of the Savoys and Mussolini has held, and Italian divisions are real but not dominant factors in Italian political life.

It is in Spain where nationalism has clearly failed and where regional fractionalism continues as a dominant political force. Few leaders have as assiduously pursued national unity as Franco, who banned regional dialects, jailed separatist leaders, and even outlawed dancing the Catalan sardana. But Franco's brutal suppression still left strong regional identities in Galicia, Catalonia, and the Basque country. The best explanation of weak Spanish nationalism is the general weakness of Spanish government and its education system. While the average German had more than eight years of education in 1960, the average Spaniard had 3.6 years of education (Barro-Lee dataset). Furthermore, education was not ultimately controlled by a nationalist bureaucracy, but by the church, which (while friendly to the Franco regime) was not likely to push nationalism at the expense of piety. Spanish transportation infrastructure was weak. Furthermore, the separatist regions within Spain were generally wealthy (industrialization came first to Catalonia and the Basque country), and separatist leaders often had the resources to fight nationalism.

However, while separatism is a powerful force in Spanish politics, regional prejudices are not a natural tool against welfare because the minority groups have tended to be rich. As the Catalans and Galicians are relatively well off, welfare cannot be attacked as being too friendly to these groups. The leaders of these areas may attack the redistribution that the welfare state involves to the rest of Spain, but so far they have been too weak to eliminate the Spanish welfare state.

Among the smaller countries, many are truly homogeneous. Norway, Sweden, Denmark, Finland, the Netherlands, Austria, and Portugal are among the most homogeneous countries in the world. The history of these areas explains their homogeneity. All of these areas were once parts of larger, more heterogeneous nations. The current borders were defined by common culture, religion, and ethnicity. The Netherlands, for example, was a former Habsburg province that belonged to Spain because Charles V was the great-grandson of Charles the Bold of Burgundy (who had controlled the Low Countries). The Dutch revolt against their Spanish overlords both reflected Dutch regional identity and strengthened that identity. Indeed, in some respects the minor religious heterogeneity of the Dutch makes them the most heterogeneous of this group of countries.

Belgium and Switzerland are considerably more fractured than the other small western European nations. Belgium is split between Dutch-speaking Flemings and French-speaking Walloons; the common Belgian identity comes from their historical existence as the Spanish Netherlands and Belgian Catholicism. Still, over the past 200 years the Fleming–Walloon split has shown a tremendous potential for ethnic politics. In our view, the only reason why this divide has not stopped the Belgian welfare state is that the numerically dominant Flemings were also historically poorer. This combination means that Fleming nationalism was unlikely to be used against the welfare state. As the Flemings have become richer than the Walloons in recent decades, we are unsurprised to see the Fleming Nationalists, the Vlaams Blok (now Belgium's fourth largest party), opposing the welfare state because it redistributes to Walloons.

Switzerland is in some ways that exception that proves the power of ethnic politics. The Swiss are truly divided by language and religion and the potential for ethnic politics within this small country seems enormous. The Swiss have quite sensibly handled this problem with a level of political decentralization that is almost unique across the world. This decentralization gives a very large amount of power to the Canton governments, which basically rule over homogeneous populations. However, as we argued earlier, federalism is an institution that tends to limit redistribution and it appears to have done so in Switzerland as well (Obinger 1999: 32). Switzerland has an extremely small welfare state by European standards and in some ways its levels of redistribution make it look more like the United States than its European neighbors. Switzerland has dealt with its heterogeneity peacefully and with a minimum of ethnic strife by devolving power to the Cantons. However, this devolution ensured moderate levels of redistribution and in a sense reflected an acceptance that Swiss heterogeneity made a massive welfare state untenable.

6.4.5. Exploiting anti-Semitism

While right-wing politicians have only rarely been able to use large-scale ethnic divisions to oppose welfare in Europe, they have more often turned to anti-Semitic hatred. Two factors have tended to make Jews particularly attractive targets for hatemongers. First, their social segregation means that historically few European gentiles have Jewish spouses or close Jewish friends. As such, anti-Jewish hatred is unlikely to create a backlash among the larger gentile population. Second, for 2,000 years, the core documents of Christianity have depicted Jews as the killers of Christ. Since World War II, the Catholic Church has significantly reduced the anti-Semitic content of mainstream Christianity, but throughout most of history, gospel readings, standard prayers, and sermons all created a basic sense of the perfidy in the Jewish people.

While Jews may be a natural target for hatred, it is less obvious that hatred of the Jews should particularly belong to the right. Given the fact that Jews have often been wealthy, it seems that hatred of Jews would tend to lead to more redistribution, not less. Indeed, George Schonerer and Karl Lueger, early anti-Semites in Austria, were populists who turned anti-Semitism against the reigning Habsburgs. While Karl Lueger's anti-Semitism served as a model for the young Adolph Hitler, Lueger was a left-wing politician. Indeed, the origins of the National Socialist Party can also be seen as reasonably left-wing and pro-redistribution from rich to poor. After all, they did call themselves socialists.

However, the Nazis did eventually become the dominant right-wing party in Germany, and anti-Semitism in Europe has been much more a tool of the right than of the left. Given the fact that Jews were not particularly poor, how did this occur? The key to understanding the right-wing tones of anti-Semitism lies in the political divisions of nineteen-century Europe. Before World War I, the key left/right divide was not over redistribution but rather over the power of the traditional monarchy. In Germany, Austria, Spain, Italy, and even France, the right still clung to the idea that monarchs (and their nobles) had a right to govern without relying on popular support. As this ideology eschewed the view that power was bestowed from below, it clung to the idea that power was bestowed from above. In other words, God gave kings their authority. Naturally, the church was deeply involved in this political world view and outside of Italy, where the house of Savoy had permanently alienated the pope by seizing his lands, priests stood behind kings. The Austrian emperor's full title was "His Imperial and Royal Apostolic Majesty, Emperor of Austria and Apostolic King of Hungary." The last Bourbon king of France was anointed with pre-revolutionary holy oil. The Hohenzollerns always relied on their pliant Lutheran priests.

Given the connection between crown and church, and given the rightists' belief in religion-based legitimacy, secularism and liberalism became strongly connected. Anti-clericalism was a core left-wing creed. Indeed, among liberal extremists, atheism became common. But given the absence of debate in the U.S. over crown and church, it is not a surprise that American traditions of anti-clericalism are much weaker than those in Europe. In Europe, the battle lines between left and right had the church on one side and the secularists on the other, it was natural that Jews (in continental Europe) ended up over-whelmingly on the left. After all, it was the French Revolution that first emancipated Jews. The left favored equality before the law in an attempt to free countries from ancient noble privileges, but there was no group that would benefit more from equality before the law than Jews. The wealth and talents of many Jews meant that they not only supported the left, but in many cases became particularly prominent leftists (Karl Marx, Leon Blum).

Just as in the United States, hatred proved to be a powerful tool. Weiss (1996: 146) writes, "From Stoecker to Hitler, rightists rarely attempted to refute socialism, preferring to cite the high percentage of intellectuals of Jewish origin among socialist publicists as proof of its subversion." Right-wing success in Germany and Austria owed at least something to the power of anti-Semitism in those countries. In the French Third Republic, successful leftists Emile Zola and George Clemenceau successfully challenged the right's attempt to use anti-Semitism in the Dreyfus Affair by using their own tools of anti-clericalism and anti-monarchist prejudice. Since World War II, anti-Semitism has become seriously discredited and it is no longer a key weapon in right-wing arsenals, but before 1945, this form of division was a regular tool of European rightists.

But while anti-Black hatred seriously stemmed the growth of redistribution in the United States, anti-Semitic hatred appears to have had much less of an effect on the European welfare state. In many places, anti-Semitism did not develop in large part because they just did not have enough Jews. For while Jews were only 1 percent of the German population, they were a much smaller share of the population in Scandinavia. Even in Germany, where anti-Semitism flourished and supported the right-wing Nazis, this hatred only modestly impacted the welfare state. The most natural explanation for this fact is that while blacks were extremely poor in America, Jews were not particularly poor in most of Europe (outside of Russia and Poland). Indeed, popular anti-Semitic diatribes emphasized the wealth of Jews and not their poverty. Thus, individual socialists could be disparaged with anti-Semitism, but the whole pro-redistribution agenda could not be. Indeed in a sense the essential idea of Nazism is the fusion of formerly right-wing anti-semitism with income redistribution.

6.4.6. Exploiting hostility to immigrants

Anti-immigrant rhetoric is a longstanding element in both U.S. and European politics. In the 1850s, American know-nothings achieved some startling political successes by attacking immigrants, particularly those who were Irish and Catholic. In more recent years, the 1980s and 1990s, anti-immigrant rhetoric increasingly became a mainstay of extreme right politicians in Europe. Attacking immigrants has proven a successful strategy in France, Austria, Denmark, Belgium, and the Netherlands. In Austria and the Netherlands, anti-immigrant parties have become so successful that they have become significant parts of governing parliamentary coalitions. These ruling coalitions have also, not incidentally, been committed to rolling back the European welfare state. Europe's new immigrant-based heterogeneity may eventually push the continent toward more American levels of redistribution.

Postwar immigration has introduced into a number of European countries a significant number of poor, ethnically distinct immigrants who have made tempting targets for demoguery. These immigrants have tended either to come from former colonies (as in France or England) or because of policies meant to increase the number of low wage workers (as in Germany and Sweden). These visible minorities have generally been poor and as a result, they disproportionately benefit from the welfare state. It would almost be surprising if right-wing politicians did not try to build hatred against these groups as a means of building support.

The most successful anti-immigration party has been Joerg Haider's Freedom Party in Austria. They took thirty-three seats in the

Austrian Parliament in 1990, fourty-two in 1994, and fifty-two in 1999, their high-water mark. On February 3, 2000, they joined a governing right-wing coalition, which was committed to reducing the size of Austria's welfare state. Anti-immigrant rhetoric was the most salient aspect of the party and "stop the over-foreignisation" was one of their election slogans. Their erstwhile leader Joerg Haider is noted for exploiting racial stereotypes in remarks such as "the Africans who come here are drug dealers and they seduce our youth." In Austria's most recent election, they lost ground and it remains to be seen if being against immigrants is enough of a basis for a permanently powerful political party in Austria.

In the Netherlands, Pim Fortuyn's party received twenty-six seats in Parliament in the May 2002 elections and also joined the governing coalition. The Netherlands has a famous history of commercially profitable tolerance, so the Pim Fortuyn phenomenon was particularly surprising. Fortuyn, a former Marxist, distinguished himself by being a somewhat unusual right-wing politician who combined anti-immigrant hostility with free market immigration policies and open homosexuality. His hostility has been particularly oriented towards Islamic immigrants and he wrote a book called "Against the Islamicisation of Our Culture." Apparently, Muslim intolerance of homosexuality partially motivated his dislike of Islam. While Fortuyn shows the power of anti-immigrant politics in the Netherlands, it seems unlikely that his already unraveling party will long survive his assassination.

The power of anti-immigrant politics in France shocked the world when Jean-Marie LePen bested Lionel Jospin in the first round of the Presidential election in 2002. LePen received 16.86 percent of the vote. LePen makes the link between immigrants and redistribution explicit. He said "there are simply too many immigrants, and they make who knows how many children whom they send into the streets and then claim welfare." While LePen had no chance of defeating Chirac in the general election, his popularity did successfully eliminate Jospin and the Socialists from contention. It is certainly reasonable to believe that Jospin would have been defeated in the run-off in any event, but LePen's anti-immigrant appeal ensured the victory of the more moderately right-wing Chirac.

Right-wing politicians with a strong anti-immigrant bent have also been successful in Belgium and Denmark. Filip Dewinter of the nationalist Vlaams Blok in Belgium urges his supporters: "we must stop the Islamic invasion." Pia Kjaersgaard and the Dansk Folkeparti are Denmark's third largest party and are not part of the ruling moderately right-wing coalition, but do provide them crucial support.

While these politicians are particularly oriented against immigration, anti-immigrant rhetoric has also been a part of the message of far more successful and mainstream conservative politicians. For example, Silvio Berlusconi is certainly seen as being anti-immigrant and he has declared "In no time we'll be thrown out of our own country by masses of immigrants." Moreover, his ruling coalition includes Umberto Bossi's Northern League, which preaches antipathy both against southern Italians and against immigrants. Even Margaret Thatcher was openly sympathetic to Englishmen who felt threatened by immigration. So far, anti-immigrant rhetoric has not led to an end to the European welfare state, but it seems quite likely that it will continue to be used against redistributive policies in the future. The views of Haidar, Fortuyn, LePen, and the Vlaams Blok are extremes in Europe, but the popularity of these politicians is growing. Their strength illustrates the point that racism is not some unusual American trait, but the natural result of minorities who are disproportionately poor and politicians who can push hatred to get elected on an anti-welfare ticket.

6.5. Why does racial heterogeneity matter?

The previous sections have provided the evidence on the connection between racial heterogeneity and redistribution. The simplest interpretation of these facts is that human beings are just less sympathetic to people who are different from them. This view would predict that voters might empathize with a poor single mother with two children who looks like them, but once that mother has a different skin color, empathy declines dramatically.

Indeed, there is significant evidence supporting the notion that people dislike or distrust individuals of different races. Alesina and

LeFerrarra (2000) show that civic participation declines in more heterogeneous communities. Glaeser et al. (2000) show that individuals are more likely to cheat people from a different race. There is a rich body of psychological research documenting the significant impact that race can have on sympathy and affection (Allport 1954 is the early classic summary).

But, there is another body of evidence that suggests that racial attitudes can be surprisingly malleable. Over the history of the GSS, there has been a remarkable decline in both racial attitudes and segregationist behavior. In 1972, 37 percent of respondents said that they thought interracial marriage was wrong. In 1998, only 11 percent of respondents thought interracial marriage was wrong. In 1972, 39 percent of respondents said that they believed white people had the right to keep blacks from moving into their neighborhoods. In 1998, only 11 percent of respondents said the same thing.

One can argue that these changes in survey responses reveal more about norms of political correctness than about true underlying preferences, but there have been accompanying changes in behavior as well. In 1973, 20 percent of whites had even had dinner at home with a black. In 1996, 42 percent of whites had dined with a black. In 1978, 34 percent of whites attended an integrated church. In 1994, that figure had risen to 48 percent. These figures are matched with evidence on intermarriage and residential segregation. While black–white mixed marriages are still rare in America, they have risen substantially from 0.12 percent of all marriages in 1960 to 0.46 percent of all marriages in 1992. Cutler et al. (1999) document the striking decline in the level of segregation. This decline follows a seven decade rise in segregation in American cities, which appears to have been accompanied by a hardening of racial attitudes in northern cities. Taken together, these facts seem to suggest a relatively fluid process where racist attitudes ebb and flow over time.

Differences across space seem as dramatic as differences across time. Almost all observers of race relations suggest that Europe has a much weaker tradition of racism than the United States. After all, prominent American blacks such as Paul Robeson and Josephine Baker fled the racially segregated United States for acclaim in more tolerant Europe. These anecdotes are born out by opinion surveys and by intermarriage figures. In Brazil, racist attitudes certainly exist, but the racial boundaries are far different and far more fluid than in the U.S.

Just as racial attitudes differ across space and time, anti-Semitic hatred, or hatred of many other groups has waxed and waned. No one living in Nazi Germany can suggest that attitudes towards Jews have not changed since 1945. No one would argue that Jews faced comparable hatred in pogrom-filled nineteen-century Russia and Disraeli's England. While the ability to hate seems to be universal, the objects of hatred are not and groups are not disliked invariably because they are different. Indeed, the best piece of evidence supporting this claim is the existence of commercial entrepots that have regularly allowed for the non-hostile mixing of different groups.

If racial differences do not necessarily lead to hatred, then why are these differences so strongly correlated with lower levels of redistribution? Our view is that these groups create the potential for hatred. Following Glaeser (2002), we suggest that hatred is the outcome of a political equilibrium where politicians supply hate when hatred is a complement to their policies. As such, Bourbon Democrats will stoke the fires of racial hatred if by making blacks out to be villains they discredit the pro-black policies of their Populist opponents. Likewise, socialists may use class hatred to engender support from their own rank and file.

In principle, hatred can be built against any person or group by making up (or exaggerating) the past crimes of this group and by hinting at future crimes in the making. As such, hatred can be built against individual politicians or against nameless special interest groups that support one's opponent. Race hatred becomes particularly appealing as a strategy for two reasons. First, the racial group must be particularly tied to one side of the political aisle. Blacks must be closely tied to the Democratic party or to the Populists. Jews must lie on the left of European politics. Second, the racial group must be relatively small or segregated socially. It is counterproductive to try and engender hatred against a group that is well integrated and large. The hatemonger will make more enemies than friends.

As such, racial minorities tend to be attractive targets when they are small or isolated and when they are closely tied to one side or the other of the political aisle. Blacks in America have generally been just such a target. Their poverty has meant that they serve as a permanent means of discrediting left-wing politics. Their isolation means that few whites are married to blacks or have them as close friends. As such, building hatred against blacks creates little blowback among the white population. Likewise, while it is often alleged that Jews were a well-integrated segment of the German population, this claim is somewhat misleading. First, the Jews were never more than 1 percent of Germany's population; as such, many Germans would have never come into contact with Jews. Second, Jews tended to locate disproportionately in a few large cities (which generally were not seedbeds of anti-Semitic hatred) and in the areas of the east. Third, the social isolation of Jews in Germany was still high, and few gentiles would have had close Jewish friends.

Our belief in the endogeneity of racial hatred offers some hope for a world where heterogeneity does not lead to hatred, but it does not eliminate the basic tendency of heterogeneity to support hate. One way of thinking about this is that heterogeneity lowers the cost of building hatred against specific groups. These lower costs do not automatically lead to hatred, but they do make hatred more likely. And when politicians see hatred as tool that can achieve a political goal, such as fighting the welfare state, then they are likely to use this tool. As such, our works suggest some hope that hatred towards blacks may really diminish in the future, but it also offers a caution about current directions in European politics. Currently, anti-immigrant hatred is a marginal phenomenon. It may not be in the future.

6.6. Conclusion

Europe is a continent filled with homogeneous countries. In many cases, the homogeneity is the result of concerted, and often bloody, work on the part of central governments to build a national identity. As a result of this homogeneity, the opponents of the welfare state have found it difficult to demonize the poor as being members of some hated minority. In this way, homogeneity made redistribution easier and more natural.

The United States, by contrast, is a highly heterogeneous society that is particularly distinguished by the overrepresentation among the poor of the most visible and socially distinct minorities. As such, it has always been easy for the opponents of welfare to use racial and ethnic divisions to attack redistribution. The southern opponents of the Populists in the 1890s relied on racial rhetoric. Ronald Reagan's election relied on the southern revolt against the Civil Rights movement. By our estimates, American racial fractionalization can explain approximately one-half of the difference in the degree of redistribution between the United States and Europe.

The recent rise of anti-immigrant politicians in Europe illustrates our claim that U.S.–Europe differences have more to do with the racial divisions than with deep cultural difference. As Europe has become more diverse, Europeans have increasingly been susceptible to exactly the same form of racist, anti-welfare demagoguery that worked so well in the United States. We shall see whether the generous European welfare state can really survive in a heterogeneous society.

Chapter 7

The Ideology of Redistribution

7.1. Introduction

In Chapter 2, we reviewed the evidence on economic inequality and income mobility in the United States and Europe. We found that before tax income inequality was higher in the United State than in Europe. Income mobility is similar on the two sides of the Atlantic today and, as far as we can tell, in much of the past as well. Indeed, today the poorest Americans appear to be more likely to stay poor than the poorest Europeans despite the fact that they often work longer hours.

Regardless of the economic facts, survey respondents in the United States and Europe express wildly different opinions about the level of mobility in their societies. Europeans are much more likely to believe that the poor are trapped in poverty and that their poverty is the result of forces beyond their control. Americans, by contrast, believe that effort, not luck, determines income and that the poor are not trapped. Table 7.1 shows results from the World Values Survey on the United States and Europe. In the United States,

Table 7.1. Beliefs About Poverty in the United States and Europe

Belief	United States	European Union
Believe that the poor are trapped in poverty	29%	60%
Believe that luck determines income	30%	54%
Believe that the poor are lazy	60%	26%

Source: Authors' calculations from the 1983–97 World Values Survey.

29 percent of respondents believe that the poor are trapped in poverty and 60 percent of respondents believe that the poor are lazy. In Europe, 60 percent of respondents believe that the poor are trapped in poverty and only 26 percent believe that the poor are lazy. In Europe, 54 percent believe that luck determines income. Only 30 percent of Americans share that view.

The American and European world views are quite different. The Europeans maintain a belief that birth determines status and the poor are trapped. Americans believe that they live in a land of opportunity where the people who stay poor are those who are too lazy to pull themselves up by their own bootstraps. We will refer to these different sets of beliefs as different ideologies, and in this chapter we will try to understand the relationship between these ideologies and the welfare state.

Regardless of whether or not these views reflect reality accurately, they certainly are at least correlated with political outcomes and behavior. Across countries, places that believe that the poor are trapped are much more likely to redistribute than countries that do not have this belief. Across the United States, the states where more people believe that achievement is determined by family background are more likely to have more generous welfare payments. Across individuals, there is a strong link between supporting more welfare, and being generally left-wing, and believing both that the poor are trapped, and that luck and family background determine income. These beliefs may not cause support for redistribution, but they certainly are correlated with support for welfare. Logically, it is unsurprising that people who believe that the poor are trapped through no fault of their own, are more likely to support redistribution. Indeed, we believe that it would be foolish to try to understand the differences between European and U.S. politics without recognizing the strong differences in beliefs between the two areas. However, there are two ways of thinking about the differences that plainly exist in these ideological beliefs. First, beliefs may be first causes, shaped either by economic reality or other exogenous forces (such as religion), that precede the welfare state. This view suggests that ideology is an important causal mechanism driving the redistribution between rich and poor.

Our competing hypothesis is that ideology is more of an effect of the political success of the right than a cause of that success, and that the root causes of right-wing political success are institutions and heterogeneity. The central claim of this hypothesis is that ideology is created by political actors who use it to support their agendas. The forces that gave the right more power within the United States also gave them the ability to push their own distinctive way of understanding economic opportunity. Furthermore, European beliefs about the poor came about in order to justify welfare, and were not based on reality. As such, our competing hypothesis is that ideology is a byproduct of, or at best a natural accompaniment to, national policies on welfare, and not a separate cause.

Our evidence supports the second hypothesis. Differences in popular beliefs about income mobility are shaped by politics and indoctrination, not by reality. The European beliefs about income immobility have more to do with a century of left-wing political power than real immobility. American beliefs about opportunities for the poor also have as much to do with indoctrination as with reality. One piece of evidence supporting this view is that factors which increase the political power of the left, but which are not necessarily correlated with income mobility (such as proportional representation), are strongly correlated with popular beliefs about income mobility.

Beliefs about income differ substantially between the United States and Europe, and these differences in beliefs surely matter to the political outcomes of the two countries. But, these beliefs do not reflect any underlying economic truth. Instead, indoctrination appears to trump reality in forming beliefs about social mobility. We suspect that this is true for many other political beliefs as well.

7.2. The connection between redistribution and beliefs about income mobility

We now focus on the correlates of the questions about social mobility shown in Table 7.1, which notes the extreme differences in beliefs about the poor between the United States and Europe. Few differences between the United States and Europe are as striking as these survey results.

While it is clear that these questions have something in common, they are not conceptually the same. One could certainly believe that luck determines income and that the poor are not trapped. Indeed, if income is randomized at some regular interval, then luck determining income would be related to a lower degree of being trapped. There is a common thread, though, which runs through all of these questions: The image of the poor. If the poor are trapped and unlucky, then they are poor souls, intrinsically the same as the rest of us, who are worthy recipients of government aid. If the poor are lazy, then they are intrinsically different from other productive members of society. As such, given their unworthiness, there is little reason to subsidize them.

Now we turn to evidence on the link between these beliefs and the level of redistribution. Figure 7.1 shows the correlation between the share of respondents who believe that luck determines income and the level of redistribution across nineteen countries with per capita GDP above $15,000 dollars in 1998, a cut off which roughly corresponds to the OECD group. There is a striking 61 percent correlation between these beliefs and redistribution. The relationship is almost a straight line. The fitted line suggests that as 10 percent more of a nation's population believes that luck determines income, the share of GDP spent on social services rises by 5 percent. If we include

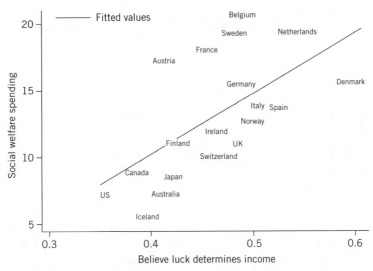

Fig. 7.1. Belief that Luck Determines Income and Welfare Spending
(*Source*: Calculations from GSS Data.)

our entire sample, and control for income, we estimate the following relationship:

$$\frac{\text{Spending on Welfare}}{\text{Total GDP}}$$
$$= \underset{(0.05)}{-14} + \underset{(0.0009)}{0.004} \bullet \text{GDP} + \underset{(0.10)}{0.35} \bullet \text{Luck Determines Income} \qquad (1)$$

Standard errors are in parentheses. There are 30 observations and the *r*-squared is 59 percent. Thus, a 10 percent increase in the share of the population that believes that luck determines income is associated with a 3.5 percent increase in the share of GDP spent by the government on redistribution. Alesina and Angeletos (2005) present additional evidence using the same data and confirm that these results are quite robust to various statistical checks.

Other variables are similarly impressive. The correlation between spending on social welfare and the belief that poverty is society's

Fighting Poverty in the US and Europe

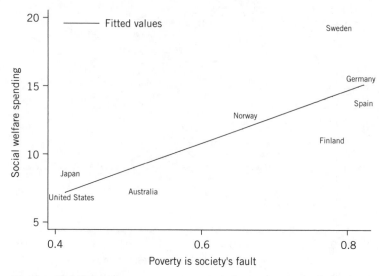

Fig. 7.2. Redistribution and the Belief that Poverty is Society's Fault
(*Source*: Calculations from GSS Data.)

fault is 82 percent among countries with GDP greater than $15,000 in 1998; this relationship is shown in Fig. 7.2. For the entire sample of countries, the correlation is 43 percent. Across countries, there is an extremely robust relationship between beliefs about the causes of poverty and the degree of redistribution.

What about correlations within countries? Within the United States, beliefs about the laziness of the poor correlate quite strongly with beliefs about whether the United States should spend more on welfare. Alesina and La Ferrara (2005), using the General Social Survey, show that the Americans who believe that luck, family connections, etc. determine an individual's income are more favorable to redistributive policies.

Table 7.2 shows these relationships. The number of observations is in parentheses. We have split the sample into people who think that what the United States is spending on welfare is about right, too little, and too high. In the table, we see that 88 percent of those who think that spending on welfare is too high say that the poor are poor

Table 7.2. Beliefs About Poverty

People's belief	The government's response to poverty		
	Too much	About right	Too little
Share the belief that need is caused by laziness (as opposed to society)	88% (N = 388)	63% (N = 294)	35% (N = 454)
Share the belief that there is a chance to escape poverty	88% (N = 456)	74% (N = 374)	55% (N = 546)

Source: Authors' calculation from the General Social Survey.

because of laziness as opposed to society in the United States. Only 35 percent of those who think that spending is too little believe that the poor are poor because of laziness. Those who think that spending on welfare is about right sit in the middle. The overall correlation between views on welfare spending and belief that the poor are poor because of laziness is 41 percent.

Similar results appear for the question of whether the poor are trapped. With this variable, 55 percent of those who think that welfare is too low think that the poor have no chance to escape poverty; 88 percent of those who think that welfare is too high think that there is a chance to escape poverty. Again, those who think that welfare is about right share that opinion. It is worth noting that even those Americans who want more spending on poverty are more likely to believe that the poor have a chance to escape poverty than the European average. Only 40 percent of Europeans thought that the poor had a chance to escape from poverty. Overall, these correlations again support the view that ideology is at least closely correlated to support for welfare.

A final demonstration of this correlation involves looking across states within the United States. In this case, we are limited to using the General Social Survey, since the World Values Survey has too few observations to form state-level means within the United States. Even with the GSS, we only have forty states where we have more than twenty observations. As such, these data are much noisier than

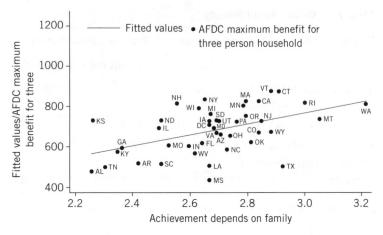

Fig. 7.3. U.S. AFDC Payments and the Belief that Achievement is Determined by Family Background

the cross-country evidence. Still, for those forty states, there is a 26 percent correlation between the belief that family background causes poverty and the maximum AFDC benefit in 1990.

This relationship is shown in Fig. 7.3, which regresses maximum welfare benefit on the state average of belief that effort can bring the poor out of poverty. There is also a 25 percent correlation between this belief and support for higher levels of redistribution. This again confirms the view that welfare spending is at least correlated with beliefs about the economy and beliefs about whether the poor can raise themselves up by their own bootstraps.

Different perceptions about the poor can also lead to a different tolerance of inequality. Europeans may be more offended by inequality because they perceive it as intrinsically unfair. Americans, on the ther hand, may be more tolerant because they see inequality as a fair result of individual effort. Alesina et al. (2001) present empirical results consistent with this interpretation. They examine survey answers to questions regarding "happiness" and show that Americans are much less bothered by inequality than Europeans. Interestingly, they find a large difference among the poor. The European poor are strongly averse to inequality while the American poor are not. This finding may reflect different beliefs in the perception about the possibilities of escaping poverty.

7.3. Myth and the reality of poverty in the United States and Europe

The simplest explanation of the differences in beliefs is that these differences reflect reality. As such, Europeans believe that the poor are trapped because indeed the poor are trapped in Europe. Conversely, Americans believe that they live in a highly mobile society because they do indeed live in such a society.

There is certainly some objective truth to the view that America has been a land of opportunity, not in the sense that Americans are all that more mobile, but just in the sense that Americans both today and historically have been richer than Europeans. After all, the millions of immigrants who came to North America traveled from their homes in part because they expected to earn more money. Even if Americans are not more socially mobile than Europeans, most American family histories include an episode where some first American left a poorer European country (especially Ireland, Italy, and Eastern Europe) for much richer America. This experience was real and one might think that it must play some role in the beliefs about the bounty of the American economy.

But, while America has historically been richer than Europe, there is little evidence to suggest that America is more mobile than Europe, either today or even in the past when the foundations of the welfare state were laid out. As we discussed in Chapter 3, Gottschalk and Spolaore (2002) find that 31 percent of Germans and 34 percent of Americans in the middle quintile moved to the either of the top quintiles between 1984 and 1999, and 60 percent of the bottom quintile of the American population stayed in that class nine years later in the United States, while only 46.3 percent of the bottom quintile in Germany stayed in that group. Checchi et al. (1999) compare Italy and the United States. They find more mobility among middle income Americans, but less among the American poor. While we accept the limits on our ability to measure income mobility across countries, we are unaware of a study that can document substantially greater amounts of mobility in the United States than in Europe today.

The historical evidence suggests that even in the past, the differences between the United States and Europe were small. Kaelble (1985) summarizes a wide range of studies (including Thernstrom) on social mobility in the United States and Europe in the nineteenth century. Upward mobility among the poor appears to have been somewhat lower in Germany, England, and France than in the United States, but somewhat higher in Scandinavia. These facts give us two reasons to doubt that differences in perceptions are the result of historical differences in reality. First, the differences appear small. Second, Sweden appears to have been the European country (in Kaelble's sample) with the most mobility, but today Scandinavians are among the strongest believers that the poor are trapped. More recent work by Long and Ferrie (2002) shows higher rates of upward mobility in the U.S.

The view that these beliefs reflect reality could be saved with the argument that the poor could escape poverty in the United States, but choose not to. If the poor in the United States were particularly lazy, while the European poor were hardworking, then the survey differences between the United States and Europe might still make sense. Evidence on high effort levels among the European poor might help us to understand why the Europeans believe that their poor are trapped. Unfortunately, only the coarsest measures of effort actually exist. Perhaps the best available measure is just hours worked per week, which we take from the Luxembourg Income Study. On an average, Americans work more than Europeans, but for our purposes, the important fact is not the national average but the distribution of hours worked among income groups.

To avoid issues related to retirement and childbearing, we focus entirely on prime age (25–54 years old) males. In Table 7.3, we show the hours worked by income quintile across seven countries. For each quintile, we show both the median hours worked and the mean. The means are often higher than the median, reflecting the long upper tail of the hours worked distribution.

Table 7.3. Median (Mean) Hours Worked by Income Quintile

Income quintile	Switzerland	France	Germany	Italy	Netherlands	Sweden	USA
1	55	39	12	50	0	39	35
	(62)	(38)	(26)	(50)	(16)	(35)	(27)
2	44	39	40	40	40	39	40
	(50)	(41)	(39)	(41)	(35)	(38)	(42)
3	42	39	40	40	40	39	40
	(46)	(41)	(41)	(40)	(40)	(39)	(44)
4	42	39	40	40	40	39	40
	(46)	(42)	(42)	(40)	(41)	(39)	(45)
5	45	45	44	40	40	39	45
	(50)	(47)	(45)	(42)	(44)	(40)	(48)
Survey year	1992	1994	1994	1995	1994	1995	1997

Source: Luxembourg Income Study. Samples include males aged 25–54 years.

Fighting Poverty in the US and Europe

While there are unusual aspects to the U.S. data, the intra-Europe differences are at least as large as the differences between the United States and Europe overall. Switzerland and Italy have the unusual pattern that the poorest work hardest. We suspect that the large informal sector in Italy makes it possible for poorer Italians to work hard without losing welfare benefits. In Germany and the Netherlands, the median person in the poorest income quintile does not work at all. The average (mean) hours worked among the German poor is 26 hours, which is comparable to the U.S. mean hours worked in that income quintile. France and Sweden are notable mainly for homogeneity across income groups. Except for the top income quintile in France, the median number of hours worked in every quintile in the two countries is 39. Labor market regulations in the two places appear to ensure a great deal of homogeneity.

When we compare the United States with the European countries, several facts emerge. First, the median American, that is the American men between the top and bottom quintiles, is working as many hours as his European equivalent. The average prime age male in the United States is not so overworked relative to his European counterparts. When we look at mean hours worked, as opposed to median hours, the Americans are working harder than their European counterparts, outside of Switzerland and except for the bottom income quintile. Together, these facts suggest that the biggest difference between the United States and Europe comes from the fact that in the United States there are some people who work many, many hours and there are many fewer of these in Europe.

Do the American poor work much less hard than the poor of European countries? It is true that the bottom quintile of the income in the United States works much less than the bottom quintile in Italy and Switzerland, who put in quite long hours. However, the differences between the United States and France and Sweden are not all that great, and the poor in the United States work much harder than the poor in Germany and the Netherlands. Notably, in Germany less than 20 percent of respondents say that the poor are lazy, and in Germany, the poor work many fewer hours than the poor do in the United States.

Perhaps the important thing is whether the difference between hours worked of rich and poor and the differences between countries in the belief that luck determines income is based on people observing the rich working much harder than the poor. Certainly, within the United States, the rich work much harder than the poor. The median hours worked increases by 10 as we move from the bottom income quintile to the top income quintile. The mean hours worked increases by 21 as we move from the bottom to the top quintile. In principle, the massive difference in hours of work across income groups could explain the American tendency to attribute poverty to laziness.

But the United States is hardly unique in having hardworking elites. For example, both Germany and the Netherlands have a comparable difference in hours worked between the rich and the poor. These countries do not share the American world view about the causes of poverty and they certainly have strong welfare states. These places are more, not less, likely than most of their fellow Europeans to believe that luck determines wealth. Figure 7.4 shows the relationship between the belief that luck determines income and

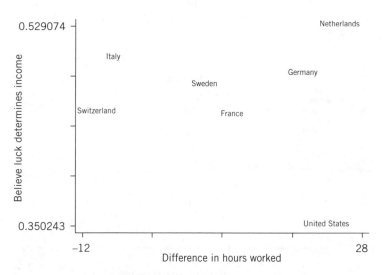

Fig. 7.4. Difference in Mean Hours Worked Between Top and Bottom Income Quintiles and the Belief that Luck Determines Income

the difference in mean hours worked between the top and bottom income quintiles within the seven countries. The figure shows that there is no relationship between the hours of work difference and opinions about the poor. The poor in many countries work less than the rich; this is not unique to America. But America's beliefs about the poor do differentiate it sharply from the European Union.

As we must conclude that economic realities do not drive beliefs about the poor, we now ask whether American beliefs perhaps reflect some other longstanding aspect of American culture. Following Max Weber, it is possible that Protestantism encouraged the belief that worldly success was related to moral worth. Perhaps it is American Protestantism that generated the view that the poor are lazy. To test this hypothesis, we looked across countries at the relationship between Protestantism and the belief that income is the result of luck.

This relationship is shown in Fig. 7.5, which considers countries with income per capita greater than $15,000 in 1998. As the graph shows, there is no relationship whatsoever. Given the vast difference in beliefs between Switzerland or the Netherlands and the

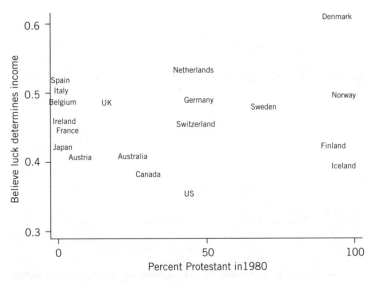

Fig. 7.5. Beliefs and Protestantism

United States, it is hard to believe that longstanding religious differences have much to do with these beliefs.

As such, beliefs about the poor are caused neither by underlying economic realities nor by religion. Now, we turn to an alternative possibility, raised by Alesina and Angeletos (2005) and Benabou and Tirole (2002), that the beliefs about the poor are as much effect as cause. As such, beliefs about the immobility or laziness of the poor are certainly related to having a welfare state. After all, it is comforting if you do not give money to the poor to believe that the poor are undeserving. But, according to this view, beliefs about mobility and laziness reflect indoctrination more than reality.

7.4. An alternative view: Ideas about the poor are shaped by politics

America has long seen itself as the land of opportunity. After all, in the 1830s, Tocqueville wrote, "In America, most of the rich men were formerly poor; most of those who now enjoy leisure were absorbed in business during their youth" [1835] (1959: 54). As we have discussed, Tocqueville appears to be somewhat misleading in terms of describing reality, but nonetheless, he captures the American self-image perfectly. The opinion surveys confirm that Americans believe that (1) they live in a land of abundant opportunity, (2) there are no social classes and as a result, (3) anyone who remains poor, pretty much deserves to be poor. Europeans do occasionally believe that their countries have opportunities, but they are much more likely to believe in social classes and they are much more likely to believe that the poor are unfortunate victims of society. Where did these beliefs start?

In this section, we analyze the hypothesis that the differences in beliefs about the economy have more to do with politics than with economics. This hypothesis suggests that differences in beliefs are the result of different types of indoctrination. Many Europeans have been exposed to almost a century of left-wing indoctrination in the capriciousness and power of the class system. Marxist theories have been taught in classrooms and the media repeats these dominant left-wing mantras. Conversely, since the days of Horatio Alger, Americans have been exposed to a right-wing, almost nationalistic indoctrination that focuses on American opportunity. Indeed, while European nationalism is often focused on a common ethnic or cultural identity, American nationalism is oriented around a land of liberty and opportunity. Moreover, some successful right-wing politicians have worked hard to ram home the idea of the poor as morally feckless layabouts. As such, American beliefs about the poor should be seen as the result, not the cause, of successful American anti-redistribution politicians. European beliefs are the direct result of the dominance of European socialism.

In this section, we focus on the history of indoctrination in the United States and Europe. We discuss the role of top-down belief formation through the school systems, but also through political campaigns and the media. In the next chapter, we turn to statistical tests, which show how politics appears to drive beliefs about the poor.

7.4.1. The image of the United States as the land of opportunity

From the first, America's boosters have presented it as a land of opportunity. In 1624, John Smith (of Pocahontas fame) wrote that if a settler in New England "have nothing but his hands, he may set up this trade; and by industrie quickly grow rich." In 1656, John Hammond wrote that in Virginia "It is knowne (such preferment hath this Country rewarded the industrious with) that some from being wool-hoppers and of as mean and meaner employment in England have there grown great merchants, and attained to the most eminent advancements the Country afforded. If men cannot gaine (by diligence) states in those parts (I speake not only mine owne opinion; but divers others, and something by experience) it will hardly be done. . . ." In 1732, a promotional tract for Georgia described that colony as "a land of liberty and plenty, where [the poor] immediately find themselves in possession of a competent estate."

While America certainly did have cheap land, and wages usually have been significantly higher on the American side of the Atlantic, even in the heady eighteenth century, the image of America as a land of opportunity was less than accurate. The Georgia colony, so boosted by James Oglethorpe (whose assistant wrote the above tract) initially failed miserably. America was neither all that remunerative nor all that mobile. Breen and Foster (1973: 213) wrote, "For most of the 1637 migrants prominence in the New World had followed substance in the Old." Indeed, many of the early leaders of the American republic seem to illustrate the importance of dynasties, or even membership in English noble families (Patrick Henry was Lord Brougham's cousin and John Marshall benefited from his blood relation to Lord Fairfax).

Yet, it is certain that the image of the land of opportunity was ubiquitous, and this is easy to understand. The descriptions of the colonies were written by boosters who had strong financial interests pushing them towards inducing migrants to come from Europe. It is hard not to think that the origins of America's self-image as a land of opportunity have as much to do with self-interested (and often misleading) advertisements than with reality.

If the view of America as a land of opportunity had its origins in promotional tracts written by large landowners like William Penn and James Oglethorpe, this view was bolstered in the ideological battle associated with the American Revolution. Pro-revolution advocates vaunted America's virtues: "a land of Liberty, the seat of virtue, the asylum of the oppressed" (Joseph Warren 1772). Alexander Hamilton (1774) argued that British "oppression" occurred out of "a jealousy of our dawning splendour."[1] Moreover, advocates of revolution argued that America, unlike England, disliked monarchy and aristocracy. The net result of this earthly paradise of material possibility and an absence of social barriers was that "if their Citizens should not be completely free and happy, the fault will be intirely [*sic.*] their own." It is hard to miss the connection between this phrase, written by George Washington himself in 1783, and the overwhelming view in America today that the poor are lazy.

In the second quarter of the nineteenth century, the battle between the Whigs and the Democrats began to have a connection to income redistribution. As opposed to more modern redistributive debates, the Democrats (the more pro-poor party) were relatively

---

[1] Adam Smith and Edmund Burke also shared this view.

laissez-faire. The Whigs favored a more aggressive government policy towards the economy, which was perceived as supporting the rich, through policies like tariffs. The Whigs fervently supported their policies with rhetoric about social mobility. For example, their pamphleteer, Calvin Colton, wrote in 1844 that "the wheel of American opportunity is perpetually and steadily turning, and those at the bottom today, will be moving up tomorrow and ere long be at the top." Whig candidates were presented as self-made men who epitomized the rags-to-riches potential in the American economy. In the particularly slick 1840 Presidential campaign, William Henry Harrison (a well-born war hero) claimed common tastes and a log cabin lineage and defeated his opponent Martin Van Buren, who was alleged to have aristocratic tastes and ancestry (he did not).

But, while the Whigs were pushing the vision of American mobility, their Democratic opponents were hardly pushing a contrasting vision of class immobility. Given the number of Democratic leaders who were themselves self-made men, including both Van Buren and more famously Andrew Jackson, this would have been a hard case for them to make. Moreover, their ideology did not need a basis in a complex Marxist system of rigid classes. The Democrats just argued for freedom. In words that would cheer a modern Reagan Republican, Van Buren said: "The less government interferes with private pursuits the better for the general prosperity" (Holt 1999: 66). This pro-liberty line was surely a much more effective ideology for a party dedicated to limiting redistribution to the rich, than attempting to create some form of class consciousness. As such, notions of social mobility became entrenched during the era of Tocqueville when the Whigs, through their words, and the Democrats, through their own lives, tended to further American notions of social mobility.

In the latter half of the nineteenth century, the Social Darwinism of Herbert Spencer became the reigning right-wing ideology of the Republican Party and during this era: "conservatism and Spencer's Philosophy walked hand in hand" (Hofstadter [1955] 1969: 46). Social Darwinism still emphasized mobility, as evolution relied upon competition and a dynamic society. But the novelty of the world view of Spencer and his economist acolyte William Sumner was that "Millionaires are the bloom of a competitive civilization," unusually endowed with "courage, enterprise, good training, intelligence, perseverance" (Hofstadter [1955] 1969: 58–9). Harking back to the Calvinist connection between material prosperity and moral worth, Spencerism implied that the poor had opportunities and their failure to capitalize on them showed their essential unworthiness. There can be no surprise that Sumner was "a prime minister in the empire of plutocratic education" (Upton Sinclair's words cited in Hofstadter [1955] 1969: 63). Indeed, the dominance of Social Darwinism during this era clearly owes much to the dominance during this period of self-made millionaires who backed Spencer and funded Sumner.

Spencerism faded and the American left began to preach sentiments that sound similar to the predominant views in Europe today. For example, the enormously influential Henry George [1887] (1973) wrote that "the injustice of society, not the niggardliness of nature, is the cause of want and misery." Thorstein Veblen [1899] (1934: 236) argued that men became millionaires not because of innate superiority but through "shrewd practice and chicanery." Marxism, which we will discuss later, emphasized both the fixed nature of one's class and the arbitrariness of class identity and became a dominant left-wing ideology. American socialists joined with their European counterparts in preaching a different view of the economy, which emphasized immobility and luck, not mobility and the unworthiness of the poor.

But, in the twentieth century, despite the Progressive Era, the New Deal, and the Great Society, ultimately the right proved more dominant in American politics, at least relative to Europe. For the reasons discussed earlier—American political institutions, military success, and racial divisions—socialism did not become a powerful force in American society. As a result, right-wing ideology, which had its roots in the view of America as land of opportunity and Social Darwinism, continued to hold sway over the American population. How did this come to be?

America's self-image as the land of opportunity was perpetuated in the twentieth century through both political discourse and the education system. The political efforts to push belief in opportunity are easier to spot. In many cases, America as a land of opportunity is a vein that runs through almost every Republican's rhetoric. As Warren Harding said in his inaugural address in 1921, "No one justly may deny the equality of opportunity which made us what we are." Calvin Coolidge said in his inaugural address, "The wise and correct course to follow in taxation and all other economic legislation is not to destroy those who have already secured success but to create conditions under which every one will have a better chance to be successful" (1925). Herbert Hoover's inaugural address (1929) echoed the claims of John Smith 300 years earlier: "Ours is a land rich in resources; stimulating in its glorious beauty; filled with millions of happy homes; blessed with comfort and opportunity."

As the left rose in power during the Great Depression, political discourse became less focused on American opportunity, and took on a more European twist. Franklin Roosevelt at his first inauguration (1933) described "a host of unemployed citizens fac[ing] the grim problem of existence, and an equally great number toil[ing] with little return," not because of their laziness or lack of fitness, but because "the rulers of the exchange of mankind's goods have failed, through their own stubbornness and their own incompetence." The New Deal was certainly the heyday of this type of rhetoric. Huey Long (1935) justified his "Share Our Wealth" program because "extreme inequalities in the distribution of wealth have closed the doors of opportunity to millions of our children." Henry Wallace, FDR's second vice president and a Progressive candidate for the presidency in 1948, argued that the luck of one's parents determined one's economic outcome: "I wonder if any scientist would care to claim that 100,000 children taken at birth from [poor white] families would rank any lower in inborn ability than 100,000 children taken at birth from the wealthiest one percent of the parents of the United States" [1939] (1944). These sentiments echoed through the 1960s, when Lyndon Johnson put forward his Great Society plan by saying, "There are millions of Americans—one fifth of our people—who have not shared in the abundance which has been granted to most of us, and on whom the gates of opportunity have been closed."

But, long before Nixon defeated Humphrey in 1968 and began the thirty-six year era of Republican dominance, New Deal rhetoric about limited opportunity and a class-based society was attacked. Because

America faced a Marxist regime in the cold war, anti-Marxist discourse was not just a tool of the right, but a fundamental part of American foreign policy. Moreover, the fight against Communist Russia gave the American right a tool to discredit anyone pushing left-wing views within the United States. Joseph McCarthy himself enjoyed only a fleeting moment of success, but anti-Communism became firmly entrenched. Unsurprisingly, the anti-Communists took particular aim at those with the ability to spread their ideas: Teachers, the media, and the entertainment industry.

In the post-Nixon era, when Republicans returned to power on the basis of white, southern votes, the image of the United States as land of opportunity has been stressed continuously. Richard Nixon's second inaugural stated, "Our system has produced and provided more freedom and more abundance, more widely shared, than any other system in the history of the world" (1973). Reagan's optimism is specifically linked to limits on government in his second inaugural address (1985): "We believed then and now there are no limits to growth and human progress when men and women are free to follow their dreams." George H. W. Bush's inaugural (1989) echoes these sentiments: "Men and women of the world move toward free markets through the door to prosperity."

Republican politicians have also emphasized mobility through more than just rhetoric. Republican leaders have often themselves had humble origins and have presented themselves as living proof of the opportunity that exists in America. Indeed, Hoover, Eisenhower, Nixon, and Reagan were Republican self-made men who ran against far more aristocratic Democratic opponents. Richard Nixon's "Checkers Speech" was a particularly extreme example of a Republican emphasizing his humble origins.

Republican rhetoric since 1960 has not just emphasized mobility, but has also suggested the moral limitations of the poor. Ronald Reagan's Welfare Queen who drove a welfare Cadillac with $150,000 stolen from the system is the most obvious example of political rhetoric aimed to suggest that the poor were both morally weak and lazy. In George H. W. Bush's inaugural (1989) he discussed "those who cannot free themselves of enslavement to whatever addiction—drugs, welfare, the demoralization that rules the slums." While this statement is coupled with a call for sympathy, the speech also clearly suggests the moral failings of the downtrodden.

As important as political rhetoric can be, public education surely provides more effective indoctrination than inaugural addresses. From its beginnings, American public education was politically motivated. In George Washington's farewell address, he said "as the structure of a government gives force to public opinion, it is essential that public opinion should be enlightened," and this creates a need for "institutions for the general diffusion of knowledge." Cremin (1951) writes:

The first, and perhaps the most widespread, demand on education grew out of the new pattern of republicanism. It was increasingly argued that if there was to be universal exercise of the rights of suffrage and citizenship, all of society would have to be educated to this task. Although the liberal intellectual envisioned such education as a means of equipping the citizenry to make intelligent political choices, his conservative counterpart saw it largely as a propaganda agency to save society from the 'tyranny of democratic anarchy.'

While direct political indoctrination on current political contests was generally kept out of the classroom, teachers were generally pushed towards the prevailing Whig view of the United States as a land of abundance and opportunity.

Kaestle (1983) describes "the semi-official, articulated ideology of America's native Protestant middle class writers, and in particular common school reformers," as including "the equality and abundance of economic opportunity in the United States." Thus textbooks, like McVickar's *First Lessons in Political Economy for the Use of Primary and Common Schools* (1835) included pieces of wisdom like "every man is the maker of his own fortune," and authoritatively states that "even the poorest boy in our country. . . has as good a chance of becoming independent and respectable, and perhaps rich, as any man in the country." But these lessons were not limited to economics texts; McGuffey's reader, the dominant text of nineteenth-century schools, declared "The road to wealth, to honor, to usefulness and happiness is open to all, and all who will may enter upon it with the almost certain prospect of success" (1848).

We should not be surprised that this ideology was ubiquitous in nineteenth-century schools. After all, the wealthier citizens who funded the schools wanted this ideology preached. Moreover, schoolteachers who wanted their pupils to show up would hardly tell them that they were doomed to lives of crushing poverty on the basis of the randomness of their birth.

Unsurprisingly, the more left-wing twentieth century saw an increase in the number of teachers who did not think that America offered infinite opportunity, and that poverty showed only moral weakness and laziness. First, American universities included professors like Veblen who taught a more left-wing view. Then, other schools became increasingly receptive to more socialist teaching. In general, colleges (especially those whose endowments make them independent) remain full of social scientists who dismiss the view that the United States is filled with equal opportunity.

But in lower grades still ultimately hold to be the basic American dogma of opportunity. Even in California (hardly the most right-wing of states), a model history lesson plan of the 1980s urged "a course should assess the role of optimism and opportunity in a land of work: The belief that energy, initiative and inventiveness will continue to provide a promising future" (1985: 568).

Why did right-wing ideology continue to dominate schools? Surely, the most general answer is local funding and control over public schools. In the United States, public schooling has always been a local affair and as a result, prominent local citizens have been able to ensure that the curriculum does not directly attack their interests or counter their views. In some instances, this general control was assisted by genuine purges of leftward leaning teachers, such as during the era of anti-Communism, but far more important than these obvious interventions are the daily monitoring of teachers by parents who do not want Marxist ideas about class immobility taught in public schools. We shall see how in the case of Europe, centralized control over schools made it much easier for social democrats to change the curriculum to fit their own ideology. Thus, federalism once again made it difficult for the left to push through their objectives, in this case the indoctrination of America's youth.

Fighting Poverty in the US and Europe

The overall story of the American belief in mobility suggests that the belief in economic mobility has been a prop of the right, and that right-wing politicians have assiduously furthered that belief. Their ability to do so has hinged ultimately on institutions and race, the two deeper causes of why America does not have a welfare state. These institutions have kept right-wing forces in power and enabled them to invest over the past centuries in creating a widespread American belief in the mobility of U.S. society and the laziness of the poor.

As a coda, it is worth mentioning that these are not the only ideologies that have been taught by the right within the United States. America's fondness for the death penalty and its belief about the validity of war are other examples of views that have been inculcated by the right. In general, these views also tend to support the electoral success of right-wing politicians and should be seen as further reasons why the welfare state did not take root in the United States.

7.4.2. The rise of class consciousness in Europe

The story of European ideology mirrors that of the United States. Just as in the United States, European politicians used rhetoric and the education system to push their own view of the world. In the nineteenth century, relatively right-wing European politicians emphasized the opportunity that existed within their own countries. The gradually expanding European left increasingly pushed the view that outcomes are determined by class, which is itself determined at birth. The difference between the United States and Europe lies in the relative success of the right and the left. For the reasons discussed above, in the United States the right has been triumphant. In Europe, the left has been much more successful, and they have used both political discourse and the education system to push their own view of economic mobility.

Late nineteenth-century European politicians used the education system to push a vision of a mobile society. Weber (1979) writes that nineteenth-century schools taught that "hard work and rectitude were bound to bring improvement, internal and external." He cites a shoemaker, Gregoire, who is the hero of moral tales for children, who says "my father had nothing, I have something; my children, if they do like me, will double, triple what I leave behind. My grandchildren will be gentlemen." The pace is slower than in America's Horatio Alger stories, but the theme is the same. France is full of opportunities and with hard work, anyone can rise in the world.

Schooling in Wilhelmine Germany was also deeply political, and while, as we have discussed, its primary goal was building a national identity, a secondary goal was fighting socialism. As Lamberti (1992: 73) writes, "On 1 May, 1889, the king of Prussia and German emperor demanded that the schools make a greater effort to refute socialist theories and to impart to the pupils a 'healthy' view of society and the state." As such, teachers were at least supposed to emphasize that " 'workers can expect justice and security only under the protection and care of the king at the head of state.' " Of course, the right in Germany was much more concerned with the king and army than it was with protecting the property of the wealthy bourgeois. It should not be then surprising that their indoctrination was less focused on the fairness of the economic system, and more focused on the greatness of the German nation.

If the image of the economy as being full of opportunity was naturally espoused by those who supported the status quo, then the image of the economy as being rigid and capricious was just as naturally espoused by their opponents, who favored radical redistribution. Indeed, it is none other than Karl Marx who is the great proselytizer of the view that the poor are oppressed ("the proletarians have nothing to lose but their chains") through no fault of their own. The *Communist Manifesto* [1848] (1998) describes the working classes: "Not only are they slaves of the bourgeois class, and of the bourgeois state; they are daily and hourly enslaved by machine, the overseer, and, above all, by the individual bourgeois manufacturer himself" (1998: 43–4). Workers do not occupy a land of opportunity: "The modern laborer, on the contrary, instead of rising with the progress of industry, sinks deeper and deeper below the conditions of existence of his own class" (1998: 49).

In the communist world view, workers are enslaved and have no chance of bettering their position. Moreover, according to Marx [1886] (1964), membership in the proletariat is arbitrary, determined at birth: "Determinate individuals, who are productively active in a definite way, enter into. . . determinate social and political relations." Marx's writings were, of course, not just abstract social science, but were seen by him and used by his followers as the intellectual basis for a revolution. If working class people believed in the possibility of upward mobility within the current system, they would be less likely to support revolution. As such, it was strongly in the interest of these hopeful revolutionaries to ensure that the poor felt trapped and exploited. As socialists acquired political power and gave up on resolution (at least in the short run), it was also in their political interests to ensure that the bourgeois would have sympathy for the poor.

How did this Marx-inspired world view, that the poor are locked in poverty through no fault of their own, come to dominate Europe? Certainly, the ability to convince Europeans that they lived in a class-based society was surely abetted by the vestiges of feudalism that still remained in Europe through World War I. The classes that Karl Marx used in his schema were intellectual constructions that may or may not be valid, but in pre-democratic Europe, there were legal differences between classes that were actually well defined. Nobles had defined legal rights, and in some cases political power, that were different from the rights of non-nobles. In some cases, legal differences existed between classes of commoners as well. Marx and Engels begin the *Communist Manifesto* by making an analogy between current class differences between the bourgeois and the proletariat with the traditional class differences in feudal Europe.

The real triumph of Marxist ideas did not depend on feudal vestiges, but on the ability of socialists to dominate political discourse and the schools. While right-wing American political leaders extolled American opportunity, European left-wing leaders discussed the hopelessness of the lives of the poor and the randomness of the system. Leon Blum (1946) wrote: "socialism is born of the concern for human equality because the society in which we live is founded on privilege. . . it is born of the contrast, scandalous and heart-rending, between the luxury of some and the privation of others, between crushing toil and insolent idleness." In Blum's world view, it is the poor who are hardworking and virtuous, while the rich are wastrels. In England, Lloyd George (1929) echoed similar sentiments: "unemployment, with its injustice for the man who seeks and thirsts for employment, who begs for labour and cannot get it, and who is punished for failure he is not responsible for by the starvation of his children . . ." And Lloyd George was a Liberal; the Labour Party was much more extreme. In Germany, Karl Kautsky writes, "In countries where the capitalist system of production prevails the masses of the people are forced down to the condition of proletarians."

These statements are not surprising. American leftists said similar things. The difference is that in Europe, socialists actually got elected. Their political statements were not the rantings of a fringe group, but rather the full-blown statements of the nation's leaders.

Left-wing leaders also used their own lives to emphasize the permanence of class. While Richard Nixon and Herbert Hoover were living embodiments of upward mobility, left-wing politicians in Europe made it clear that despite their political success, they were still profoundly working class. In this manner, they ensured that their voters would understand that class identity was immutable and the only way forward was class-based redistribution. Thus, labor and socialist politicians wrapped themselves in the clothes and symbols of workers. Leaders from Keir Hardie to Vladimir Lenin adopted the cloth worker's cap as their preferred headgear. They generally spoke in recognizably lower class accents. Despite the fact that left-wing political leaders had reached the pinnacle of power in their society, they often did all that they could to deny that fact.

Of course, the propagation of left-wing ideas about society occurred in European schoolrooms at least as often as the propagation of more right-wing ideas occurred in U.S. classes. Even before the left ran the government, teachers' unions, which were after all part of the labor movement, worked to move the curriculum to the left, or to stop right-wing indoctrination in the schools. Lamberti (1992: 87) describes how the German Teachers' Association fought the Kaiser's attempt to move the curriculum rightward: "The political outlook of the Left Liberals in the German Teachers' Association also made them unwilling to ally with and serve the forces of antisocialism in Wilhelmine Germany." Before World War I, Social Democrats tried to shift the curriculum of elementary schools: "The radicals suggested specific curricular reforms to instill values compatible with the tenets of socialism" (Olson 1977: 3).

But these pre-war efforts were minor relative to the much more enduring impact that socialism had on European schools after World War I. Just as before the war, the attempts to shift the curriculum came from both the top (socialist politicians pushing for curricular reform) and the bottom (the teachers' unions advocating views connected to their own political interests). In France, World War I "profoundly changed the [teaching] profession, radicalizing the formerly non-committal and throwing the formerly radical into key positions of power" (Singer 1977: 420). Further, in the early 1930s, "Teachers *syndicats* [unions] now collaborated on nominations and promotions, not to mention salary negotiations, and increasingly, *instituteurs* moved into politics and became a power within the Socialist party itself" (Singer 1977: 423). Left-wing control of the schools in France did not wait for Blum's premiership; it started with the unions themselves who dominated the schools and pushed the curriculum to the left.

In Sweden, the Social Democrats have been a dominant party since 1932, and "since the early 1950s the entire Swedish school system has been undergoing radical restructuring and has come to take on a self-consciously democratic, egalitarian and secular, value system" (Tomasson 1965: 203). In Germany, Italy, and the Low Countries, there has also been a considerably greater leftist orientation of basic education than in the United States. As in Sweden and France, to some extent this was the top-down result of government policy, and to some extent it was the result of left-wing teachers' unions. Education served both to create skills and to create a world view conducive to social democracy.

This exploration into beliefs about income mobility has suggested great similarities between the United States and Europe, not only in the reality of mobility but also in the political roots of economic beliefs. In both countries, politicians used rhetoric, symbols, and schooling to propagate their own world view. Everywhere, the left emphasizes class solidarity and sympathy for the downtrodden. The right emphasizes economic mobility and the sins of the poor. The difference between the United States and Europe is that in Europe, the left won, and then used the tools of power to impose their ideology on the nation. Because of the forces described earlier—political institutions and racial homogeneity—the left has had steady control over European states and the ability to control the education of Europeans. Likewise, in America, the right has more often controlled the government. Marxist theory or at least Marx-inspired ideas, which are common in European schools, are rare in the United States. Ideology appears, to us at least, to be the result, not the cause of political success.

This view is linked to the model of hatred proposed by Glaeser (2002) which argues that reality rarely troubles the stories that are told by politicians in order to build hatred against their neighbors. In this context, the model suggests that the anti-redistribution forces will try to vilify the poor. The pro-redistribution forces will emphasize the crimes of the rich. The model argues that the superior political power of the anti-redistribution forces in the United States combined with the social isolation of the poor in America (because they are minorities and because of the geographic spread of the United States) made it possible for the politicians of the right to be more successful in their vilification efforts. While this model suggests that negative attitudes about the poor are certainly a complement to lower levels of redistribution, it also suggests that these attitudes are more likely based on political aspects of the country than on anything real about the poor.

7.5. Testing the idea that politics drives beliefs about the poor

We have argued that beliefs about mobility are driven by political indoctrination, not reality. We have examined the evidence on one part of this claim, that beliefs do not reflect reality. In this section, we will examine whether political differences are correlated with, and perhaps cause, differences in beliefs about economic mobility. In a world where people's beliefs are completely based on reality, there would be little reason to suspect that institutions like proportional representation would be correlated with beliefs about income

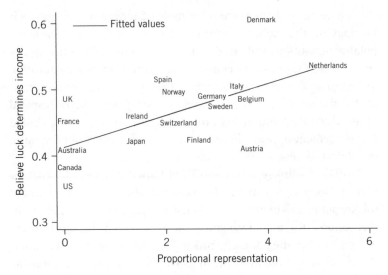

Fig. 7.6. Beliefs About Luck Determining Income and Proportional Representation

mobility. However, in a world in which beliefs about income mobility are the result of successful indoctrination by either the left or the right, we would expect to see a correlation between proportional representation and beliefs.

To test this hypothesis, in Fig. 7.6, we show the relationship between proportional representation and the belief that luck determines income across countries with per capita income greater than $15,000 in 1998.

As the figure shows, there is a high correlation between these variables. The countries with proportional representation, which we already know predicts more welfare, are much more likely to believe that luck drives income. The overall correlation between the two variables across these countries is 61.5 percent.

The correlation between belief that the poor are lazy and proportional representation, shown in Fig. 7.7, is even stronger. While we have only eight countries in the sample, the correlation between the two variables is 84 percent. Places with more proportional representation, that have as a result been more generous to the poor,

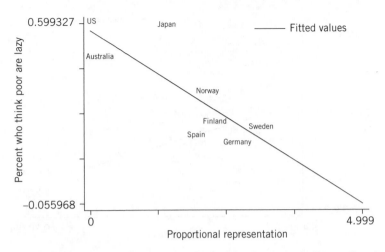

Fig. 7.7. Beliefs About the Poor Being Lazy and Proportional Representation

end up thinking that the poor are more deserving than majoritarian societies, which give less to the poor. There is also a strong correlation between proportional representation and the belief that the poor are trapped (48.6 percent). Insofar as we can treat institutions as being predetermined, the causal link appears to run from institutions to redistribution to belief.

We argued that large land area is one exogenous variable that made it harder for left-wing movements to shape governments. If our hypothesis is correct, then bigger countries should be more likely to believe that luck determines income. This is shown in Fig. 7.8 (again for countries with per capita GDP over $15,000). The correlation coefficient is 59 percent. The correlation between land area and the belief that the poor are lazy is even higher: 66 percent. We know of no innate reason why countries with more land area should have a lazier set of poor people. Yet people in bigger countries are much more likely to think that the poor do not work hard. Our solution to this puzzle is that in places that are bigger, politics has tended to favor the right, and as a result, right-wing views have become more dominant.

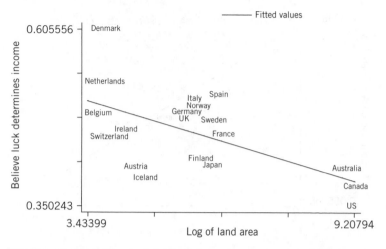

Fig. 7.8. Country Size and the Belief that Luck Determines Income

As a final test of this hypothesis, we can look at our other primary causal variable—racial fractionalization. The logic of this test is much the same. If beliefs about the poor occur mainly to justify redistributive policies, then we should expect countries with more fractionalization—which we already know predicts less redistribution—to have lower opinions about the poor. This test is somewhat complicated by the fact that racial heterogeneity means that racism may confound the results. People in racially fractionalized societies are as likely to have negative assessments of the poor because they come from a different race as they are to have negative assessments of the poor because such opinions justify their low levels of redistribution. In this case, the correlation is almost 50 percent. While this relationship is certainly subject to multiple interpretations, it appears to further the view that exogenous variables which shift the level of redistribution appear to have a strong impact on attitudes towards the poor.

We take away from these graphs the view that exogenous variables, which have tended to empower the left, have also ended up producing an ideology where the poor are seen in a more positive light and where classes are determined by birth. Even within this view that exogenous political factors drove beliefs about mobility,

214

there are two explanations. The first is that these beliefs are irrelevant and simply *ex post* rationalizations. According to this view, there is a market for ideas and individuals will listen to ideas when it makes them feel good about themselves. Societies that have a large welfare system are likely to be open to ideas about the general worthiness of the poor. People in a less generous system are going to prefer listening to stories about how the poor are lazy. This view suggests that these views are basically irrelevant, *ex post* rationalizations.

A second view, which we prefer, is that these views are endogenous, but not irrelevant. Hatred of the poor is a tool in the arsenal of the opponents of redistribution. Hatred of the rich is a tool in the arsenal of those who favor large-scale redistribution. Both of these tools matter and they help to shape elections. However, the degree to which society tends to hate the poor or hate the rich depends on the political power of the friends and enemies of redistribution. In societies where pre-existing factors, such as racial heterogeneity or majoritarian government, have made the enemies of redistribution politically strong, then we should not be surprised to see that they have been more successful in pushing their tool—beliefs that the poor are undeserving.

As such, this view does accept the idea that these world views are important, but argues that they are endogenous and ultimately the outcome of different levels of proportional representation and racial heterogeneity in the United States and Europe. Because the pro-redistribution forces were strong in Europe, their ideology, which emphasizes that income comes from luck, has been dominant. Because the anti-redistribution forces were strong in the United States, their ideology, which emphasizes the connection between effort and income, has been dominant. These ideologies are not irrelevant, but they are the result of innate political and social characteristics of the countries.

7.6. Conclusions

In this section, we have documented the very considerable differences in attitudes towards the poor between the United States and

Europe. We have shown across countries, states, and people that areas with more redistribution tend to believe that luck determines income, that the poor are trapped, and that the poor are not lazy. Most notably, there are huge differences in these attitudes between the United States and Europe.

However, current income mobility data suggests that economic realities offer little basis for these differences. Income mobility appears to be roughly the same in the United States and Europe and if anything, today, the poor are less upwardly mobile in the United States. Historical differences show greater disparities, but still the United States appears to be less mobile than some, particularly Scandinavian, countries. Moreover, the countries in Europe that were more mobile in the past are no more likely to believe that the poor are lazy, or that income is determined by factors other than luck. We are left with the view that these attitudes towards the poor are not explained by current realities and are unlikely to be determined by past economic realities either.

Instead, we have argued that these attitudes reflect the political realities of the United States and Europe. Because of racial fractionalization and American institutions, there was never a socialist government in the United States. As a result, socialist ideas, such as class consciousness, never made significant headway in the United States, while ideas that were amenable to low levels of redistribution such as a belief in social mobility and the laziness of the poor were successfully propagated. Conversely, in Europe, where left-wing groups were able to reshape institutions and gain power, left-wing ideas became ascendant. In neither case do these ideas reflect economic reality. Instead, they are the legacy of the political success of different groups.

Chapter 8

Conclusions

At the beginning of this book, we asked a very specific question: Why is it that in the United States the welfare state is much more limited than in Europe?

As economists, our first instinct was to use our home field advantage and search for a purely economic explanation. After exploring well-traveled economic theories based on pre-tax income inequality, openness, the efficiency of the tax structure, and social mobility, we came out almost empty handed. Then we looked for an answer by moving to other fields, like history, poltical science, sociology, and even psychology, and we found greater success.

Ultimately, we believe the welfare state in the United States did not develop as much as in Europe because of American political institutions, such as majoritarianism (as opposed to proportional representation), federalism, and checks and balances, American ethnic heterogeneity, and different beliefs about the nature of poverty in the United States. American institutions are ultimately the product of an eighteenth-century constitution, which was crafted by men of property, determined to stop the state from expropriating their wealth. After all, they had just fought a revolution motivated, in part, by aggressive taxation. European current constitutions have more recent origins, and they were often written by representatives of the socialist left, in the wake of labor-led uprisings. It should not surprise us that they are far less conservative than the much older American system. American laissez-faire is also supported by an American belief system where a much larger fraction of Americans relative to Europeans believe that the poor are lazy and could escape poverty if they tried hard enough.

Institutions and ideology underpin the differences between the United States and Europe, but these forces, while powerful, are not first causes. They are themselves the result of the profoundly different geographies and ethnicities of America and Europe. America is sprawling and strikingly diverse. It is separated from other nations by two immense oceans. European countries are denser, far more homogeneous, and far more likely to have fought wars on their own soil. To us, these are the first causes: The roots of the gap between America and Europe.

This importance of ethnic fractionalization cannot be over-emphasized. The ethnic and racial fragmentation of the United States' working class interfered with the formation of a unified and powerful labor movement and Socialist Party. Racial fragmentation is correlated with income differences: Blacks and Hispanics are poorer than whites. Experimental evidence shows that people tend to be more sympathetic to individuals of the same race, so a less generous welfare state is in part due to the fact that the white majority does not want to redistribute in a way that would favor racial minorities. Racial differences between rich and poor facilitated the propagation of views such as "all poor are lazy" precisely because racist views associate laziness with different skin colors. In Sweden, say, where 95 percent of the population has the same race, ethnicity, and religion, it is much more difficult to identify the poor with some racial characteristics.

Once again, racial conflicts can also be used strategically by political entrepreneurs interested not so much in "hating blacks" but in preventing redistribution. By convincing even the not so rich whites that redistribution favors minorities, they have been able to build large coalitions against welfare policies. In other words, some poor whites are willing to vote against redistribution that would favor them because their racial animosity wants to prevent blacks from getting the same redistribution.

The ethnic and racial mix of western Europe is changing. Immigration from North Africa and Eastern Europe will make western Europe less homogenous. In fact, the extreme right in Europe is already using the race card to oppose welfare policies. We predict that as racial heterogeneity in Europe increases, even the more "respectable" right will move in that direction.

But, even if all Americans were Lutheran Swedes, America would still have a much less generous welfare state because of its political institutions. Conservative predominance within the United States was associated with a nonproportional electoral system, a presidential system, a powerful system of checks and balances enforced by the Senate (a millionaire's club until the early twentieth century), and a powerful Supreme Court with a mission to defend private property. All of these political institutions were heavily influenced by the desire to limit the amount of redistribution that the poor could impose on the rich.

But when we examined the histories of these countries, we began to understand that the right question about the differences in institutions is not "why did the United States choose conservative institutions and Europe did not?" After all, almost all European countries in 1890 had institutions that were far more conservative than those in the United States. The right question is "how were the conservatives in the United States able to keep conservative, eighteenth century institutions, while the European right was not?" American institutions have evolved, but they are far more stable than their European counterparts, which often changed drastically in "revolutionary" periods.

Why did Europe have these revolutionary periods and the United States did not? To this our answer is geography. Why is geography so important? First, America was much less congenial to the formation of cohesive labor movements and socialist parties. Its low density and vast size interfered with communication and diffused social conflict. Vast distances between the corridors of power and the factories meant that unions had difficulty threatening the government. Furthermore, the open frontier allowed for geographic and social mobility. Thus, it should not surprise us that the Belgian labor movement was able to force constitutional change in the 1890s, but the American labor movement was not.

Even more importantly, America's geography ensured that the Unites States has never fought a war on its own territory. European wars, especially World War I, created grievances, poverty, and a fertile ground for Socialist and Communist parties to establish themselves. Perhaps even more importantly, in the aftermath of these conflicts, defeated or disorganized armies lost the ability to suppress leftist insurrection, partly because the armies were in disarray after the war and partly because soldiers themselves were sympathetic to the revolutionaries. It is difficult to imagine the Russian Revolution, the Spartacist revolution, and Germany's subsequent left-wing constitution, or even Italy's move to proportional representation in 1919, without the military weakness that came from World War I. This did not happen in the United States.

For instance, proportional representation, which is strongly associated with more generous welfare states, was introduced in most countries in Europe after World War I and in the aftermath of the Russian Revolution, when the left was extremely powerful. Also, in Europe new constitutions were written (and rewritten) *ex novo* in the twentieth century under the influence of a powerful left. In contrast, the relative stability of the U.S. Constitution makes the United States a country governed by a (revised) document written by a minority of white, wealthy men.

We also believe that two other forces surely helped ensure conservative dominance. First, America started off at least at the very beginning as a classless society, compared to Europe with its tradition of nobility, hereditary wealth, and status. An added factor is America's status as an immigrant nation. Those immigrants who came from Europe were almost by definition taking their economic destiny in their own hands. Many of those who stayed in the Old Continent believed more in a political or even revolutionary solution to their grievances.

A final factor is ideology, supported by some sort of indoctrination. Americans believe that they live in a mobile society in which individual effort can lift people up the social ladder. Likewise, the European welfare states are supported by European beliefs that the poor are unfortunate and would be stuck in their poverty without government intervention. Indicators of actual social mobility do not seem to support the idea that these strong differences in views reflect true differences in mobility across the Atlantic. Probably the middle class is a bit more upwardly mobile in the United States than in Europe and probably the poor in the United States are somewhat less mobile, but the differences are not very large.

So how can one reconcile these very large differences in beliefs with reality? One answer is that the poor have in fact more opportunities in the United States and they do not take advantage of them because, precisely as a majority of Americans think, they are lazy. The other explanation is that conservative forces have an interest in propagating in the United States the notion of a self-made person without any need for government intervention. Conversely, in Europe, an often centralized education system, in many cases heavily influenced by the left, has all the invectives to instill the opposite ideological view. In other words, opposing ideological biases are present on the two sides of the Atlantic. Incidentally, these biases may be "self-fulfilling." That is, a belief that the poor are stuck may lead to heavy taxation and redistribution that may interfere with market incentives and make it in fact more difficult for the poor to take advantage of markets to escape poverty.

To the extent that our explanation of differences in the welfare state has to do with a different predominance of left- and right-wing views on the two sides of the Atlantic, this may help us to understand some of the recent conflicts between the United States and Europe. The world views of both places are shaped by different histories and institutions. The European left has been able to push its ideas much more widely than its American counterpart. This inevitably leads to differences in opinion across the Atlantic in many areas, including over wars, equality, and international institutions. If we are to avoid more conflict, we would do well to remember how much of all of our views are formed by indoctrination, not reality, and to recognize that there is usually a significant amount of truth in the opposing viewpoint as well.

References

Acemoglu, D. and Robinson, J. (2000). "Why Did the West Extend the Franchise? Democracy, Inequality, and Growth in Historical Perspective," *Quarterly Journal of Economics*, 115: 1167–99.

—— —— and Johnson, S. (2001). "The Colonial Origins of Comparative Development: An Empirical Investigation," *American Economic Review*, 91: 1369–401.

Aghion, P., Alesina, A., and Trebbi, F. (2004). "Endogenous Political Institutions," *Quarterly Journal of Economics*, May.

Alesina, A. and Angeletos, M. (2005). "Fairness Redistribution: U.S. versus Europe." *American Economic Review*, forthcoming.

—— and Ardagna, S. (1999). "Tales of Fiscal Adjustments," *Economic Policy*, 27: 489–545.

—— ——, Nicoletti, G., and Schiantarelli, F. (2005). "Regulation and Investment." *Journal of the European Economic Association*, forthcoming.

—— Baqir, R., and Easterly, W. (1999). "Public Goods and Ethnic Divisions," *Quarterly Journal of Economics*, 114: 1243–84.

—— —— and Hoxby, C. (2004). "Political jurisdictions in heterogeneous communities," *Journal of Political Economy*, 112: 348–96.

—— Danninger, S., and Rostagno, M. (2001). "Redistribution through Public Employment: the case of Italy," *IMF Staff Papers*, 48: 447–73.

—— Devleeschauwer, A., Easterly, W., Kurlat, S., and Wacziarg, R. (2003). "Fractionalization," *Journal of Economic Growth*, 8: 155–94.

—— and Drazen, A. (1991). "Why are Stabilizations Delayed?," *American Economic Review*, 81: 1170–88.

—— and LaFerrara, E. (2000). "Participation in Heterogeneous Communities," *Quarterly Journal of Economics*, 115: 847–904.

—— and —— (2005). "Preferences for Redistribution in the Land of Opportunities," *Journal of Public Economics*, 89: 897–931.

—— and —— (2002). "Who Trusts Others?" *Journal of Public Economics* 85: 207–34.

—— Glaeser, E. L., and Sacerdote, B. (2001). "Why Doesn't the U.S. Have a European-Style Welfare State," *Brookings Papers on Economic Activity*, Fall, 187–278.

References

Alesina, A. and Mare, M. (1992). "Evasione e Debito" in M. Monorchine (ed.) *La Finanza Publica Italiana dopo la svolta del 1992.* (Bologna: Il Mulino).

—— and Perotti, R. (1997). "The Welfare State and Competitiveness," *American Economic Review*, 87: 921–39.

—— ——, and Tavares, J. (1998). "The political economy of fiscal adjustments," *Brookings Papers on Economic Activity*, Spring, 197–226.

—— and Rodrik, D. (1994). "Distributive Politics and Economic Growth." *Quarterly Journal of Economics*, 109: 465–90.

—— and Rosenthal, H. (1995). *Partisan Politics Divided Government and the Economy* (Cambridge, U.K., Cambridge University Press).

—— Roubini, N., and Cohen, G. (1997). *Political Cycles and the Macroeconomy* (Cambridge, MA, MIT Press).

—— and Spolaore, E. (1997). "On the Number and Size of Nations," *Quarterly Journal of Economics*, 112: 1027–56.

—— and —— (2003). *The Size of Nations* (Cambridge, MA: MIT Press).

—— Di Tella, R., and MacCulloch, R. (2001). "Inequality and Happiness: Are Europeans and Americans Different?" *Journal of Public Economics*, forthcoming.

—— and Wacziarg, R. (1998). "Openness, Country Size and the Government," *Journal of Public Economics*, 69: 305–21.

Allport, G. (1954). *The Nature of Prejudice* (Cambridge, MA: Addison-Wesley).

Ashenfelter, O. (1972). "Racial Discrimination and Trade Unionism," *Journal of Political Economy*, 80: 435–64.

Atkinson, A. (1995). *Incomes and the Welfare State: Essays on Britain and Europe* (Cambridge: Cambridge University Press).

Banabou, R. and Tirole, J. (2003). "Belief in a Just World and Redistributive Policies," Unpublished manuscript.

Barber, Kathleen L. (1995). *Proportional Representation and Election Reform in Ohio* (Columbus, OH: Ohio State University Press).

Barro, R. (2000). "Inequality and Growth in a Panel of Countries," *Journal of Economic Growth*.

Barro-Lee dataset. Available online at www.nber.org/pub/barro.lee.

Barton, D. Scott and Cantrell, G. (1989). "Texas Populists and the Failure of Biracial Politics," *Journal of Southern History*, 55: 659–92.

Bassanini, A. and Ernst, E. (2002). "Labor Market Institutions, Product Market Regulations and Innovation: Cross Country Evidence." *OECD Economics Department Working Paper*, No. 316.

References

Becker, G. (1957). *The Economics of Discrimination* (Chicago: University of Chicago Press).

—— (1983). "A Theory of Competition Amongst Pressure Groups for Political Influence," *Quarterly Journal of Economics*, 98: 371–400.

—— and Mulligan, C. (2003). "Deadweight Costs and the Size of Government," *Journal of Law and Economics*, forthcoming.

Benabou, R. (1996). "Inequality and Growth," in B. Bernanke and J. Rotemberg (eds.), *NBER Macroeconomics Annual 1996* (Cambridge, MA: MIT Press).

—— (2000). "Unequal Societies," *American Economic Review*, 90: 96–129.

—— and Ok, E. (2001). "Social Mobility and the Demand for Redistribution: The POUM Hypothesis," *Quarterly Journal of Economics*, 116: 447–87.

—— and Tirole, Jean (2002). "Belief in a Just World and Redistributive Politics," Unpublished manuscript.

Besley, T., and Coate, S. (1991). "Public Provision of Private Goods and the Redistribution of Income," *American Economic Review*, 81: 979–84.

—— and —— (1995). "The Design of Income Maintenance Programs," *Review of Economic Studies*, 62: 187–211.

Blanchard, O. and Katz, L. (1992). "Regional Evolutions," *Brookings Papers on Economic Activity*: 1–75.

—— and Wolfers, J. (2000). "The Role of Shocks and Institutions in the Rise of European Unemployment: The Aggregate Evidence," *Economic Journal*, 110.

—— and Giavazzi, F. (2003). "Macroeconomic Effects of Regulation and Deregulation in Goods and Labour Markets," *Quarterly Journal of Economics*, forthcoming.

Blum, L. (1946). *For All Mankind* (New York: Viking Press).

Boeri, T. (2000). *Structural Change, Welfare Systems, and Labour Reallocation* (Oxford: Oxford University Press).

—— and Perotti, R. (2002). *Meno Pensioni e più Welfare.* (Bologna, Italy: Il Mulino).

Breen, T. H. and Foster, S. (1973). "Moving to the New World: The Character, of Early Massachusetts Immigration," *William and Mary Quarterly*, 3rd Series, 30(2): 189–222, quote from p. 219.

Brennan, G. and Buchanan, J. (1980). The Power to Tax: Analytical Foundations for Fiscal Constitutions (Cambridge: Cambridge University Press).

Brinkley, A. (1995). *The End of Reform: New Deal Liberalism in Recession and War* (New York: Alfred A. Knopf).

Buchanan, J. and Tullock, G. (1962). "The Calculus of Consent." (Am Arbor: University of Michigan Press).

References

Burrows, Edwin G. and Wallace, M. (1998). *Gotham: A History of New York City to 1898* (New York: Oxford University Press).

Bush, G. (January 20, 1989). Second Inaugural Address. Available online at gi.grolier.com/presidents/aee/inaugs/1989bush.html.

Cameron, D. (1978). "The Expansion of the Public Economy: A Comparative Analysis," *American Political Science Review*, 72: 1243–61.

Caro, R. (1982). *The Years of Lyndon Johnson 1982* (New York: Knopf).

Checchi, D., Ichino, A., and Rustichini, A. (1999). "More Equal and Less Mobile? Education Financing and Intergenerational Mobility in Italy and in the US," *Journal of Public Economics*, 74: 351–93.

Colton, C. (1844). *Junius Tracts* (New York: Greely & McElrath).

Conde-Ruiz P. and Profeta, P. (2002). "What Social Security: Beveridgean or Bismarkian?" Unpublished manuscript.

Coolidge, C. (March 4, 1925). Inaugural Address. Available online at gi.grolier.com/presidents/aee/inaugs/1925cool.html.

Coppa, F. (1995). "From Liberalism to Fascism: The Church–State Conflict over Italy's Schools," *The History Teacher*, 28(2): 135–48.

Cremin, L. (1951). *The American Common School: An Historic Conception* (New York: Bureau of Publications, Teachers' College, Columbia University).

Cutler, D., Glaeser, E. L., and Vigdor, J. (1999). "The Rise and Decline of the American Ghetto," *Journal of Political Economy*, 107: 455–506.

D'Souza, D. (1995). *The End of Racism: Principles for a Multicultural Society* (New York: Free Press).

Deininger, K. and Squire, L. (1996). "A New Data Set Measuring Income Inequality," *World Bank Economic Review*, 10: 565–91.

Department of Geodesy and Cartography of the State Geological Committee of the USSR. (1964). *Atlas Narodov Mira*. Moscow.

DiPasquale, D. and Glaeser, E. L. (1998). "The L.A. Riots and the Economics of Urban Unrest," *Journal of Urban Economics*, 43: 52–78.

Disney, R. and Johnson, R. (eds.) (2001). *Pension Systems and Retirement Investment across OECD Countries* (London: Edward Elgar).

—— and Whitehouse, E. (2002). "Cross-National Comparisons of Retirement Income," in S. Crystal and D. Shea (eds.), *Annual Review of Gerontology and Geriatrics, Economic Outcomes in Later Life*, (22): 60–94.

Djankov S., La Porta, R., Lopez de Silanes, F., and Shleifer, A. (2002). "The Regulation of Entry," *Quarterly Journal of Economics*, 1–37.

DuBois, W. E. B. (1903). *The Souls of Black Folk: Essays and Sketches* (Chicago: A.C. McClurg).

Easterly, W. and Levine, R. (1997). "Africa's Growth Tragedy: Policies and Ethnic Divisions," *Quarterly Journal of Economics*, 111: 1203–50.

References

Enikopolov and Zhuravskaya (2002). "Decentralization and Political Institutions" (unpublished).

Fehr, E. and Schmidt, K. (2001). "Theories of Fairness and Reciprocity– Evidence and Economic Applications." Prepared for the 8th World Congress of the Econometric Society.

Fields, G. and Ok, E. (1999). "Measuring Movement of Incomes," *Economica*, 66: 455–471.

Flora, P. and Heidenhemeier, J. (1981). (eds) *The Development of Welfare States in Europe and America* (Transection Books: New Brunwick, NJ).

Gavin, M. and Perotti, R. (1997). "Fiscal Policy in Latin America," in B. Bernanke and J. Rotemberg (eds.), *NBER Macroeconomics Annual*. (Cambridge, MA: MIT Press).

George, H. [1887] (1973). *Progress and Poverty: An Inquiry into the Cause of Industrial Depressions, and of Increase of Want with Increase of Wealth. The Remedy* (New York: AMS Press).

Gilens, M. (1999). *Why Americans Hate Welfare: Race, Media, and the Politics of Antipoverty Policy* (Chicago: University of Chicago Press).

Glaeser, E. L. (2002). "The Political Economy of Hatred," *Harvard Institute of Economic Research Discussion Paper*, No. 1970.

—— and Shleifer, A. (2002). "Legal Origins." *Quarterly Journal of Economics*, 117: 1193–230.

—— and —— (2001). "Not-for-profit Entrepreneurs," *Journal of Public Economics*, 81: 99–115.

—— Laibson, D., Scheinkman, J., and Soutter, C. (2000). "Measuring Trust," *Quarterly Journal of Economics*, 115: 811–46.

Gottschalk, P. and Spolaore, E. (2002). "On the Evaluation of Economic Mobility," *Review of Economic Studies*, 69: 191–208.

Gregory, F. and Neu, I. (1974). "The Industrial Elite of the 1970s: Their Social Origin," in E. Pessen (ed.), *Three Centuries of Social Mobility in America* (Lexington: D.C. Heath).

Grilli, V., Masciandaro, A., and Tabellini, G. (1991). "Political and Monetary Institutions and Public Finance Policies in Industrial Countries," *Economic Policy*, 13: 341–92.

Grusky, D. (1986). "American Social Mobility in the Nineteenth and Twentieth Centuries," *University of Wisconsin Center for Demography and Ecology*. Working Paper No. 86–28.

Gruber, J. and Wise, D. (2001). "Social Security Programs and Retirement Around the World." NBER Working Paper, No. 9407.

Hamilton, A. (1774). *Pamphlet, in response to Samuel Seabury.*

References

Hamilton, A. Jay, J., and Madison, J. [1787] (1982). *The Federalist Papers* (New York: Bantam Classic Books).

Hammond, J. (1656). *Leah and Rachel, or the Two Fruitfull Sisters, Virginia and Mary-Land: Their Present Condition, Impartially Stated and Related. With A Removall of such Imputations as are scandalously cast on those Countries, whereby many deceived Souls chose rather to Beg, Steal, rot in Prison, and come to shamefull deaths, then to their being by going thither, wherein is plenty of all things for Humane subsistance* (London: T. Mabb).

Harding, W. (March 4, 1921). Inaugural Address. Available online at gi.grolier.com/presidents/aee/inaugs/1921hard.html.

Hauser, R. (1997). "Adequacy and Poverty Reform among the Retired." Paper presented to the joint ILO-OECD Workshop "Development and Reform of Pensions Schemes." Paris, 15–17 December.

Hayek, F. (1960). *The Constitution of Liberty*. (New York: Routledge).

Heinrich, G. (2000). "Affluence and Poverty in Old Age: New Evidence from the European Community Household Panel." *IRISS Working Paper Series*.

Hibbs, D. (1987). *The American Political Economy Macroeconomics and Electoral Politics in the United States* (Cambridge, MA: Harvard University Press).

Hofstadter, R. (1955). *The Age of Reform: From Bryan to F.D.R* (New York: Random House).

—— [1944, rev. 1955] (1969). *Social Darwinism in American Thought* (New York: George Brazillier) (Revised edn.).

Holt, M. (1999). *The Rise and Fall of the American Whig Party: Jacksonian Politics and the Onset of the Civil War* (New York: Oxford University Press).

Hoover, H. (March 4, 1929). Inaugural Address. Available online gi.grolier.com/presidents/aee/inaugs/1929hoov.html.

Huber, E. and Stephens, J. (2001). *Development and Crisis of the Welfare State* (Chicago: University of Chicago Press).

Jackson, Kenneth T. (1967). *The Ku Klux Klan in the City: 1915–1930* (New York: Oxford University Press).

Jenkins, R. (2001). *Churchill: A Biography* (New York: Farrar, Straus & Giroux).

Johnson, Lyndon Baines (March 16, 1964). "The War on Poverty."

Joskow, P. and Rose, N. (1989). "The Effects of Economic Regulation," in R. Schmalensee and R. D. Willig (eds.), *Handbook of Industrial Organization* (New York: Elsevier Science).

Kaelble, H. (1985). *Social Mobility in the 19th and 20th Centuries: Europe and America in Comparative Perspective* (Dover, NH: Berg).

Kaestle, C. F. (1983). *Pillars of the Republic: Common Schools and American Society, 1780–1960* (New York: Hill and Wang).

References

Kautsky, K. (1910). *The Class Struggle* (Chicago: Charles H. Kerr & Co.).

Key, V. (1949). *Southern Politics in State and Nation* (New York: Alfred A. Knopf).

Kohl, J. (1992). "The Public/Private Mix in the Income Package of the Elderly: A Comparative Study." *LIS Working Paper No. 78.*

Kolesar, R. (1996). *Communism, Race and the Defeat of Proportional Representation.* Available online at www.mtholyoke.edu/acad/polit/damy/articles/kolesar.htm.

Lamberti, M. (1992). "Elementary School Teachers and the Struggle against Social Democracy in Wilhelmine Germany," *History of Education Quarterly*, 32: 73–97.

Lindbeck, A. (1997). "The Swedish Experiment," *Journal of Economic Literature*, 35: 1273–319.

Lipset, S. (1996). *American Exceptionalism* (New York: W. W. Norton & Co.).

—— and Marks, G. (2000). *It Didn't Happen Here: Why Socialism Failed In the United States* (New York: W.W. Norton & Co.).

Lloyd George, D. (1929). "We Can Conquer Unemployment" (Pamphlet), London: Cassell and Company.

Long, H. P. (1935). *My First Days in the White House* (Harrisburg, PA: Telegraph Press). Available online at www.ssa.gov/history/hueywhouse.html.

Long, J. and Ferrie, J. (2002). A Tale of Two Labor Markets, Career Mobility in the U.K. (1851–81) and U.S. (1850–80), Minieographed.

Luttmer, E. (2001). "Group Loyalty and the Taste for Redistribution," *Journal of Political Economy*, 109(3): 500–28.

Luxembourg Income Study.

Luxemburg, R. [1906] (1971). *The Mass Strike, The Political Party and the Trade Unions; and the Junius Pamphlet* (New York: Harper Torchbooks), p. 72. Available online at www.marxists.org.

Marx, K. and Engels, F. [1848] (1998). *The Manifesto of the Communist Party* (New York: Verso).

—— (1964). *Selected Writings in Sociology and Social Philosophy* (London: McGraw-Hill).

—— [1869] (1975). "The Belgian Massacres. To the Workmen of Europe and the United States" (leaflet). Published in *Karl Marx and Frederick Engels: Collected Works.* Volume 21 (New York: International Publishers), p. 47. Available online at www.marxists.org.

Mauro, P. (1995). "Corruption and Growth," *Quarterly Journal of Economics*, 110(3): 681–712.

References

Mayer, J. (2002). *Running on Race: Racial Politics in Presidential Campaigns, 1960–2000* (New York: Random House).

McGuffey, William Holmes (1848). *Newly Revised Eclectic Third Reader* (Cincinnati: W.B. Smith & Co.).

McVickar, Rev. John (1846). *First Lessons in Political Economy for the Use of Schools and Families* (Boston: Hillard, Gray & Co.).

Meltzer, A. and Richards, S. (1981). "A Rational Theory of the Size of Government," *Journal of Political Economy*, 89(5): 914–27.

Milesi-Ferretti, G., Perotti, R., and Rostagno, M. (2002). "Electoral Systems and Public Spending," *Quarterly Journal of Economics*, 117: 609–58.

Miller, W. (1974). "American Historians and the Industrial Elite of 1900" in E. Pessen (ed.) *Three Centuries of Social Mobility in America* (Lexington: D.C. Heath).

Model Curriculum Standards for U. S. History and Geography: The California Experience (in The State of the Profession) (1985). *The History Teacher*, 18: 555–80.

Moore, B. (1966). *Social Origins of Dictatorship and Democracy: Lord and Peasant in the Making of the Modern World* (Boston: Beacon Press).

Musgrave, R. (1959). *The Theory of Public Finance* (New York: McGraw-Hill).

Nardinelli, C. and Simon, C. (1990). "Customer Racial Discrimination in the Market for Memorabilia: The Case of Baseball," *Quarterly Journal of Economics*, 105: 575–95.

National Opinion Research Center, General Social Survey, 1972–1994.

Nickell, S. (1997). "Unemployment and Labor Market Rigidities: Europe versus North America," *Journal of Economic Perspectives*, 11: 55–74.

—— and Layard, R. (1999). "Labor Market Institutions and Economic Performance," in O. Ashenfelter and D. Card (eds.), *Handbook of Labor Economics*, Volume 3B: 3029–84 (Amsterdam: North Holland).

Nicoletti, G. and Scarpetta, S. (2003). "Regulation, Productivity and Growth," *Economic Policy*, 37: 43–95.

——, Scarpetta, S., and Boyland, O. (2001). "Summary Indicators of Product Market Regulation with an Extension to Employment Protection Legislation," *OECD Economics Department Working Papers*, No. 226.

Nisbett, R. and Cohen, D. (1996). *Culture of Honor: The Psychology of Violence in the South* (Boulder: Westview Press).

Nixon, R. (January 20, 1973). Second Inaugural Address. Available online at gi.grolier.com/presidents/aee/inaugs/1973nixo.html.

References

Oates, W. (1972). *Fiscal Federalism* (New York: Harcourt Brace).

—— (1999). "An Essay on Fiscal Federalism," *Journal of Economic Literature*, 37: 1120–49.

Obinger, H. (1999). "Minimum Income in Switzerland," *Journal of European Social Policy*, 9: 28–47.

Oglethorpe, E. (1733). *A New and Accurate Account of the Provinces of South-Carolina and Georgia: With Many Curious and Useful Observations on the Trade, Navigation and Plantations of Great-Britain, Compared with Her Most Powerful Maritime Neighbours in Ancient and Modern Times* (London: J. Worrall).

Olson, J. (1977). "Radical Social Democracy and School Reform in Wilhelmian Germany," *History of Education Quarterly*, 17: 3–16.

Peltzman, S. (1980). "The Growth of Government," *Journal of Law and Economics*, 19: 211–40.

Perlstein, R. (2001). *Before the Storm: Barry Goldwater and the Unmaking of the American Consensus* (New York: Hill and Wang).

Perotti, R. (1996). "Growth, Income Distribution and Democracy: What the Data Say," *Journal of Economic Growth*, 1: 149–87.

—— and Kontopoulos, Y. (2002). "Fragmented Fiscal Policy," *Journal of Public Economics*, 27: 191–222.

Persson, T. and Tabellini, G. (1994). "Is Inequality Harmful for Growth?", *American Economic Review*, 84: 600–21.

—— and —— (2000). *Political Economics: Explaining Economic Policy* (Cambridge, MA: MIT Press).

—— and —— (2003). *The Economic Effects of Constitutions* (Cambridge, MA: MIT Press).

Pessen, E. (1974). "The Myth of Antebellum Social Mobility and Equality of Opportunity" in E. Pessen (ed.) *Three Centuries of Social Mobility in America* (Lexington: D.C. Heath).

Pflanze, O. (1955). "Bismarck and German Nationalism," *American Historical Review*, 60: 548–66.

Picketty, T. (1995). "Social Mobility and Redistributive Politics," *Quarterly Journal of Economics*, 110(3): 551–84.

Populist Party Platform (1892). In Tindall, George B., David E. Shi and Thomas Lee Pearcy (2000). *The Essential America* (New York: W.W. Norton & Co.).

Program of the National Socialist German Workers' Party (1920). Available online at http://fcit.coedu.usf.edu/holocaust/resource/document/program.htm.

Putnam, R. (2000). *Bowling Alone: The Collapse and Revival of American Community* (New York: Simon & Schuster).

References

Rawls, J. (1971). *A Theory of Justice* (Cambridge, MA: Harvard University Press).

Reagan, R. (January 21, 1985). Second Inaugural Address. Available online at gi.grolier.com/presidents/aee/inaugs/1985reag.html.

—— (October 26, 1987). Executive Order 12612.

Ritchie, A. (1998). *Faust's Metropolis: A History of Berlin* (New York: Carroll & Graf).

Rodrik, D. (1998). "Why Do More Open Economies Have Bigger Governments?" *Journal of Political Economy*, 106: 997–1032.

Romer, T. (1975). "Individual Welfare, Majority Voting and the Properties of a Linear Income Tax," *Journal of Public Economics*, 7: 163–88.

Romer, P. (1996). "Preferences, Promises, and the Politics of Entitlement," in V. Fuchs (ed.), *Individual and Social Responsibility: Child Care, Education, Medical Care, and Long-Term Care in America* (Chicago: University of Chicago Press).

Roosevelt, F. D. First Inaugural Address. March 4, 1933. Available online at gi.grolier.com/presidents/aee/inaugs/1933roos.html.

—— (March 9, 1937). Fireside Chat.

Roubini, N. and Sachs, J. (1989). "Government Spending and Budget Deficits in the Industrial Economies," *Economic Policy* 8.

Rozwenc, E. "Captain John Smith's Image of America," *William and Mary Quarterly* 3rd Series, 16: 27–36.

Sidanius, J., Pratto, F., and Bobo, L. (1996). "Racism, Conservatism, Affirmative Action, and Intellectual Sophistication: A Matter of Principled Conservatism or Group Dominance?" *Journal of Personality and Social Psychology*, 70: 476–90.

Simon, J. (2002). *What Kind of Nation: Thomas Jefferson, John Marshall, and the Epic Struggle to Create a United States* (New York: Simon & Schuster).

Singer, B. (1977). "From Patriots to Pacifists: The French Primary School Teachers, 1880–1940," *Journal of Contemporary History*, 12: 413–34.

Skocpol, T. (1992). *Protecting Soldiers and Mothers: The Political Origins of Social Policy in the United States* (Cambridge, MA: Harvard University Press).

—— Ganz, M., and Munson, Z. (2000). "A Nation of Organizers: The Institutional Origins of Civic Voluntarism in the United States," *American Political Science Review*, 94: 527–46.

Skowronek, S. (1982). *Building a New American State: The Expansion of National Administrative Capacities* (Cambridge: Cambridge University Press).

Smith, J. (1624). *The Generall Historie of Virginia, New-England, and the Summer Isles* (London: I. D. and I. H. for Michael Sparkes).

References

Sombart, W. (1905). *Socialism and the Social Movement* (Chicago: Charles H. Kerr).

—— (1976). *Why Is There No Socialism in the United States?* (London: Macmillan).

Spero, S. and Harris, A. (1931). *The Black Worker: The Negro and the Labor Movement* (New York: Columbia University Press).

Taeuber, K. and Taeuber, A. (1965). *Negroes in Cities: Residential Segregation and Neighborhood Change* (Chicago: Aldine).

Tanzi, V. and Schuknecht, L. (2000). *Public Spending in the Twentieth Century: A Global Perspective* (Cambridge: Cambridge University Press).

Therenstrom, S. (1970). "Working Class Social Mobility in Industrial America." in Richter, M. (ed.) *Essays in Theory and History*. (Cambridge, MA: Harvard University Press: 221–38).

—— (1973). "Poverty and Progress: Social Mobility in a Nineteenth Century City." (Lexington: D.C. Heath).

Tideman, N. and Richardson, D. (2000). "Better Voting Methods through Technology: The Refinement-Manageability Trade-Off in the Single Transferable Vote," *Public Choice*, 103: 13–34.

Tocqueville, A. (1835). *Democracy in America* (London: Saunders and Otley).

—— [1835] (1959). *Democracy in America* (New York: Doubleday).

Tomasson, R. F. (1965). "From Elitism to Egalitarianism in Swedish Education," *Sociology of Education*, 38: 203–23.

Tornell, A. and Velasco, A. (1995). "Fiscal Discipline and the Choice of Exchange Rate Regime," *European Economic Review*, 39: 769–70.

Trivers, R. (1971). "The Evolution of Reciprocal Altruism," *Quarterly Review of Biology*, 46: 35–57.

Veblen, T. [1899] (1934). *The Theory of the Leisure Class: An Economic Study of Institutions* (New York: Modern Library).

Virtanen, S. and Huddy, L. (1998). "Old-Fashioned Racism and New Forms of Racial Prejudice," *Journal of Politics*, 60: 311–32.

Wagstaff, A. *et al.* (1991). "Redistributive Effects, and Treatment: Personal income tax in 12 OECD Countries," *Journal of Public Economics*, 57: 72–98.

Wallace, G. (1963). Gubernatorial Inaugural Address. Available online at www.archives.state.al.us/govs_list/inauguralspeech.html.

—— (1968). "American Independent Platform." Available online at www. pbs.org/wgbh/amex/wallace/filmmore/reference/primary/68plaform. html.

Wallace, H. [1939] "The Genetic Basis of Democracy." (Speech) Printed in Wallace, Henry A. Russel Lord (ed.), (1944). *Democracy Reborn* (New York: Reynal and Hitchcock).

References

Warren, J. (1772). "An Oration Delivered March 5th 1772 at the Request of the Inhabitants of the Town of Boston to Commemorate the Bloody Tragedy of the Fifth of March, 1770" (Boston: Edes and Gill).

Washington, G. (June 8, 1783). Circular to the States.

—— (September 19, 1796). Farewell Address. Available online at gwpapers.virginia.edu/farewell/.

Watson, T. (1892). "The Negro Question in the South," *The Arena*, VI: 540–50. Available online at www.chss.montclair.edu/english/furr/spl/tomwatson.html.

Weber, E. (1979). *Peasants into Frenchmen: the Modernization of Rural France, 1870–1914* (London: Chatto & Windus).

Weingast, S., Shepsle, K., and Johnsen, R. (1981). "The Political Economy of Benefits and Costs: A Neoclassical Approach to Redistributive Politics," *Journal of Political Economics*, 89: 642–66.

Weiss, J. (1996). *Ideology of Death: Why the Holocaust Happened in Germany* (Chicago: Elephant).

Wilenski, H. (1981). "Leftism, Catholicism and Democratic Corporatism" in Flora P. and Heidenhemeier, J. (eds.)

Wilentz, S. (1990). "The Rise of the American Working Class, 1776–1877: A Survey," in J. Carroll Moody and Alice Kessler-Harris (eds.), *Perspectives on American Labor History* (DeKalb, IL: Northern Illinois University Press).

Woodward, C.V. (1938). "Tom Watson and the Negro in Agrarian Politics," *Journal of Southern History*, 4: 14–33.

—— (1971). *Origins of the New South, 1877–1913* (Baton Rouge: Louisiana State University Press) (Revised ed.).

Woodward, C.V. [1955, rev. 1973] (2002). *The Strange Career of Jim Crow* (New York: Oxford University Press) (3rd edn.).

World Values Survey 1981, 1990, 1995.

Wright, G. (1995). *France in Modern Times: From The Enlightenment to the Present* (New York: W.W. Norton & Co.) (5th edn.).

Name Index

Name Index

Subject Index

Subject Index

Subject Index

Subject Index

Subject Index

Subject Index